Environmental Action in Eastern Europe

Environmental Action in Eastern Europe

Responses to Crisis

Edited by
Barbara Jancar-Webster

M.E. Sharpe
**Armonk, New York
London, England**

Library of Congress Cataloging-in-Publication Data

Environmental action in Eastern Europe: responses to crisis /
edited by Barbara Jancar-Webster.
p.   cm.
Includes index.
ISBN 1-56324-036-X (cloth).
ISBN 1-56324-187-0 (pbk.)
1. Environmental policy—Europe, Eastern—Congresses.
2. Europe, Eastern—Economic policy—1989- —Congresses.
I. Jancar-Webster, Barbara, 1935–
HC244.Z9E52   1992
363.7′056′0947—DC20
92-37852
CIP

Printed in the United States of America

The paper used in this publication meets the minimum requirements of
American National Standard for Information Sciences—
Permanence of Paper for Printed Library Materials,
ANSI Z39.48–1984.

BM (c)   10   9   8   7   6   5   4   3   2   1

BM (p)   10   9   8   7   6   5   4   3   2   1

Contents

Part II
The Influence of Environmental Movements

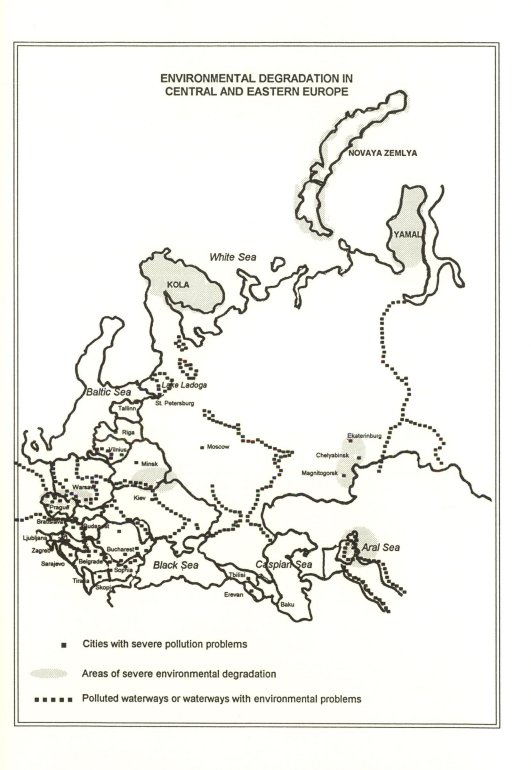

ENVIRONMENTAL DEGRADATION IN
CENTRAL AND EASTERN EUROPE

NOVAYA ZEMLYA

YAMAL

White Sea

KOLA

Lake Ladoga

Baltic Sea

Tallinn

Riga

St. Petersburg

Vilnius

Ekaterinburg

Minsk

Moscow

Chelyabinsk

Warsaw

Magnitogorsk

Kiev

Prague

Bratislava

Budapest

Ljubljana

Zagreb

Bucharest

Aral Sea

Sarajevo

Belgrade

Tirana

Sophia

Black Sea

Caspian Sea

Skopje

Tbilisi

Erevan

Baku

■   Cities with severe pollution problems

        Areas of severe environmental degradation

■ ■ ■ ■ ■   Polluted waterways or waterways with environmental problems

1

Introduction

Barbara Jancar-Webster

In 1989 the people of Eastern Europe threw off the communist yoke, and with it, forty years of Soviet hegemony. The principal issue that became symbolic of the arbitrary and dictatorial nature of the communist system was the environment. In every East European country and in republics of the Soviet Union the population rallied to demand the end of the regime which had brought them to the brink of environmental catastrophe. The elections of 1990 brought to power parties that promised swift environmental remediation; yet to date, no government has given more than lip service to environmental projects. The environmental issue receded into the background as old nationalist scores demanded settlement and new economic concerns pushed to the forefront. At the beginning of 1992, the former communist countries found themselves deep in the process of transition. It was clear where they had come from; but the future was shrouded in uncertainty. Yugoslavia and the Soviet Union faded from the map, to be replaced by sovereign states formed from the constituent republics of the communist federations. There was much talk of democracy and human rights, but in most countries these were far from being implemented. The toll from the war between Croatia and Serbia was estimated at $15 billion, with over half a million people driven from their homes and some 15,000 killed.[1] In Nagorno-Karabakh, battles raged between Azeri and Armenian nationalists. In Czecho-Slovakia, the government instituted a five-year moratorium on the employment of former members of the

1

Communist Party, and then negotiated its own demise as the country broke in two. Much was written about the need to create a free market economy, but in every country in the region, the bulk of economic activity remained in state hands.

This book was developed from papers presented at the World Slavic Congress held at Harrogate, England, in July 1990. At that time, there was general euphoria regarding developments in Eastern Europe. In June of that year, Czechs and Slovaks had gone to the polls in the first free elections since 1946. The Civic Forum and its Slovak counterpart won handily. Throughout the region that summer, the air was electric with change, reform, and new beginnings. The papers presented at the Congress reflected the positive atmosphere. But like all new beginnings, it takes time for seeds to bear fruit, and the first flowers can appear a long way off. The papers presented here mirror the uncertainties and doubts that accompanied the end of the democratic honeymoon and present a sober assessment of the chances for ameliorating the region's serious environmental problems any time soon.

The chapters that follow address the current uneasy time of transition in a similar pattern. Each attempts to explain why and how the old regime brought such environmental destruction, why and how the opposition utilized the environmental theme to bring down the communist government, and what new legislation and organized action on the part of environmental groups are needed to remedy the existing negative environmental conditions.

These problems are arranged under two separate categories and treated on a country-by-country basis: legislation or environmental remediation from the top down, and the environmental movement, or environmental remediation from below. The authors are specialists in the area or government officials from the East European countries, Russia, and the West. The mix of authors was deliberate. While the Western experts base their analyses on observations from outside the system, the East European and Russian specialists write from their life experiences within. The tone and seriousness of the chapters vary widely from the ironic humor of Sandor Peter of Hungary and Evgenii Shvarts of Russia to the drier scholarly prose of Michael Kozeltsev of Moscow University and Evaldas Vebra of Lithuania's Department of Environmental Conservation.

There may be objections that not all the countries of the region are represented here. Attempts to secure the participation of Bulgarian and

Romanian experts were frustrated by difficulties in communication. Nevertheless, the problems discussed in this collection of essays may be considered representative of those faced by all the new democratic governments in developing effective environmental programs.

Several common themes run through all the chapters. First and foremost, while admitting the validity of the more general categories of problems causing environmental deterioration, such as inefficient use of energy, old plant equipment, forced use of coal for fuel, and poor enforcement of environmental regulations, all the authors insist that environmental degradation must be seen as endemic to the communist system *qua* system. The East European experts are virtually unanimous in the opinion that the command method of rule, or what East Europeans commonly call "real socialism," was the root cause of the environmental problems of their country. Szacki, Głowacka, Liro, and Szulczewska baldly state: "The ecological crisis in Poland and other countries coming out of 'real socialism' is the result of a disastrous doctrine of economic development implemented over the past 45 years." According to Peter, "The system of state socialism and its philosophical basis, the communist ideology, are factors of pollution themselves." Seserko talks of the "economic monopolies" in Slovenia, lulled into comfort under communist rule and practicing "barbarism" on the environment. According to Kozeltsev, "Marx and Lenin paid very little attention to environmental issues. . . . The protection of nature . . . was treated in the classic way, simply as a factor increasing productivity."

The Westerners share similar views, although expressed in somewhat different language. Fisher identifies the key features of the communist system as the exclusion of society from the decision-making process and the restriction of information flows. Censorship permitted the creation of what he terms a façade of order over a reality of disorder, which increasingly appeared in its environmental form. Kabala describes the system as one based on "the extensive pattern of development," which saw the creation of heavy industry and the achievement of import substitution as the road to socialism.

A second general finding is that the power of the environmental movement during the downfall of the system was more symbolic than real. First of all, the official mass organizations, particularly in Hungary and Czechoslovakia, had engaged large segments of the population in solid conservation efforts, and in the case of Czechoslovakia were increasingly taking on the role of environmental conscience, particularly in Slovakia. Second, in every country, by the mid-1970s, a core of environmental scientists had emerged with access to environmental data who were working within the system to put the environment on the political agenda. Finally, the unofficial environmental groups that proliferated after the Chernobyl disaster did not receive mass support until after other opposition groups had joined them and the environmental problem had been transformed into a political issue. Persanyi, among others, notes the existence of a great many unofficial environmental groups in the 1980s. Only one of these, the Danube Circle, received massive popular support, and only after the conflict over the construction of the Danube dams was transformed into an open political fight between the old regime and the opposition. Szacki notes the tactical role of the environment in the roundtable talks that led to the first relatively free elections in 1989, pointing out that the environmental talks were broken off by the opposition, not the government. Shvarts gives us a feeling of the public's perception of the political nature of the Soviet student environmental movement during the 1970s: "When every tenth poacher was a party, Soviet, or Komsomol official, . . . the work of the student groups was regarded as the embodiment of people's democracy, as the realization of societal control over the party and state aristocracy. . . ."

The symbolic role of the environmental groups as defenders of democracy was the principal reason in the minds of virtually all the authors for the movement's rapid loss of power and fall from public view. All the authors express disappointment with the new governments' prosecution of environmental problems. Election rhetoric notwithstanding, no government has yet undertaken any serious remedial environmental program. Several reasons are offered for the lack of government action: the priority of the economy, the need for stability to preserve democracy, the government's ignorance concerning the importance of a healthy environment for economic growth, the population's lack of awareness of environmental problems, the complexity of environmental issues.

Finally, both East Europeans and Westerners stress the importance of Western assistance in three critical areas: intergovernmental assistance, foreign financial aid, and help from the international environmental nongovernmental organizations (NGOs). Fisher pays particular attention to the role of the international NGOs in providing the stable organizational structure and financial base upon which NGOs in Eastern Europe and the former Soviet Union can build. Both sides apparently concur in the view that Western know-how, institutions, and money are the appropriate successors to the old Stalinist organizational and financial instruments. Only Seserko seems to reserve opinion on this matter. He chastises the big-business interests of Austria, Italy, and Germany on their eagerness to profit from the building of what he believes to be unnecessary and environmentally unsound highways. Eastern Europe's almost unquestioning acceptance of the Western political and economic model may be alarming to those who believe that current Western institutional arrangements must be radically changed if the world is to progress toward sustainable development. But the fact is that today, Eastern Europe especially looks towards Western Europe as the standard for the good life, and will not be content until it enjoys the same luxuries. The failure of "real socialism" has automatically been translated into the victory of "real free market capitalism."

More important than these similarities are the differences between the East Europeans and the Western academics. One difference is in the tone of their writings, and may be attributed to the impact of censorship in Eastern Europe. The chapters written by authors from the former socialist countries express more outrage, more frustration, in short, more emotion than do those written in the West. Kozeltsev talks of the "ecological crimes" of the old system that only now are coming to light, and categorically states that reform begins with access to information. In a few sparse phrases, Peter condemns a situation in which the state held a monopoly on information but in which neither the populace, nor the academics, nor the authorities had real or accurate indices of environmental quality and pollution. Szacki stresses the enormous propaganda effort undertaken by the former socialist regimes to convince people that pollution was the price to pay for industrialization. He forcefully describes the activities of official environmental agencies as "formal motions" that erected "a screen to conceal the antienvironmental policy of the government." There is real and deep anger over the way censorship enabled the regimes to erect a façade of environmental concern around approaching environmental disaster.

A second difference that separates the East European from the Westerner is the different perspective on recent history. Both sides see a watershed in the democratic transition, but East Europeans place the decisive moment within the context of the last twenty or thirty years. Shvarts, for example, speaks of the "democratic embryo" started by Khrushchev. Szacki, Persanyi, Seserko, and Shvarts trace the beginnings of the environmental movement to the 1960s. All insist that not only were environmental problems becoming visible by the 1960s, but that conditions were ripe to force them to the leadership's attention. The environmental legislation of the 1970s is seen as the result of this initial activism. Shvarts especially stresses that strategy and tactics developed by environmental groups under the old regime were inappropriate under democratic conditions. Before the changes, tactics were intrinsically linked with bureaucratic practices. The success of the student movement lay in revealing the environmental wrongdoings of officialdom because the bureaucracy systematically prevented the students from tackling real environmental problems. As a result, when the scientists in the student movement were coopted into the government, the students found themselves pushed to the sidelines, watching the scientific institutes assume the task of providing the much-needed environmental solutions.

Persanyi, Szacki and Shvarts all emphasize the role of strong personalities in the formation of environmental groups under the old regime, as well as the importance of single issues, particularly on a local level. Szacki's description of the sociopolitical nature of the groups may be usefully compared to Shvarts's description of the defenders of democracy. The fact that tactics for the environmental movement were developed in a situation in which environmental activism was considered subversive made it difficult for the movement to survive the transition to democracy intact. Hence, in contrast to the Western authors, the East Europeans tend to present the environmental explosion at the end of the 1980s as the culmination of a long process, not the herald of a new political regime.

Finally, the East Europeans provide valuable insight into the politics behind the environmental movement both before and after the democratic revolution. In Hungary and Poland, we see the inability of the various groups to coalesce and take joint action. Attempts are made to develop coordinating umbrella structures, but none is successful. While the strong personality of a group leader was doubtless a mitigating factor, over and over again, the East Europeans express in various ways the lack of trust between the groups. Far from erasing the distrust, transition politics seems to have increased it. There is no trust in the government. The East Europeans seem to concur on the inability of government to address environmental issues under the current unstable economic and political situation. But if the government cannot be looked upon as a source of redress, neither can any group apparently rely on another to initiate common action. On the contrary, each group looks at another's success or cooperation with a Western environmental group as proof of the power of money over environmental values. Peter, Szacki, and Shvarts are particularly illuminating in this regard. Jancar sees a lack of trust as a major reason for the failure of the Green candidates in the East European elections in 1990. The election results explain the reluctance of local environmental groups to cooperate among themselves, and they explain the passivity of the population regarding environmental issues after the transition.

We in the West who have never lived under a communist regime may comment on the system's success in developing anomie and a sense of isolation among the peoples subjected to it. Havel's "The Power of the Powerless" speaks to this very problem. People did what the regime expected them to do, just to be left in peace. Everyone acted the same way in public, so that you could not be sure of who your friends or enemies were except within a very small group of intimate acquaintances. Even then, as the opening of the East German Stasi records is showing, life-long friends turned on one another, husbands denounced their wives and wives their husbands. The climate of suspicion encouraged and fostered by the system made long-term organized political opposition difficult if not impossible. The rapid decline in influence of the East European environmental movement is testimony to the success of the old system in preventing the emergence of a strong and coherent opposition. The system was brought down by the brief and virtually spontaneous fusion of many strands of opposition, as people poured into the streets to demonstrate their frustration with their leaders. But when the demonstrations ended, the seeds of distrust sown under the old regime sprouted anew.

As we move into the murky world of who knew whom and who trusts whom, we begin to understand the enormity of the problems confronting the former communist countries in their efforts to build democratic societies: fragmented political parties, low voter turnout, absence of a strong victory for any one political party, splintered non-governmental organizations.

Facing the initial attempts at pluralism are the old bureaucratic structures, determined to hold on to power at any cost. As Seserko, Shvarts, and Peter make clear, they are not easily dismissed. They will use all their political wiles to transform their former political power into economic power, and in so doing, undermine any governmental effort to tackle the environmental problems. Their arguments are persuasive and common to every public contest of political will: We stand for order, for security, for jobs. The country does not need revolution, but evolution. Nothing should be done in haste, and so on and so on. In Moscow, some people are asking for the old days back. The conclusion is inescapable that a strong popular environmental movement with wide public participation is essential if the transformation of the political and economic structures of these countries is to be successful.

We thus invite you to read this book, bearing in mind the symbolic character of the pretransition environmental movement. The new directions in environmental management are all to the West, from the West, and, to a large extent, must be by the West. Moreover, they must be constructed on the ruins of a system in which powerful bureaucratic interests ran roughshod over individuals and institutions they did not like, as well as their countries' environment and natural resources. They were successful because they were able by force and propaganda to sow sufficient distrust to prevent people from organizing on anything higher than an immediate personal level, and by making knowledge a privileged commodity, to keep most people from realizing the full scope of the harsh reality around them.

Hopefully, the reader will come away with a better appreciation of the enormity of the task confronting both the peoples and the governments of Eastern Europe, and of the necessity to make the environmental issue an integral part of any solution. We may well share the pessimism about the future expressed in many of the chapters, but we cannot fail to endorse the optimism implicit in the East Europeans' determination to move forward.

Note

1. *Christian Science Monitor*, January 17, 1992.

PART I

Problems and Changes in Environmental Management

2

Political and Social Changes in Poland

An Environmental Perspective

Jakub Szacki, Irmina Głowacka, Anna Liro, and Barbara Szulczewska

The Anti-Ecological Policies of "Real Socialism"

The ecological crisis in Poland and other countries coming out of "real socialism" is the result of a disastrous doctrine of economic development implemented over the past 45 years. This doctrine was based on the principle of granting priority to the development of two key branches of industry: raw materials and heavy industry. The output of these two types of industry was used to fuel further production, mainly of armaments, rather than consumer goods. This emphasis on the expansion of industries turning out the means of production was promoted to the rank of an "economic law" of socialism that was used to shape the economy in its characteristic branch-trade structure, eliminate markets, and institutionalize central planning.[1]

The implementation of this principle led to the rise of a high energy-

The authors are associated with the Institute of Physical Planning and Municipal Economy in Warsaw.

and material-intensive form of industrial production with low efficiency in the use of available natural resources, causing systematic
deterioration of the natural environment. The functioning of this economic system, so harmful to the environment and human life, was
maintained by its inherently anti-environmental policies.[2] These bred a
legal system that, in land use planning and regulation, ignored all
interests other than those that catered to the siting of industrial installations. The economic sanctions that were adopted regarding the use of
natural resources and their impact on the environment failed to stimulate pro-environmental strategies in the operation of economic enterprises and played only a marginal role in their financial management
(some 1 percent). Moreover, the adoption of the global output of an
enterprise as the yardstick of profit assessment rewarded material-intensive economics that were more immediately profitable to enterprises than cost effective, pro-ecological policies. Such policies also
included the cancellation of expenditures for environmental protection
needs when these violated the reigning definition of investment effectiveness. Government waivers were always available to prevent the
enforcement of environmental regulations. In short, the system of legal
and economic controls rooted in economic voluntarism rather than in
market forces did not ensure the achievement of the state's environmental goals nor the citizen's right to a life in a clean environment.

Environment protection policies were viewed by the governments of
the socialist states as an unimportant element of economic and social
life. However, the increasing visibility of environmental degradation in
the 1970s began to obstruct economic development and provoked a
growing public resistance.

While the importance of pro-environmental policies was appreciated, in the socialist countries these policies existed mainly in a symbolic way in propaganda. In practice, there was a sharp contradiction
between environmental slogans and actual programs, and the constantly worsening ecological crisis was ignored. There existed various
environmental principles that were publicly declared to govern numerous fields of activity. In reality, however, economic policy favored the
continued expansion of specific branches of industry and hence determined the scope of environmental degradation. A very narrow approach to the concept of environment protection was adopted.
Pollution control was reduced to measures geared to prevent or eliminate environmental damage that affected industry. The message was

drummed into the public mind that environmental degradation had to be taken in stride as the price to be paid for accelerated industrialization if one wanted to reap the various benefits of civilization.

Until the 1980s the mouthpiece for this approach was the government agency responsible for environmental protection, the Ministry of Forestry. Instead of creating a conscious, rational ecological strategy linked to economic and social objectives, the ministry merely went through the motions, erecting a screen to conceal the anti-environmental policy of the government.

The few environmental organizations of the period were also just showpieces. The League for Nature Protection, the Polish Hunters Association, and the Polish Anglers Association carried on the 1918–39 tradition of a primarily conservationist approach. Although the hunters and the anglers associations declared themselves to be concerned with environmental protection, as a rule, neither the representatives of these organizations nor members of elite research institutes were appointed to sit on the relevant consultative and constitutional bodies in the government. Deprived of any opportunity to warn against possible environmental threats, environmental organizations were unable to influence government decisions. The regime's *modus operandi* precluded any real protest by environmentalists, and when such did occur, it was construed by officialdom as an activity that was hostile to Poland and that threatened to undermine the foundations of the system and its alliances. Environmental warnings and activities in the field of environment protection were a political problem closely controlled by censorship.

The Breakthrough in Ecological Thinking: The "Round Table"

The awakening of popular environmental awareness after the period of fascination with the development of heavy industry may be said to have begun in the 1960s, when the first echoes of "ecological shock" experienced by West European societies reached Poland. Publications on this subject were used by the government as propaganda to show the dark side of the capitalist economic system. The culmination was the release in 1969 of the famous U Thant report. At the same time, the perceptible deterioration of Poland's natural environment, coupled with the absence of official information on environmental problems, sparked public interest in the subject.

The next important period in the development of environmental awareness was the sixteen months in 1980–81 during which the Solidarity movement operated legally. It was a time of intense public political involvement accompanied by a marked relaxation of censorship and increased activity on the part of underground publishers. During this period, a substantial part of the public came to realize the scale of the country's ecological problems and the dangers involved, and the public achieved what was probably its first environmental success in post-1945 Poland. As a result of the August 1980 agreements between the government and the nascent Solidarity organization, one of the most noxious divisions of the Skawina aluminum smelting plant near Cracow was shut down.

Of primary importance for the awakening of public environmental awareness was the Chernobyl disaster and the considerable delay in the release of relevant information, especially in those regions either directly threatened or already contaminated by radiation. The information lag generated a veritable tide of fear regarding the effects of radiation and focused public attention on the problems of contamination in general. Public concern found expression in the inclusion of pro-environmental demands in the programs of opposition organizations, Solidarity in particular, and in the birth of grass-roots "unofficial" organizations that later obtained legal status.

The imposition of martial law in December 1981 may have hindered public action but did not end it. In the course of the next few years, opposition groups who had gone underground produced numerous clandestine publications. Some of these specialized in problems of environmental protection. In nearly every region of the country, activists secretly released and disseminated occasional or regular bulletins exposing the real state of the environment. They sought to explain the inside manner in which decisions had been made in the most glaring cases of abuse, involving the construction of industrial plants particularly harmful to the surrounding area. The sincerity and the clandestine nature of these publications contributed to their credibility as compared to the censored data carried by the official press. They also influenced the lawful media, forcing them to compete against the underground and increasingly to feature environmental problems.

Gradually, ecological problems developed into a unique "safety valve" issue for social discontent and were written into the program of the ruling Communist Party as one of the foremost social problems. Then, unofficial environmental groups obtained the right to exist openly. Permission to function legally was largely due to the increasingly active involvement of international "green" movements and to pressures exerted by West European states. As the pollution generated within their borders gradually became more manageable, these saw Poland and the other "socialist" countries as the largest source of air- and waterborne pollution. Increasing grass-roots pressure for political change in Poland ultimately led to the initiation of talks between the ruling team and the not yet fully legal opposition, known as the "Round Table Talks." At the talks, environmental issues were featured separately from the other political and social problems, and assigned to the Round Table Ecology Sub-Team. The government side was represented by members of the Ministry of Environment Protection and Natural Resources and invited experts. The opposition, or "Solidarity," side was composed of representatives of unofficial environmental groups and their experts. The official record of the sub-team debates contains the guidelines for immediate action that both sides agreed to. The opposition eventually tabled their demands, with the government representatives consenting to them (with one exception). The controversial demand on which no consensus was reached concerned the discontinuation of the construction of the Zarnowiec nuclear power plant. The guidelines that were agreed on and adopted were set forth in the "Proceedings of the Civic Committee to the Chairman of the IATU 'Solidarity'," no. 2, 1989 (in Polish):

1. The restructuring of the economy and its further development would take into account the protection of the human environment, natural resources, and the efficient use of energy.

2. Amendments would be made in legislation, and economic and administrative mechanisms established that would really promote environmental protection.

3. International cooperation in the protection of the environment and natural resources would be a priority.

4. A system of citizen involvement in environmental protection would be set up, which would provide citizens with access to information on the state of the environment and give them a share in all decisions regarding the economic development of their communes, townships, and counties.

5. The system of values would be changed to give natural resources the same ranking in the order of cultural values as the architectural heritage of the country.

The guidelines were intended to give citizens an opportunity to participate in shaping the natural environment and to persuade the government to take measures to ameliorate the disastrous environmental conditions. The itemization of the basic environmental problems and the articulation of the need to restructure the entire socio-economic system were important for activating the public and developing public awareness of the role environmental problems play in human society in general and in the country's future in particular.

The Round Table brought together twelve of the strongest grass-roots organizations. In the period immediately following, many new associations, clubs, and parties came into being. Their objective was to improve the state of the environment and help influence public attitudes toward an appreciation of the environment and a harmonious coexistence with nature. However, subsequent rapid political change that brought about a transition to democracy also brought economic recession and a restructuring of the economy. This process adversely affected the efficacy of the fledgling environmental groups. Some of the pressure that they could have brought to bear on the government was therefore lost. As a result, only some of the demands that had been agreed on during the Round Table were met. Others became irrelevant due to changes in administration and the transition to private property. In addition, no legislation or economic mechanisms are yet in place that are consonant with the new reality. Thus, in some respects the situation has become worse compared to the period before the Round Table Talks. Popular initiatives and environmental organizations continue to carry little weight apart from their opinion-making role.

The Grass-Roots Environmental Movement

The Polish environmental movement emerged as a typical protest movement.[3] Its chief characteristic is the highly disparate nature of its participants: Although the intelligentsia predominate, all social strata are present, members of the clergy, professionals, and local officials as well as ordinary people. The common unifying trait is the willingness to renounce violence. Two main branches of the movement may be distinguished: the "conservationists," motivated by fear of the aftereffects of environmental degradation, whose movement is sometimes dubbed the "ecology of fear," and followers of the "deep ecology" trend, who seek new cultural values, question the consumer life-style, and stress man's unity with nature.[4] According to Glinski,[5] the ecological movement in Poland, unlike those in the West, is more socio-political than cultural in nature. This feature is probably attributable to the specific character of the socio-political system in Poland in the 1980s rather than being a peculiarity of the movement itself.

Given the rapid changes that have taken place in Poland in recent years, it is difficult to provide a full list of grass-roots environmental organizations, let alone classify them. Changes in the country's political structure have been accompanied by changes in grass-roots organizations. Moreover, given the current "fashion" for ecology (often, unfortunately, only verbal), numerous organizations claim to be active ecologically that are actually not.

A recent study by Czajkowski[6] lists the following types of environmental organizations:

• 70 environmental non-governmental organizations (NGOs), such as the League for the Preservation of Nature, the Polish Ecological Club, Nature Conservation Guard, Pathfinders Environmental Protection Movement, the Polish Green Party.
• 60 organizations that list environmental problems on their agenda, mainly civic and professional societies (political, youth, tourist, religious organizations). These include the Polish Sailing Association, the Peasant Youth Union, Popular Knowledge Society, the Polish Tourist and Country-Lovers Society.
• 35 environmental groups: REFA, St. Francis of Assisi Ecological Movement, the Green Federation, Ecology and Peace Movement, "Wole byc" (I prefer to be), the Silesian Ecological Movement.
• 20 groups that include environmental concerns in their activities, such as WiP (Liberty and Peace), the ZEN-Czogie Buddhist Association in Poland, *Pomaranczowa Alternatywa* (the Orange Alternative).
• A dozen-odd environmental foundations.

The mushrooming of environmental organizations is generally related to the activities of certain individuals or milieux. The youth movement "Wole byc" came into being in Silesia as a result of letters to the editor of a weekly newspaper following its publication of a report on the devastation of the region, accompanied by an appeal to the readers. The editor's office helped the readers concerned to get in touch. Cases of local ecological danger have frequently stimulated the formation of environmental organizations. The Citizens' Ecological Committee at Darlowo is a case in point. Unofficial information kept secret by the government leaked out to the effect that a nuclear plant was to be built in the area. An information-gathering meeting of local people was broken up by the militia and the participants were detained, thus giving the people two reasons for protest. In the 1980s similar conflicts provoked by the arrogance of the authorities were very common.

The environmental organizations in Poland have six basic goals:

- to study environmental problems
- to educate the public
- to assess the nature of a threat to the ecology
- to form groups with a specific function, such as the monitoring of a given area. Good examples are the Biebrza Society and the Civic Committee for Protection of the Great Mazurian Lakes.
- to exert pressure on the authorities
- to change the public's attitudes toward nature

In most cases, activities undertaken by the environmental organizations are legal, for example, lectures, meetings, ecological church services, publications, legal consulting, cooperation with self-government bodies, "nature" activities such as tree planting. Some organizations have also engaged in illegal activities, such as unauthorized demonstrations and the blocking of access roads. Most of these unauthorized demonstrations have been against nuclear power plant construction, notably that at Zarnowiec.

Although the number of NGOs that have an environmental focus is high, "green" parties in Poland carry little weight. The Polish Green Party was the most politically ambitious and ran in the parliamentary elections. However, torn apart by internal strife, it splintered into three parties and hence failed to play any role in the elections. Aware of their slim chances at the polls, the two splinter parties refrained from campaigning.[7]

Other environmental parties did not participate in the campaign, claiming they had no interest in winning power. One such was the Green Federation. The Federation's political program included: an ecological perception of the world, the promotion of eco-development ideas, ecological and social security, the renunciation of violence, and demilitarization. The goal of the organization is what it terms "spokesmanship," or alerting the bureaucracy and public leaders rather than governing. The Federation's groups send their liaison officers to the Federation's coordinating committee, which is vested with two functions only: the exchange of information and the coordination of supra-local activity. Members of the Federation favor legal activities in the belief that attempts to secure permission to hold a demonstration serve to "educate" civil servants.

The Independent Party "Ruch Zielonych" (The Green Movement) embraces a different political concept. Its members do not plan to run in elections, nor do they consider themselves a political party. Instead, they demand the institution of a new type of authority, called "environmental authority," that would parallel the already existing institutions but be independent from the state administration. The concept is to be realized through a system of Environmental Dietines or assemblies (on the local, regional, and national level). These would conduct their activities in accordance with the Polish Ecological Program (the *sui generis* Ecological Constitution) and would be authorized to make definitive investment decisions.

Characteristically, the grass-roots environmental movement avoids any dependence on the authorities. Its reluctance to do so is based on experience: in the 1980s the authorities attempted to control the environmental organizations by establishing the Civic Ecological Movement under the aegis of the progovernment organization PRON. However, while extreme caution in forming relations with other organizations and the avoidance of formal structures within the environmental movement have enabled it to preserve its identity and to survive, they also have been major contributors to the movement's political weakness.

Conceivably, the emergence of a new, democratic government could have facilitated the operation of ecological pressure groups by opening up new opportunities for action to all civic groups. Unfortunately, these hopes have proved largely illusory. Although it is true that demonstrations are no longer dispersed by the militia, new problems have arisen while some old ones have persisted.

Many members of grass-roots environmental groups that were linked with Solidarity have accepted positions in the state administration and have lost interest in civic work promoting the environment. Although Solidarity itself greatly contributed to environmental protection in its initial period of legal operation (1980–81) and during martial law (e.g., by aiding in the release of underground environmental pamphlets), it no longer pays sufficient attention to environmental problems. In Parliament many members who were very vocal about the environment during their election campaigns became oblivious to them once they were elected. During the presidential campaign in the fall of 1990, environmental issues were almost completely forgotten. The ecological group in Parliament, which largely comes from various pro-environmental grass-roots organizations, is unimpressive in number and is constantly losing out to both the "pure" economists and the industrial lobby.

The proposed tax on gasoline is a case in point. This legislation would have funded the environmental protection fund, but it went nowhere. The program of debt-for-nature swaps could not be carried out to any satisfactory degree because some economic decision-makers considered it inflationary.[8] The "victory" over the Zarnowiec nuclear power plant appears to be a result of the country's financial problems rather than legislative concern for the environment. Recently a Sub-committee for the Support of Ecological Initiatives was formed in Parliament to oppose anti-ecological tendencies in the legislature and government.

Another obstacle diminishing the effectiveness of the environmental movement is what sociologists at the Institute of Philosophy and Sociology of the Polish Academy of Sciences term "the barrier of public environmental awareness."[9] The effect of this barrier is seen in the public prosecutors' inability to prosecute environmental offenders while government officials side with enterprises in their conflict with environmentalists. In addition, legislation on environmental protection is also imperfect. For instance, the 1980 bill on environmental protection permits NGOs to approach administrative organs and request the application of measures designed to eliminate a threat to the environment, repair environmental damage or prohibit activities endangering the environment. In practice, a restrictive principle has been adopted that permits NGOs to come forward only in situations where such a possibility follows clearly from other legal regulations.[10]

The environmental organizations' scope of influence is further limited by financial problems. The minimum outlay required annually for environmental protection stands at some 3 trillion zlotys. In 1990, the Parliament allocated 7 billion.[11] There is reason to fear that the reasonable proposals on the principles of environmental policy elaborated by the Ministry of Environmental Protection and Natural Resources, that are largely consonant with popular demands, will not be implemented.[12]

Environmental Awareness in Times of Political Change

The impact of the environmental movement on national environmental policy will depend on the level of public awareness.

It is difficult to gauge the state of public environmental awareness in Poland. Research since 1980 has produced a highly varied and incoherent image.[13] A survey conducted in 1988–89 enabled Burger and Stojek[14] to develop the following propositions regarding public environmental awareness in Poland at that time.

1. In the popular mind, instrumental environmental values rank highest (pure water, clean air, etc.).

2. People generally recognize, at least intellectually, that environmental problems exist.

3. The realization of threat goes hand in hand with very little knowledge of its causes and effects. The realization tends to bring a reaction of fear rather than a rational counterresponse.

4. The level of ecological awareness is closely associated with personal experience of environmental degradation in one's community.

5. There is a generally negative assessment and distrust of the value of government or official institutional action.

Since the survey was taken, there have been changes in all areas of public and private activity. These will not fail to influence Poland's environmental future and already are affecting the role that the state and government agencies play in shaping it.

New Directions in Environmental Management

If there is to be a new direction in environmental management, several conditions must be met. First and foremost, there will have to be a fundamental shift in national priorities, and development objectives will have to be reformulated so that ecology takes precedence over the economy. Poland needs to implement the ideas of sustainable development. Given the legacy of technologically backward and energy-intensive industries left by the previous regime, this kind of restructuring is certainly no easy task, particularly when we are in the midst of an economic crisis. However, unless we begin to restructure industry along ecologically sustainable lines, environmental degradation cannot be checked.

Second, environmentally friendly legal and institutional arrangements must be developed. The transition from a centrally planned economy to a market economy is fraught with new perils. The expansion of economic initiatives uncontrolled by appropriate, responsible, and authoritative agents of environment protection could lead locally to further environmental degradation. Suitable legal and organizational instruments are therefore necessary. Current legislative work seeks to amend our basic regulations on environmental management based on a mutually reinforcing set of goals:

1. A radical departure from the former declarative formulation of principles of environmental protection and a shift to practical directives backed up by concrete sanctions.

2. The recognition of a fundamental environmental protection strategy based on foresight and planning, compliance with the principle of the long-term use of the environment, a ban on further environmental degradation, implementation of "the polluter pays" principle, incorporation of environmental impact assessment (EIA) procedures, and compliance with international legal norms on environmental protection.

3. The introduction of the mandatory prosecution of polluters, irrespective of personal or legal interests.

4. The introduction of a "right to know" provision, giving the public general access to information on environmental conditions.

5. Extension of the jurisdiction and responsibilities of self-governing bodies, with respect to environmental protection.

6. Significant changes in the economic system linked to environmental protection.

The implementation of these assumptions in legal and institutional form will be a long-term process. But the halt to environmental degradation depends on the effectiveness, consistency, and adaptability of the new arrangements.

The third condition for the translation of the new environmental thinking into action is environmental education. This important aspect of environmental policy is still very much undervalued. It should be national in scope and should be included as an integral part of the formal curricula of grade schools, universities, and technical schools.

Public education via the mass media (radio, television, and press) should also be implemented.

Environmental education in Poland today earns rather poor marks.[15] The primary error lies in the very narrow way in which specialists in specific disciplines are trained. Since environmental knowledge by its nature is interdisciplinary, a different educational approach is needed to stimulate both the growth of the individual's creative and innovative abilities, and his capacity to grasp environmental processes at work.

Environmental Policy at the Local Level

Another condition for the implementation of new principles of environmental protection is the acceptance of responsibility for environmental policy by local self-government bodies all the way to the grass-roots level. There are two views on the future role of self-government in environmental protection. One view is that the best guarantee that due care will be taken concerning the environment are democratically elected local authorities, because they are most aware of the importance of environmental issues and are responsible for dealing with them. The other view holds that local government responds only to local needs and hence will only implement a local environmental policy that represents the convergence of interests of various local groups and organizations. An additional argument bolstering this opinion is the belief that many environmental problems cannot be appreciated or solved at the local level. The management of environmental problems in all their complexity thus requires a wider, regional outlook and supra-local action, including action by the central government. This view argues with justification that local government is not always ready, does not have the expert capability to assess the environmental impact of various economic activities, and does not have a uniform legal system adjusted to change in place. The transfer of decision-making from the center to the commune level thus opens up the possibility for various groups to organize and bring pressure to bear on local government bodies. In the absence of the availability of domestic capital, powerful foreign investors are increasingly moving in, supported by the local population demanding tangible economic benefits. Moreover, the dominant type of investor up to now has been the small industrial enterprises and small producers bent upon obtaining high and rapid returns. The result is the formation of groups indifferent to the value of protecting natural resources. In the struggle to obtain their objectives, these pressure groups tend to utilize environmental slogans even if they do not share the environmental thinking behind them.

A case in point is the current controversy over the site of a large housing development in Warsaw around a small lake that had originally been intended as a nature reserve. In the blueprint plans, the development completely hems in and isolates the lake. If constructed, the birds and plants are doomed, and the lake will disappear with the lowering of the ground-water table. To encourage buyers to acquire relatively low-cost real estate, the developers claim that the reserve will be protected and cared for by interested residents. Similar arguments are fielded by those involved in developing a large residential district in the woods inside a landscape park. The developers promise to redress the damage by constructing a sewage-treatment unit. Others would make up for the destruction of a park in the city center by planting trees in a national park elsewhere in the country.

Grass-roots environmental groups, particularly those which have sprung up in the wake of decisions by local government to curtail all economic activity in their area, have also resorted to such demagoguery. The felling of one or two trees is blown out of proportion and claimed to be a problem of ecological devastation, while the clearing of vegetable allotments in the center of the city becomes a "crime perpetrated on the body of living nature," even when the area is to be turned into a park. While spontaneous grass-roots environmental groups greatly benefit the environment and contribute to "ecological ethics,"[16] their use of demagoguery for their own self-interest or for settling personal accounts is immoral and saps their credibility. The only way to avert such behavior is to restructure the legal system in Poland as swiftly as possible and to engage in universal environmental education while simultaneously expanding the use of expert services.

The Need for International Agreements

The disastrous environmental conditions in most of the former Council for Mutual Economic Assistance (COMECON) countries coupled with their overall economic weakness precludes a rapid improvement. Poland has a multitude of problems to solve and enormous financial requirements if the country is to implement the most basic environmental protection program. Similar problems have surfaced in other postcommunist countries or will do so once the information ban of official censorship is lifted on the state of the environment and hazards to human health. Poland's frail nongovernmental environmental movement needs to contact stronger ones in Western Europe that are functioning more effectively. Their experience should be tapped and used to solve problems such as stopping the entry of foreign toxic waste into Poland. There are other problems that need the cooperation of not only governments but also the public, for example, the siting of a highly harmful industrial plant just outside the country's border in Stonava, Czecho-Slovakia.

World industry's ever-newer technologies keep creating ever-newer chemical compounds, often unknown in nature. This process calls for the evolution of ever-newer methods of neutralizing emissions and waste. The East European countries are lagging behind in neutralizing old technology waste, and are even less equipped to cope with the new ones. Without adequate knowledge and experience the nascent environmental NGOs will be incapable of realistically predicting the effects of economic restructuring or monitoring the government's environmental policies. If environmental groups cannot exert the necessary kind of pressure, the feasibility of environmental improvement could be postponed into the future. International contacts, joint conferences, and the exchange of expertise between environmentally aware companies and neophytes could bring this future closer.

Conclusion

Given the plight of the environment in Poland, its protection should become top priority for the government as well as for the public. Unfortunately, this is not the case. There are two views on the ways and means to counteract environmental threats, which are not necessarily mutually exclusive. According to the first view, the success of environmental protection is linked primarily to the progress of technology. According to the second, the resolution of the civilization-versus-the-environment conflict depends on profound changes in our system of values and public attitudes. Even if the former view, which gives more weight to technology, is closer to the truth, the key factor, decisive for the success of our efforts to save and protect nature in Poland, is the simultaneous promotion of ecological awareness among the public and the economic decision-makers.

Heightened awareness will multiply the number of those concerned with environmental matters, thereby enhancing the popular environmental movement, which, under the present democratic regime, has gained more space for pressuring the authorities on environmental issues. Such pressure is indispensable for saving what can still be saved and for redressing the damage already done. The Ministry of Environmental Protection and Natural Resources and the other official organs in the national government are dominated by the industrial lobby. An effectively functioning "environmental police" that can tackle the enormous task of improving environmental conditions in Poland has yet to appear.

Notes

1. A. Delorme, "Stalinowski paradygmat rozwoju a kryzys ekologiczny" [The Stalinist Paradigm of Development and the Ecological Crisis], *Aura* no. 10 (1990): 9–11.

2. K. A. Dobrowolski, A. Jankowska-Kłapkowska, B. Prandecka, and P. Trojan, "Polityka ekologiczna wybranych krajow socjalistycznych" [Environmental Policy of Selected Socialist Countries], in P. Trojan, ed., *Polityka ekologiczna krajow socjalistycznych* [Environmental Policies of the Socialist Countries] (Wrocław: Ossolineum, 1989), pp. 103–76.

3. P. Gliński, "Ruch ekologiczny w Polsce" [The Environmental Movement in Poland], in P. Czajkowski, ed., *Ruchy i organizacje ekologiczne w Polsce* [Environmental Movements and Organizations in Poland] (Warsaw: PAX, 1990), pp. 5–43.

4. Gliński, "Ruch ekologiczny"; also *Aura* no. 10 (1990).

5. *Ibid.*

6. P. Czajkowski, ed., *Ruchy i organizacje ekologiczne w Polsce* [Ecological Movements and Organizations in Poland] (Warsaw: PAX, 1990), pp. 1–11.

7. *Przeglad techniczny* no. 44 (1990).

8. See *Przeglad techniczny* no. 49 (1990).

9. Personal communication from A. Wyka of the Institute.

10. See A. Wasilewski, "Ustawa a praktyka" [The Law and Practice], *Aura* no. 10 (1990): 31.

11. *Przeglad tygodniowy* no. 9 (1990).

12. E. Garscia, "Polityka ekologiczna" [Environmental Policy]. *Aura*, no. 11 (1990): 2.

13. T. Burger, "Uwagi o świadomości ekologicznej" [Remarks on the Environmental Conscience], *Przeglad powszechny* no. 12 (1986): 374–89; P. Gliński, "Świadomość ekologiczna społeczeństwa polskiego, dotychczasowe wyniki badań" [Ecological Conscience of Polish Society: Results of Existing Studies], *Kultura i spoleczeństwo* no. 3 (1988): 183–96.

14. T. Burger and T. Stojek, *Wstepna koncepcja programu edukacji*

ekologicznej [Preliminary Concept of Ecological Education] (Warsaw: Ekoplan, 1990, printed manuscript), p. 15.

15. *Ibid.*

16. W. Szymański, "Kodeks podstawowych zobowiazań etyki ekologicznej" [The Code of Ecological Ethics], *Aura* no. 1 (1988): 15–16.

3

New Directions in Environmental Management in Hungary

Sandor Peter

Introduction

At the time when I began writing this paper[1] the economic and social system of Hungary and of all Eastern Europe was entirely different from what it is now. I was honored to be asked to present this paper in 1989, when there were "socialist" countries in Europe even if under various "reforms." Today, most East-Central European countries have pluralistic, democratic governments, and they seem to have given up the idea of communism and even socialism.

The idea and practice of Marxist socialism has disappeared from Europe, with a few exceptions. Most of the changes in economic systems cannot be called "reforms" any more, because the current systems are not the same ones that existed in 1989. A definite and uniform change in the social, political, and economic system, often a quite sharp "right-turn," can be observed in countries like Hungary, Poland, Czechoslovakia, let alone East Germany, which no longer exists. Other countries, like Romania and Bulgaria, show more ambiguous, slower, and less sure directions of transformation.

The author is a research consultant based at the International Management Center in Budapest.

Unfortunately, unlike the changes in the field of politics, the transformation in environmental management seems to be unclear. In this chapter I shall give an overview of some of the possible and most likely changes and directions for environmental management in Hungary as a result of the current course of social and political events. My focus is on some controversial issues at the very turning point of the system, related both to micro- and macroeconomic aspects of environmental management.

Environmental Pollution under State Socialism

During the forty years of communist rule in Hungary, environmental pollution became a major problem. Unfortunately, it was not seen as such at the government level. Although environmental issues were always paid lip service, especially from the late 1970s on, in general, East Europe was in fact the most polluted region on the continent in the era of state socialism.[2] Today, eight of the ten most polluted European cities are in this region, in spite of the fact that the countries of East Central Europe are industrially and economically less developed than those in Western Europe. There is a great deal of data that document the tragic environmental condition of Eastern Europe, whether the issue be air, water, or any other element of the environment.

The cause of this situation verging on catastrophic environmental degradation may only partly be attributed to the obsolete technology used. To state the problem more precisely, it is not the final reason. The system of state socialism and its philosophical basis, the communist ideology, are factors of pollution themselves. This is, of course, a strong statement that requires more explanation.

The myth of the superiority of central planning and state ownership has gradually evaporated as time has demonstrated it to be a set of axioms resting on the pillars of Marxism rather than on proven facts. The falling out of favor of central planning ran parallel with the progressive failure of socialism. Some socialists in the West and in the East argue that socialism has not failed since it never really existed. In opposition to this view, we maintain that socialism did exist and that it failed. This position seems to be a reasonable one until a long-term and desirable socialist system is observed somewhere in the world.[3]

The official belief was that protecting the environment was in everybody's interest. But in fact, just like property, it was in nobody's interest. The rationale for existing pollution was usually that "the theory is basically right but there are still some secondary, practical, political, human, external factors and problems that have to be overcome." The superiority of planning over the "chaos of the free market" was often cited, and perhaps, "perfect planning" in theory would be superior if it existed. The superiority of "socialist" environmental planning and management was also proclaimed. But in fact, socialist environmental management proved to be less efficient than that in developed market economies, and considerably less effective as well.

Some people in favor of socialism might argue that it is very easy now to blame the old regime for present problems. In the first place, data and facts prove that environmental quality in Eastern Europe as compared to other European countries is worse now than ever before. In the second place, many of us warned the socialist government years ago of the seriousness of the situation, and the government paid no attention to the warnings. We are not, therefore, just blaming the old regime but also pointing out the weakness of state socialism from the environmental point of view.

The Old Regime and Environmental Degradation

During the period of state socialism environmental quality was decreasing at a faster rate than in market democracies at a similar level of economic development for the following reasons. These reasons are obviously not independent but, rather, various phenomena of the overall structure of the state socialist economy.

Quantitative Growth in a Centrally Controlled Economy

The growth of production is the major goal of planning and management even if formal documents state differently. Not only environmental controls but stricter controls on economic costs are disregarded if growth is the focus. The roots of the growth strategy lie in the very ideology of socialism. Kornai's "soft budget constraint" theory supports it, too, with the addition that environmental constraints are naturally even "softer" than economic ones, making the exploitation of the environment even more relevant. The strategy was especially obvious in the era of industrialization in the 1950s. The result was, doubtless, fast economic growth, but society paid an enormous price for it. From this point of view, the mere fact of central control over the economy is important; there does not have to be formal central planning as such. A less formal yet dominating form of central control, such as a system of political and social "expectations" on the part of one's superiors, can have the same effect of disregarding real social costs.

Closed Social and Political System

Neither the population nor the academics nor the authorities were really and fully aware of the social costs of the growth of production to society's well-being. They were especially ignorant of the real and accurate indices of environmental quality and pollution. This lack of knowledge is partly due to the traditional socialist "mystique" of handling such "strategic" indicators, and partly the inefficient system of national statistics. Information was in general monopolized.[4] Even last year the municipal authorities of Budapest refused to make public and display daily air quality data for the downtown area, arguing that "there is no need to cause panic." Such an attitude is typical of political paternalism where one group of people is supposed to "know better" what is good for the people and what is bad. In addition, lacking democratic institutions, people never had the chance to question authority or have any significant control over environmental measures. In this situation, where there were neither reliable data nor open channels for the public to act, environmental management was left entirely to the mercy of higher authorities whose preferences—as was mentioned above—did not favor environmental quality.

Inverted Economic Structure

Among other factors, the requirements of military development and the ideology of "iron-and-steel" led in the 1950s to the support of the heavy industrial sectors of metallurgy, machinery, and building and construction at virtually any cost. Not only plants but whole "socialist cities" were built upon this policy. These industries were highly polluting and, what is more, perpetuated pollution. Once built, these enterprises were never able to modernize because they never had enough money to do so. They thus continued to operate with obsolete, polluting technology. It must be understood that this obsolescence is not a result of bad marketing and business activity but of the central policy that created them for the sake of growth at any cost.

Closure to Foreign Markets

Closure to foreign markets caused basically two problems. First, products and technologies were not forced to compete with more modern and "cleaner" ones. Second, currency was not convertible, so hard currency was a scarce resource distributed by the central authorities. Under these conditions, enterprises received little funding for the importation of "nonproductive" goods, like pollution-abatement technologies, since these were among the last on the list of priorities. Enterprise managers had to bargain and fight for extra resources, and they were unwilling to spend precious bargaining power on obtaining antipollution monies, because pollution control was of secondary importance from the point of view of the major goal: the physical increase of production.

All the above factors and their effects are rooted in the fundamental ideological principles of Marxism-Leninism-Stalinism, and the various modifications of communism. Taken together, they precipitated a virtually unlimited growth of environmental degradation. Naturally, environmental protection was always part of formal plans and declarations. Many bills and acts were passed regarding the environment. But the mere analysis of official documents alone would lead the researcher to a dead end, if he was trying to document environmental efficiency in the past system. Even the Constitution proclaimed the "right to a clean environment." (Free speech and thought were also rights in each of the socialist countries.) Sadly, the citizen never was able to enjoy or use the right to a clean environment, because the system gave preference to quantitative economic growth over quality of life.

In addition to the systemic reasons for environmental degradation, there were, of course, more general ones. These included mismanagement, lack of incentive, lack of education. But the systemic factors were the dominant ones. Consider the case of leaded gas as an example. In the West, even if one could argue that its consumption is "just in the interest of big corporations," unleaded gas is widespread, whereas in "well planned" Eastern Europe it is very rare.

The Environmental Problem in Hungary Today

Let us take a quick look at some representative environmental problems in Hungary, whose environment is well known to be miserable.

Hungary is a small country, similar to Portugal in both area and population. It lies in the middle of Europe, and it has very good agricultural resources.[5] But forced industrial development under the influence of the systemic factors described above have caused such a degradation of the natural environment that today 11 percent of the area of the country is declared to be dangerously polluted. Approximately 40 percent of the population lives in these regions. Some calculations estimate that the damage caused by pollution amounts yearly to about 4 percent of the annual national income.[6]

Air pollution is very significant in most of the cities, especially in Budapest. The major cause of air pollution in most cities is heavy industry, but Budapest has a Los Angeles–type problem: traffic. The crowd of cars circulating through the narrow streets can hardly be eliminated. The only possible solution is to encourage consumers to replace the old and inefficient Soviet and East German cars with more efficient automobiles that work with unleaded fuel. This type of change requires time because the majority of the people cannot afford even a small Western car.[7]

Water pollution is most visible at Lake Balaton, which is now primarily a tourist recreation area for foreigners. It has become too expensive for Hungarians. There is another problem that, although not so spectacular, is more important for rural people: the lack of potable water in several hundred villages. Water in many places is of bad quality, and people are supposed to use the better water supplied by the regional government. However, in most of these small, underdeveloped villages people are quite uneducated and do not understand the importance of pure water and continue using the "good old" local wells. The persistence of this practice has caused in some areas significant health problems, mostly among children. This phenomenon is now beginning to change thanks to information carried by the much maligned television, which is the only entertainment of these people.

Soil erosion is a major, typically underestimated problem in a country that is preparing to base its economic future on a well-developed food industry. Soil erosion has a long-term, strongly negative economic effect that is not often emphasized even by the "green" movement. In general, the popular environmental movements have tended to focus on some contemporary regional or local issue, like the Danube dam, or on air pollution or industrial waste. This latter is becoming more important because up until now it has been left virtually unregulated.

The concentrated "socialist" style of development in certain regions has tended to let environmental, social, and economic problems pile up in so-called "crisis zones." These are principally the northeast industrial zone, the northwest with its mining and chemical industries, the southwest mining region, and the Budapest agglomeration itself. In these areas pollution, unemployment, and low income develop and increase simultaneously with shrinking capital.[8] Furthermore, because of the lack of decent communications and a road network in these regions, Western capital cannot be expected to flow in either. The improvement of these areas demands comprehensive development strategies, and these are now being worked out.

In 1989 the ruling Socialist Workers Party fell apart, and with its fall went the communist regime. In the first free elections as many as 62 political parties and movements fielded candidates to run for a parliamentary seat. Out of these, only six parties ultimately reached the "big house"; the rest did not receive the necessary 4 percent of the vote. The elections were won, with a significant margin, by the Hungarian Democratic Forum. The Forum originally started as a movement of democratic opposition forces, but gradually it has turned into a right-of-center Christian Democratic–type party. The Forum formed a majority government in coalition with the Christian Democrats and the Smallholders. The liberals (in the American meaning of the term) remained in opposition. These were the Free Democrats, the Young Democrats, and the Socialist Party.

The first free elections thus brought a uniformly center-right, quite conservative, and rather populist government to power. Since then, privatization has been in progress with the concomitant liberation of prices, foreign trade, and similar measures. (Mandatory central planning was abolished in Hungary in 1968!) Private ownership is permitted virtually everywhere, and foreign capital enjoys privileges in taxation and in many other areas. State firms are being turned into corporations, and stocks are sold both on the newly opened Budapest stock exchange and in Vienna, Austria. The extent of the transformation makes it impossible to describe the changes in Hungary as "reforms." This is not a communist regime turning social democratic, but quite a new system.

From the environmental point of view, the populist tone of the government program is important, because populism is associated with supporting rural as opposed to urban development. The new government emphasizes the role of agriculture, rural areas, rural development more than the socialist did, and probably more than the opposition would do. However, the same government inherited economic conditions that are very hard to manage, no matter which parties are in power. These adverse conditions make change slower than many people would like to see.

Several macro- and microeconomic conditions in the economy constitute the main obstacles to the new efforts to improve environmental quality. First and foremost on the macroeconomic level is the country's international debt, the per capita amount of which is the highest in Europe (about US$2100 in 1990). The second factor is the inherited obsolete economic and technical structure connected to the steel, metallurgy, and chemical sectors of heavy industry. The third most important problem that I would emphasize is the extremely poor communication and transportation network. The three macroeconomic problems are accompanied by the lack of foreign currency, or, stated another way, the lack of convertibility of the Hungarian currency.[9] Disequilibrium is about to disappear with the boom in private enterprise, and shortage is usually limited to shortage of money.

These circumstances may continue to represent serious obstacles to more efficient environmental regulation. The principal goals of current economic policy are to reach some kind of equilibrium and stability and, at the same time, repay the debts. Everything else is subordinate to these. Although there is regulation mandating the "best reasonably available technology" for new plants, circumstances may cause the national or local government to allow virtually any foreign industry to operate in Hungary, even if its environmental standards are not what they should be. In other words, the country may encourage developed Western countries to export their pollution to Hungary, at least to some extent, in exchange for reducing debts. Such a situation is highly reminiscent of the use of "green energy" by certain South American countries, the negative effects of which are felt decades after the decisions were made!

There are additional problems at the microeconomic level. Apart from the multitude of old and bad cars, which cannot be helped because people just do not have enough purchasing power no matter what favorable taxes and tariffs are implemented, the bulk of air pollution is coming from the huge plants of the big state enterprises. These can be privatized only slowly because they are neither profitable nor structurally modern. Moreover, they have large debts and an old, large, hardly convertible stock of machinery. The machinery is often so obsolete that it is technically impossible to find the proper pollution-reducing equipment for it. And developing such equipment would cost so much that it would not be worthwhile paying anyone to do it.

Perhaps an even tougher obstacle is the survival of the "socialist" managerial behavior pattern. Unfortunately, this pattern is not restricted to managers of big state firms. Many managers have carried their old behaviors and routines to new firms and corporations. The old pattern relies on utilizing personal and institutional connections. It is a product of state socialism, where connections used to be the normal way of gaining more economic and political power. As long as these behaviors persist, economic incentives and financial regulation are much less efficient than they should and could be.[10]

The same holds true for environmental regulation. The present system of air pollution control relies on effluent standards and fines, and is based on self-reporting by the polluting plants. Many economic studies point out that this is not an efficient system even in a free-market economy. Under conditions of self-reporting, even profit-motivated, free-market firms are likely to "optimize" the allocation of resources by reporting false pollution data. Furthermore, because of the persistence of the old management routines, through smart bargaining there is always the chance to "explain" the bad results and make the authorities cut the fines drastically.

Another microeconomic problem that is also part of the behavioral pattern is the fact that pollution fines do not significantly affect a firm's financial position. This is only partly due to their rate or amount. Another reason is that, just as in other former socialist countries, in Hungary the currency is not even "internally convertible." Although this problem is slowly disappearing, overall economic and financial regulations are obsolete and overly complicated. One forint has different practical values in different areas, and there are separate funds for different types of expenses. In this system investment is the hardest to realize. It is still easier to pay the fine levied for pollution than to turn the same money into investment. Since pollution abatement usually needs investment (the marginal profit value of which is quite low), firms do not spend money on it even if they can afford to, but rather spend it on production equipment if they can. This is another issue that will only be solved with full convertibility, when money will be just money without external restrictions on its use.

Actually, quite ironically, inefficiently working state enterprises can plan their pollution fines quite efficiently: First they calculate their expected net profits. From this they compute the money left after they cover all the necessary payments, and then they calculate their fines.

In summary, it appears that, besides the macroeconomic problems like debt, inflation, and regional inequalities, the old obstacles are rooted in three things: behavior patterns that can be changed only by the practice and requirements of the new economic system and not by some sort of "education"; regulation, or rather, regulation that is the product of legislation; and monetary development. This latter seems to be a key question from many points of view. A stable, strong, convertible currency could eliminate the problem of internal convertibility and could reinforce the power of regulation. As long as the currency is not real money and is not convertible, costs are not real costs. The power of any regulation is perforce limited, because the goals of managers may actually be quite diverse. Furthermore, disequilibrium is parallel with undervalued money.

New Directions in Environmental Management

The foregoing has been a brief overview of the economic and environmental conditions inherited by the new political system. Now let us look at the possible direction the new government may take and the chances for better environmental management.

The government of Mr. Antall seems to set the following priorities for its current economic policy: (1) stabilization and stopping inflation, (2) privatization and the promotion of new private ventures, (3) obtaining funds and handling international debts, (4) handling mass bankruptcies and unemployment, (5) regional development and inequalities.

The order of these priorities may change, but they all definitely take precedence over environmental considerations in the country's present situation. Making the forint convertible is especially important because it is an essential instrument to reach other goals. Right now a brand-new, comprehensive Environmental Act is under preparation and it will hopefully be taken to the Parliament early in 1991. Unfortunately, not much is known about it yet.

Indirectly, the environment does enjoy certain priorities. One such factor is the popular and rural orientation of the governing coalition, mentioned earlier. In supporting rural development, the new government supports the improvement of conditions in rural and agricultural areas. These improvements are closely connected to more efficient environmental management.

In the fall of 1990, an interesting situation developed. When local elections were held, the opposition liberal parties won in most places! So today the national government is conservative and the local and regional governments are liberal. Liberal parties emphasize environmental protection a great deal, and now they have gained power in most of the problematic, polluted big cities. Thus a sort of "division of labor" has occurred, in which the right-wing conservative national government (which has its basis in rural areas and small towns) is more responsible for the rural environment, and the problematic big cities are left to the "left": "Let's see what you can do with the air of Budapest." The division has produced results: in many cities the new mayors have restricted motor vehicle traffic in the historic downtown areas.

The new regional and local governments will have much more power and independence than they have had before now. They have the right to levy local taxes, which they did not have before, and to issue or refuse permits for certain types of businesses. Of course, independence means that local governments will receive less money from the central budget, so they will be obliged to raise funds. Once again the danger is that they may be willing to sell out some areas to whichever business pays, and then use the tax revenue to neutralize the negative (pollution) effects of the same business.[11]

It is still too early to say much about the actions of the new governments as they have been in office only a short time. But on the basis of their first two months of activity, they appear to show more definite environmental concern than the former ones, independently of party status. In rural areas and in the villages, where the Christian coalition won, more money has been more frequently allocated to water and sewage treatment systems, and in liberal urban areas, more concern has been given to traffic problems and public waste disposal. Thus, from the standpoint of environmental management, the "division of labor" between the big political groups is proving to be quite efficient. However, it must be emphasized that the picture may change entirely after the two forthcoming new laws are passed: the law on self-government and the comprehensive law on environmental protection.

Privatization and foreign capital, of course, may have a different impact. As was mentioned, the encouragement of new enterprises has high priority and may have a negative effect, or at least may neutralize other positive environmental efforts. Probably, entirely new environmental regulations will have to be elaborated after the law on enterprises is passed, because the regulations now in force are not suitable for private enterprises operating under market conditions. It is very important to keep in mind that under the old regime environmental regulation was ineffective because the economic system itself was not working. Thus, a new market economy and democracy hold out the possibility for the first time of improving environmental management. But to realize these improvements is, again, a difficult task.

On the whole, I am pessimistic for the short term and only slightly optimistic for the long term. In the short run, much cannot be expected in the way of environmental improvement in Hungary because of the very strict priorities of economic policy. A collapse of the economy must be prevented at all reasonable cost. Preventing collapse and stopping inflation are the two paramount short-term tasks. Hence, whatever new environmental law may be enacted, the old rules of behavior cannot be expected to change on either the macro or the micro level.

On the other hand, if and when the country achieves a stable democratic market economy, the importance of effective environmental management can be expected to rise sharply. Efficient environmental management cannot exist without an efficient economy. Poverty, we well know, is the most significant source of pollution. Finally, when short-term economic survival is no longer at stake, the democratic political system will encourage different movements and groups to express and promote the environmental agenda.

At present there are two positive signs: the increased role of local government, and the increasing role of monetary policy and taxation as opposed to direct regulation. Moreover, where profits govern economic activity, these can be influenced more directly than in the "soft" political economy of socialism, where nobody really knew what to regulate. Private owners are responsive to profit changes and these can be a point of reference.

Nowadays we Hungarians are often warned by some American colleagues not to have illusions about the market economy. We do not have illusions. "Socialism" has proved to be much more an illusion. Robert Begg told us in Hungary: "Don't sell your soul to the devil . . .

Or if you do, at least make sure you get a good price." Since we do not have anything else to sell, we follow his advice. This joke underscores the nature of my pessimism. The optimist believes that we are living in the best of all possible worlds. The pessimist is *afraid* that we really *are* living in such a world.[12]

Notes

The preparation and presentation of this paper was fundamentally supported by the Great Britain/East Europe Centre, London. Since it would not have been possible to present the paper without the generous help and support of the Centre, I am especially grateful to the Director, Alan Brooke Turner, and his colleagues. Further thanks are due to Barbara Jancar-Webster as well as to the Center for Regional Studies in Hungary, each of whom supported my participation.

1. At the time of writing of this paper (1990) the author was an Economic Advisor on the Board of Economic Advisors for the Prime Minister (Jozsef Antall) of Hungary. However, the article represents the personal views of the author and has no relation whatsoever to government views or policies.

2. I prefer to call these former systems "state socialism" in order to preserve the name they called themselves ("socialism"), and to distinguish them from socialism as the word is used in the West, e.g., Swedish, British socialism.

3. In my view a socialist system is feasible if it is working or existing and at the same time (for the people inside and outside) desirable, and not only temporarily but in the long term. However, as a common joke of the 1980s put it: "It is not true that there is no socialism at all. There are not one but two kinds of socialism: the working one and the existing one. Fortunately, the working one does not exist, and the existing one does not work."

4. Another common saying was that the rulers of capitalism monopolized factories and banks, and the rulers of socialism monopolized information.

5. Hungary has always had very good agricultural potential, and in contrast to some other communist countries, has managed to utilize it, too. Even in the communist era Hungary was the only net grain-exporting COMECON country.

6. We must note here that another 2 to 3 percent of the national income is estimated to be lost because of the lack of decent communication and transportation systems. Hungary ranks next to last in Europe in number of telephones per 1000 persons. Now, when the country wants to attract foreign capital, this may mean even more loss since the inefficiency of the telephone and road networks discourages foreign investment.

7. For example, in 1990 a two-year-old Ford Escort cost as much as 600,000 forints, which represented about 2.5 years of the average net family income!

8. We even were supposed to be proud of these super-industrial-concrete-jungle monsters of socialist development: the "socialist city."

9. This situation hopefully will be resolved in the near future. The forint is convertible now in a very limited way: basically for entrepreneurs, mostly for foreigners. As a joke puts it, again: There is half-convertibility now, because you can buy forints for dollars any time. Nevertheless, the ratio of the black market

rate to the official rate always shows the strength of the currency. Now it is quite low, about 1.25–1.30 to 1.

10. There are good examples, too. One of the most successful new multimillionaire entrepreneurs is a simple man who used to be a blue-collar worker ten years ago. Last year he bought a steel plant for hundreds of millions. That plant was to be shut down, because nobody saw any possibility of solving its technical and financial problems. It was an old plant employing a few hundred workers, whose lives were lived in a crisis zone and who depended on the plant. Mr. Petrenko not only made the plant profitable, and raised the workers' incomes by 30 percent (an outstanding raise in Hungary), but from the profits he opened a chain of department stores. It is just a small detail that this new tycoon happens to be a new representative in the Parliament sitting in the rows of the Socialist Party.

11. Another example: With the total elimination of censorship in Hungary, pornography boomed in 1990, openly and without inhibition. Now there are the first signs that people have had enough of it. Citizens have formed movements against it. However, the brothels and massage parlors pay good money to local governments who badly need funding, and thus waver between allowing and prohibiting them. It seems that in Budapest some districts will allow them, others not. They can decide independently of Budapest's Council. Unfortunately, independence now usually means lack of money.

12. Some people say a pessimist is just an optimist with more information. Unfortunately, while I was finishing this paper, the Gulf War broke out. Nobody knows what may happen, but if Saddam Hussein were to explode all the Kuwaiti oil wells it would cause a climatic catastrophe for half of the world, and any other environmental problem could be insignificant.

4

Environmental Management in Czecho-Slovakia

Eva Adamova

Environmental protection is regarded as one of the major problems that Czecho-Slovakia must face. The effectiveness of environmental activities depends among other things on the implementation of various economic, legal, administrative, technical, and other instruments that can promote or hinder environmental protection. This chapter first introduces a brief survey of the state of the Czecho-Slovak environment. We then discuss in detail current legal and administrative aspects of environmental management in the country today.

The State of the Environment in Czecho-Slovakia

Czecho-Slovakia is among the most polluted countries in Europe. The country at the same time is also an important "exporter" of emissions. The level of water, air, and soil pollution is considerable. In some regions of Czecho-Slovakia, northern Bohemia or northern Moravia, for example, the situation is critical. The air quality is impaired mostly by sulfur dioxide emissions, less by nitrogen oxide, carbon dioxide, and particulates. One of the main causes of these emissions is that

The author is a legal scholar at the Institute of Public Administration, Czech Academy of Sciences.

energy production is based largely on the combustion of fuel high in sulfur. Because of these emissions[1] more than 50 percent of forests in Czecho-Slovakia are dead or dying, and this trend is expected to continue in the following years. The water is polluted by insufficient waste treatment, an excessive application of industrial fertilizers, and by oil accidents. The extent of soil erosion and its declining quality is apparent too. It is the result of ill-judged building, mining, forestation, and sometimes ill-conceived farming methods.[2] The deterioration in environmental quality has had a negative impact on human health. The population's health is getting worse and resistance to various diseases, primarily on the part of the younger generation, is steadily declining.

The current problems of environmental protection are closely connected with the economic and administrative system of the previous political regime. They are visible evidence of the lack of commitment on the part of the former leaders to address environmental issues with more than declarations of intention only.

The high level of environmental degradation was the result of a distorted economic structure. After World War II the Czechoslovak economy was oriented to heavy industry. The undue emphasis on this branch of the economy together with the development of a command, administrative (bureaucratic) system of economic management led to excessive depletion of natural resources and unreasonable consumption of energy. Although there was clear evidence that environmental conditions were deteriorating, state subsidies for the necessary environmental investments were very limited.

The adverse circumstances under which environmental protection had to be implemented is well illustrated by the lack of environmental information. What might be called a state embargo on environmental data persisted virtually up until 1988. Access to these data was highly restricted and in many cases they were kept secret. The shortage of information was also a consequence of the absence of a comprehensive system of environmental information. The appropriate communications technology was nonexistent. Since 1989, public access to environmental information has substantially improved through increased publication of environmental data. But the information distribution system still is not what it should be.

At the end of the 1980s, changes in East–West relations brought changes in the political and social domestic climate. The government began to pay more attention to environmental issues. Some legal, administrative, and financial measures were taken,[3] but they were not nearly enough, and could not succeed in removing or even mitigating the environmental damage we still have to face today.

Despite severe political restrictions, there were several environmental movements that were quite active under the former regime. Various nongovernmental organizations (NGOs) in the Czech and Slovak republics tried to promote nature protection, and to a certain extent they played the role of pressure group. It stands to reason that they were regarded as an undesirable and suspicious opposition. The current position of the environmental movement might seem rather surprising at first. Under the new political conditions, the NGOs have much more opportunity to express their opinion freely and to play a more important role in environmental protection. In actual fact, they have not taken advantage of these opportunities.

There are several explanations for this development. First, many of the people involved in those movements considered their participation as a form of protest against the totalitarian system. When the political situation changed for the better, they lost their motive for joining such organizations. Some of their representatives became politically active and went to work directly in the newly formed environmental agencies of the Czech and Slovak governments or in other administrative organs.[4]

The changing economic situation is a second factor which must be taken into account. The large majority of people in Czecho-Slovakia today seek economic and social security. Environmental problems do not now seem so urgent to them. It must be understood that the entire society is confronted with new and sometimes unexpected economic, political, social, and psychological conditions, and it will take time to reach a sound balance between social and individual needs.

Environmental Law in Czecho-Slovakia

Division of Powers

Czecho-Slovakia is a federation consisting of two republics—the Czech republic and the Slovak republic.[5] Relations between the federation and the republics are defined by the division of powers set forth in the constitutional act on the Czecho-Slovak federation adopted in 1968.[6] The primary aim of this act was to give both national republics more autonomy. Due to political developments following the Soviet occupation in the second half of 1968, this principle was abandoned. At the beginning of 1970, a process towards a more rigid centralization of power at the federal level started, and the federation became more formal than real.[7] Relations between the federation and the republics changed in 1990 with the passage of an amendment to the 1968 Constitutional Act.[8] The amendment gave the republics more power and expanded their jurisdiction beyond anything they had ever had before. Despite its seemingly positive thrust, its implementation substantiated the misgivings raised during parliamentary discussions that this solution to the division of powers would bring on new disputes instead of removing the old.

Until the amendment of 1990, the federation was responsible for developing legal regulations[9] for certain specified environmental areas only, namely, the protection of agricultural land, land use planning, and the building code. At the same time, however, the federation was entitled to intervene in republican legislation on environmental protection to ensure legal consistency and unity within the environmental codex. In other words, the federation exercised discretionary power of decision over whether a specific question would be covered by a federal act or not.

Under the new constitutional act of 1990 the legislative power of the federation was simplified, although the grounds for disputes were not eliminated. The federation now has the right to pass legislation, when the environmental question is of "principal importance." This general provision turned out to be rather questionable. There have already been several discussions as to whether a certain environmental act should be passed by the federal or republican legislative bodies.

In all other cases, each republic has complete responsibility for all legal and administrative rule-making and for legislation concerning the institutional arrangements for environmental protection within its borders.

Environmental Law

The entire Czecho-Slovak legal system is currently under major "reconstruction," and environmental legislation is caught up in this process. A considerable number of acts, decrees, and orders in virtually every branch of jurisprudence must be amended or replaced by entirely new legislation. This reconstruction is one of the prerequisites for the implementation of political, economic, and social change. The legislative bodies are under enormous pressure: they are expected to pass a large number of laws of very high quality in various areas as quickly as possible.

In 1990, about 450 acts, decrees, and orders were passed. However, in spite of the immense legislative work that has already been completed, few changes have been made in environmental law. As a consequence, most of the acts and administrative regulations issued before 1989 are still in force.

The sources for environmental regulation are found throughout the main branches of jurisprudence. In the first place is constitutional law. Under the Constitution of 1960, environmental problems were limited more or less to the protection of human health.[10] The state had the obligation to protect nature and scenic areas so as to provide a more suitable environment for human health. In the 1990 amendment to the Constitution,[11] the state's responsibility was broadened to include the consideration of adverse environmental consequences that do not directly affect human health. In the 1990 amendment, the state protects nature and the environment so as to promote ecological balance. The state further is required to guarantee the "appropriate" exploitation of natural resources. The fundamental rights and duties of the citizens toward the environment are set forth in the Charter on Human Rights and Freedoms.[12] The Charter states that everyone has the right to a favorable environment and to complete and timely information on the state of the environment and the exploitation of natural resources. In the exercise of his rights, no one is allowed to endanger or violate the environment beyond the limits set forth by law. The Charter is the first constitutional act to declare the right to a clean environment one of the principal constitutional rights. However, the rather vague language of the provision on the right to a "favorable environment" may become an obstacle for its effective implementation and may prove to be a cumbersome problem for the courts.

The main emphasis of all new legislation is on economic regulation. Most of the laws enacted before 1989 would make economic reform impossible. Economic reform is an area that demands strict but sound environmental ground rules. In this connection, the reform process itself contains both positive and negative incentives. The intention to change the structure of the economy, to limit the role of heavy industry, and to reduce energy consumption, among other things, coincides in principle with environmental protection. The danger connected with economic reform, in my view, is found mainly in the overly optimistic attitude that environmental problems can be solved through the mechanism of the market alone. It would be naive to rely on the willingness of enterprises voluntarily to restrict their economic activities should they threaten the environment. The aim must be to develop such environmental regulations that it would be more efficient, from the economic point of view, to observe these rules rather than violate them.

The new legislation so far has responded very little to environmental demands. Despite the detrimental effects of a polluted environment on economic development, little effort has been made to incorporate environmental parameters into economic legislation. Both of the two fundamental economic acts, the Act on National Economic Planning and the Act on Economic Relations between Enterprises,[13] paid little or no attention to environmental protection. After 1989, several new economic laws were enacted, but these still do not guarantee the observance of environmental norms. Some impose no requirements, others impose them in such a way that they can be easily violated or bypassed. Examples of the latter case are the Acts on Agricultural Cooperatives and on Private Undertakings of Citizens. Under these acts, the subjects must protect the environment against the detrimental impact of their activity and finance the removal of the damage incurred by this activity.

Another important branch of law, criminal law, contains no special provisions relating to environmental protection. Serious violations of environmental regulations therefore have been subsumed under a more general provision of the penal code.[14] The amendment of the penal code enacted in 1990 set penalties for breaking environmental laws and made possible the more vigorous enforcement of environmental protection. Anyone who is convicted of an environmental offense is subject to imprisonment for up to three years.

Environmental protection is regulated primarily by administrative laws that cover almost all principal issues. The large number of acts, decrees, and other administrative regulations deal usually with an individual environmental area or an aspect of environmental protection. To date, there exists no general act on environmental protection. Special regulations are in force for each of the environmental categories: water, air, nature conservation, agricultural and forest land protection, land use planning, building codes, noise and vibration, nuclear safety, and waste management. The only exception to this "branch" system is the Human Health Care Act passed in 1966. The act covers the protection of air, water, and land and other questions connected with the environment. The shortcoming of this rather comprehensive act is that it addresses environmental issues strictly from the point of view of human well-being. Pollution is looked at only in relation to its impact on human health, and the law pays no attention to other negative consequences on the environment.

The negative effect of this "branch" system of regulation is that individual laws provide legal protection for a particular environmental area to the neglect of other related areas. The implementation of such provisions brings about a clash of individual environmental interests, sometimes to the detriment of the area the laws are supposed to protect. For example, the legislation on the protection of agricultural land conflicts with, and in some cases negates, legislation on water quality and water use. These conflicts usually result from poor coordination during the legislative process.[15]

Despite its drawbacks, however, the branch system of environmental law cannot be entirely replaced. Even if there were a comprehensive act on environmental protection, it could not include all the necessary details. The point is to try to create greater consistency among the special laws and to find a balance between the individual environmental interests.

Most of the environmental laws now in force were passed during the second half of the 1970s, but there are several old laws that are still valid that do not meet the new strict demands for environmental protection.[16] Even some of the laws passed in the late 1970s do not adhere to an environmental philosophy, and protect the given environmental area from a more economic point of view. For example, the Agricultural Land Protection Act of 1966 (as amended in 1976) put the main stress on the preventing the reduction in acreage of agricultural land. Its primary purpose was to secure agricultural production, and the protection of land quality was neglected.

Second, some of the laws are regarded as progressive, but they do not fulfill their primary objective: improvement in environmental quality. The Water Act adopted in 1973 may be a good example. It defined very strict conditions for water quality in connection with wastewater discharge. At the same time, the act entitled the republican governments to give variances from the wastewater discharge limits under certain conditions. Since many industrial enterprises did not have the necessary wastewater treatment plants or the financial wherewithal to construct them, they could not meet the legal requirements and asked for a variance. The result of this situation was the issuance of several thousand variances by the government and a decline in water quality. The Water Act is a case of the failure to estimate correctly the technical and economic conditions necessary to the successful implementation of a law. In this instance, underestimation virtually negated the effects of legal regulation.

In the late 1980s, the former government became more aware of the true extent of environmental degradation and the inadequacy of existing environmental legislation. Some new laws on environmental protection were proposed. After 1989, the legislative drafters continued to work on these drafts. Thanks to the new political situation, stricter conditions and progressive provisions could now be included in the drafts. In many cases the drafters tried to incorporate some basic principles from European Community regulations.

The Waste Management Act is the first important environmental act to have been passed since 1989. An air quality act and a nature conservation act are being discussed in the legislature. A number of amendments and new laws have been proposed, including the Environmental Impact Assessment act, a water act, a forest act, and the comprehensive act on the environment.

Improvement of the legal instruments of environmental protection demands not only special environmental laws and their coordination, but also the strict enforcement of environmental provisions in economic legislation and in the other branches of law.

Public Administration and Environmental Protection

Division of Powers

The division of power between the federation and the republics is the basic framework not only for legislation but also for the public administration system. Up to 1990, the administration of environmental protection was concentrated in the republics, while the role of the federation lay mainly in the legislative sphere. Nevertheless, the federal administration was responsible for certain questions, such as nuclear safety, territorial planning, building, and the protection of agricultural land. In line with the process of centralization that started in 1970, the supremacy of the federation over the republics had its impact on the relative positions of the federal and republican administrations. The federal government had the general right to suspend or even to abolish the execution of a measure adopted by the republican government if it was contrary to federal procedure.

Under the new division of power in 1990, this rule was abolished, and the federal government no longer has the right to intervene in the activities of the republican governments. As regards environmental management, the federal government is now limited mostly to conceptual and legislative activity. The only exception is nuclear safety, for which the federation takes exclusive responsibility.

The Administrative System of Environmental Protection

The old system of administrative organs involved in environmental protection on both the central and local levels has changed considerably since 1989. Before 1989, no one organ was charged exclusively with environmental problems. Instead, environmental management tasks were performed by a variety of institutions. At the central level, several branch ministries or other central agencies were responsible for the administration of individual environmental areas (water, agricultural land, air, etc.). The same features inherent in branch-based legislation were typical of the environmental management system.

At the federal level there were only a few ministries involved in environmental administration. These were:

• the State Commission for Scientific and Technical Development and Investments (responsible for the administration of federal programs on environmental protection, international cooperation, and land use planning);
• the Federal Ministry of Agriculture and Food (responsible for legislative and planning policy regarding the protection of agricultural land);
• the Federal Ministry of Mining, Heavy Industry, and Electronics (responsible for metal wastes);
• the Czechoslovak Commission for Nuclear Energy (responsible for nuclear safety and radioactive wastes).

Other authorities, such as the State Planning Commission and the Ministry of Finance, although they had an influence on environmental management, did not play a really significant role in environmental protection. Agencies responsible for the administration of central planning and other economic issues mostly neglected environmental demands.

The sectoral system of administration was more characteristic for the republics. Here the responsibilities for the different environmental areas were divided in the following manner:

• the Ministry of Water Management and Forest Industry (responsible for the protection of air, water, and forest land);
• the Ministry of Agriculture and Food (responsible for the protection of agricultural land, fisheries, hunting, and veterinary care);
• the Ministry of Culture (responsible for nature conservation, protected land, national parks);
• the Ministry of Health (responsible for all aspects relating to the impact of the environment on health);[17]
• the Central Authority of Mining (responsible for the supervision of mineral resources);
• the Ministry of Building and Construction (responsible for land use planning and construction);
• the Ministry of the Interior and Environment (charged with the environmental issues at large and with municipal waste management).

One important consequence of this branch system was a strong tendency for each ministry to enforce its own special environmental interests regardless of the needs of the environment as a whole. The lack of coordination was felt intensely even by the ministries, and some of them concluded an agreement on cooperation concerning the exchange of information and assistance in pollution control.

Another significant feature of the previous system was the double function of the branch ministries. Many of them took responsibility for the protection of one aspect of the environment, but at the same time they had to ensure the economic development of their particular industry. For instance, the Ministry of Agriculture and Food was responsible for the protection of land and simultaneously was in charge of agricultural production as well. In making a decision, the ministry was customarily involved in an inner conflict if environmental demands deviated from economic interest. The prevailing tendency was to give priority to economic requests. Hence, the outcome of this inner dispute was known before the public decision was made.

The former institutional system also provides examples of the unsuitable division of environmental responsibilities. A case in point is the Ministry of Culture. The main tasks of the ministry were quite different from nature conservation and were directed toward culture, art, and the information media. The assignment of nature conservation to this ministry demonstrated that such an institutional solution was no solution at all. In some instances responsibility for one environmental area was shared by two or more ministries, For example, the administration of soil conservation was jointly shared by three agencies, the Ministry of Agriculture and Food, the Ministry of Forestry and Water Management, and the Ministry of Health.

The ministry of the interior and environment deserves special attention. The establishment of this ministry in 1988 was a result of the increasing focus at all levels of government on the need to solve environmental problems. The existence of the ministry is one more demonstration of the formal approach to problem solving that was the trademark of official politics. The only function of the ministry was to coordinate other central authorities in environmental matters, but the conditions and manner of coordination were not defined. The ministry's position was weakened by the fact that it had no special authority nor power to make binding decisions regarding environmental protection. This power was entirely in the hands of the branch ministries.

An important part of the Czechoslovak administrative system were the so-called deconcentrated (specialized) agencies. These organs are specialized on a certain issue and are subordinated to the responsible ministry or other central authority. These agencies deal only with the individual environmental issues assigned to them, and never consider environmental protection as a whole. A variant of the deconcentrated agency is the state inspection organs. These play the role of advisory and monitoring bodies in technical inspections for air quality and water management. Their power of decision making is highly restricted, and so their influence is comparable to that of the specialized agencies. However, they have more power and a broader area of jurisdiction, covering both environmental and economic assignments.

Formerly, the institutions responsible for environmental protection at the local level were the national committees. The committees were hierarchically organized from the regional level down to the district and communal level. They had administrative authority in many areas. In addition to environmental tasks, the national committees had responsibility for the economic, cultural, and social development of their territory. Although they occupied a prominent position in their area, they experienced considerable difficulties. Like local governments the world over, a chronic lack of finances often led them to become dependent on the financial, material, or technical support of the industrial enterprises settled in their territory. The close relations between them impacted negatively on the environment. If the enterprises did not observe environmental regulations and caused environmental damage, it is because the measures taken by the national committees against them were not as strict as they should have been.

The current system of local organs responsible for environmental protection differs substantially from the previous one. Responsibility has been concentrated, with a few exceptions, in a special administrative body—the Federal Committee on the Environment, the Czech Ministry of the Environment, and the Slovak Commission on the Environment. The position of the new environmental authorities is far from easy. On the one hand, immense environmental investments are required. On the other, economic policy has priority. Whenever these agencies propose environmental measures, they must expect to face the opposition of the economic ministries.

The Federal Committee on the Environment is charged with the preparation of the national environmental policy, international cooperation, and land use planning. It also oversees the administration of nuclear safety implemented by the Czecho-Slovak Commission of Nuclear Energy.

Primary responsibility for environmental protection is entrusted to the republics. The Czech administrative system differs somewhat from that of the Slovak republic. The Czech system is based on one special environmental body with broad authority. The Ministry of the Environment is responsible for the protection of water, air, nature, agricultural and forest land, and mineral resources. It further is responsible for the monitoring of mining installations and other extractive processes, geological research, and the technical and economic aspects of waste management. In addition, the ministry has the ultimate say in the Czech lands concerning environmental matters and administers the republic's environmental information system. The aim of this high concentration of authority was to ensure the necessary integration of agencies dealing with all environmental problems and an effective coordination of all measures taken in this area. Although the original intent seems eminently reasonable, it has one negative aspect. The ministry is the highest instance of appeal. This function has overloaded it with demands on its time to make decisions on separate individual cases. The time spent on these cases has an undesirable impact on its efficiency. The ministry should be engaged primarily in environmental management, strategic planning, and conceptual activities, while the individual decisions should be left to the lower levels of administration.

The Czech ministry has recently been charged with the preparation of a new law on the environmental control of mining. The intention is to provide the ministry with power to stop a mining activity if the level of pollution in a given area is too high. This right may be regarded as an important administrative instrument against environmentally destructive economic activities undertaken by enterprises. But any decision to close a mine will doubtless be highly influenced by political considerations and will reflect the relatively weak position of the Ministry of Environment and the general attitude of politicians toward environmental/economic trade-offs.

The authority of the Slovak Commission on the Environment is not so extensive because it does not include the protection of agricultural and forest land. These questions are governed by the branch ministries—the Ministry of Agriculture and Food and the Ministry of Forest and Water Management. Responsibility for the administration of waste management is jointly held by the Slovak Commission, the Ministry of the Interior, and the Ministry of Industry. The system of assigning responsibility for administering the various environmental areas to various branch ministries has not been eliminated to the extent it has been in the Czech Republic.

One common feature of the two republican environmental authorities is the strict separation of the environmental function from the economic function, with the latter being performed by the branch ministries (the Ministry of Agriculture and Food, Ministry of Forestry and Water Management). In addition to having one responsible central authority, the new institutional structure reflects the trend toward a more efficient and specialized enforcement system. The new system is based on the old system of "deconcentrated" agencies. The state inspection organs are to be transformed into authoritative agencies with the power to impose fines. The system of inspections in the Czech Republic will be made complete by the addition of further kinds of inspections—forest inspections, waste management inspections, and inspections for nature conservation. In the Slovak Republic, a special inspection for the environment was established; inspectors have enforcement powers in those areas that fall within the jurisdiction of the Slovak Commission on the Environment.

The administrative system at the local level has changed entirely since 1990. The three-tiered national committee structure has been replaced by a two-tiered system of local authorities.[18] As far as environmental protection is concerned, there are a few important differences between the Czech and the Slovak republics. In the Czech Republic, environmental problems are administered by the organs of local government that have succeeded the national committees at the district and the commune level. The Slovak system is based on special environmental bodies: the district and local environmental authorities.[19] This approach has turned out to be an imperfect solution at best and is supposed to be changed to a system similar to that existing in the Czech Republic.

Environmental protection at the local level faces several problems. One problem has to do with the position of the communes[20] as self-governing bodies and at the same time as bodies charged with administrative functions transferred to them by the state. In its capacity of self-governing body, the commune is governed exclusively by laws and administrative regulations (decrees, orders) that are generally binding. In the case of transferred functions, the communes are subordinated to a higher administrative authority, which can interfere in their activities through the use of internal instructions and other means. The Act on Communities[21] unfortunately provides no clear and precise boundary between the two functions. Such circumstances may give rise to disputes and obstacles that may impede the proper execution of environmental protection measures.

Members of the two-tiered local government are currently in search of more convenient administrative units which would more appropriately accommodate the geophysical, economic, social, demographic, and environmental factors that occur naturally in a given region. Those districts that were formed with no consideration of natural boundaries and other basic factors appear to have the most problems.

Finding a sound balance between a community's economic and financial capacity of local government and its urgent economic, environmental, and social (health care, education) requirements is one of the crucial problems facing local government. A major part of the solution lies in the formulation of clear and reasonable legal and economic regulations.

Conclusion

The extent of environmental degradation in Czecho-Slovakia is enormous, and we cannot expect that the situation will change in a short time. According to rough estimates it will take a minimum of several years to stop the process of deterioration and to make some progress in environmental protection. The prerequisite is to improve all the necessary instruments of environmental management, especially implementation and enforcement.

The legal framework for environmental management must define strict and unambiguous rights and duties for all public authorities responsible for environmental management and stern penalties for those who pollute or degrade. The law must be implemented by an institutional system in which each level has clearly defined responsibilities, sufficient power to enforce the environmental regulations, and the monitoring capability to see that the rules are obeyed. Legal and administrative instruments should be used in close connection with economic instruments. But above all, there must be a radical change in the individual's scale of values, particularly in his approach to the environment. This last may be at least as, if not more, difficult to "restructure" than our economy.

Notes

1. About 46 percent of sulfur dioxide emissions come from the neighboring countries, above all from former East Germany and Poland, to a lesser extent from West Germany and Austria.

2. Most of the land is still in private possession, although after 1948 much of it was taken away from private farmers and transferred to the so-called "common use" of the agricultural cooperatives. The loss of a close personal relationship to the land is thought to be another reason for this ill-treatment of the land.

3. The decision on a state subsidy of about 17.6 milliards of crowns for environmental investments assigned for a five-year period (1986–90) was thought

to be a great success. To compare this provision with the real demands—according to the estimation of the current Czech government, the necessary ecological investments for the next two years only (1990–92) amounts to 40 milliards of crowns.

4. All three environment ministers were members of the ecological movement.

5. There are three legislative bodies in Czecho-Slovakia: the Federal Assembly, the Czech National Council, and the Slovak National Council; and three systems of administration: the federal system and the systems of the Czech and Slovak republics.

6. Constitutional Act No. 143/1968.

7. Constitutional Act No. 125/1970.

8. Constitutional Act No. 556/1990.

9. That is to say, the acts and the administrative regulations, such as decrees of the government and orders of the ministries or other central authorities, that are of generally binding character.

10. Constitutional Act No. 100/1966.

11. Constitutional Act No. 100/1990.

12. Constitutional Act No. 23/1991.

13. Act No. 69/1989 and Act No. 109/1964.

14. Act No. 140/1961.

15. The laws are mostly drafted by the responsible ministry or other central authority.

16. For example, the Act No. 40/1956 on Nature Protection.

17. The responsibilities were fulfilled by the Chief Health Officer, established by the Ministry of Health.

18. The Czech National Council Act No. 367/1990 and the Slovak National Council Act No. 472/1990.

19. The Slovak National Council Act No. 595/1990.

20. The district authorities do not have a self-governing character.

21. The Czech National Council Act; the Slovak National Council Act.

5

Old and New in the Environmental Policy of the Former Soviet Union

What Has Already Occurred and What Is To Be Done

Michael Kozeltsev

Each country has a unique path of development. Just as no two people are exactly alike, each state has its own specific, if sometimes unclear, patterns of growth. In the USSR, economic development was subordinated in the main to political objectives. Resources were concentrated on certain priorities, whatever the cost of their fulfillment. Yet at the same time there was very little limitation on economic development. The anti-ecological character of development was largely determined by structural disproportions in the economy and the high cost of economic growth. The ecological crisis in the former USSR can also be partly explained by more general reasons: population growth, development of new harmful technologies due to scientific progress, lack of knowledge, and so on.

Marx and Lenin paid very little attention to environmental issues. One could conclude that the protection of nature (particularly in the area of land use) was treated in the classic way, simply as a factor

---

The author is an economist at Moscow State University.

increasing productivity. If the founders were still alive today, surely they would be subjected to sharp criticism both from above and from below. But seventy years ago, communist dogmas were steadfastly carried into life by the Party leaders. As a matter of fact, there was no consistent environmental policy in the former USSR, though there were certain significant achievements in some particular areas (the establishment of nature reserves [*zapovedniki*], for example). Accordingly, it is necessary to construct such a policy, first, by reconceptualizing the strategy for development of the common ecological space of the Commonwealth, and second, by radical structural *perestroika*.

These arguments form the structure of this chapter. Economic and institutional tools of environmental policy play an important, but subordinate, role based upon forms of ownership, the aims and tasks of development, and the economic and social relations among people.

The Heritage of Communism

Under the communist system, the degradation of the environment reached an extreme due to the implementation of the extensive economic growth model. Almost the entire map of the former USSR is covered by dark spots representing ecological crises or disasters. Altogether these represent about one hundred regions covering 3.7 million square kilometers, or 16 percent of the whole territory of the former USSR.[1] Given the size of the country and the scale of its industry (third in the world in terms of gross national product), it has had a significant impact on the global environment, depleting the world's natural resources and poisoning the environment with radioactive wastes.

According to official communist thinking in the USSR, the preservation of national sovereignty and the implementation of a successful national security policy depended upon the realization of certain basic economic policies:

• rapid industrialization and militarization of the economy (Khrushchev and Brezhnev as followers of Lenin and Stalin aimed to reach parity with the United States in some kinds of weapons and to surpass it in others);

• self-isolation and the effort to achieve a self-sufficient economy;

• high priority assigned to the production of means of production at the expense of consumer goods;

• "increasing the weight" of the economy through development of the raw materials sector.

The implementation of these policies led to disproportions that would not be characteristic in the United States. Today in the Commonwealth of Independent States (CIS) one can find old equipment dating back to the late nineteenth and early twentieth centuries, as well as ultra modern machinery. The old equipment is found mostly in the textile, light, and food industries (these industries are not among the most environmentally sound), and the new machinery mostly in the military sector.

The old equipment has become obsolete, causing many accidents and emergency situations that pollute the environment to a great extent. The large number of repair operations and an unstable technological regime contribute to the pollution.

The new machinery may discharge less polluting substances into the environment, but the potential threat to human health is much greater. Twelve years ago there was a disease called "Siberian ulcer" that led to severe illness and even mortality among inhabitants. There was ulcer spore leakage at the secret military plant for biological weapons production in the Chkalovsk region of Sverdlovsk (now Ekaterinburg). According to official statements, 64 people died. Nonofficial sources number hundreds of victims. Apparently the cause was a purely technological one—a break in a filter. The second outbreak of this "epidemic" produced 18 victims because of the lack of even elementary means of protection for the clean-up crews.[2] When one considers this situation and the similar one in Chernobyl, one understands the real value of human life in the Soviet military sector.

The militarization of the economy directly and/or indirectly led to the two greatest ecological catastrophes: the Aral Sea and Chernobyl.

The Aral Sea was a highly productive reservoir with over forty thousand tons of fish harvested annually. It was once a resort area, but its picturesque beaches are a thing of the past. Since the early 1960s, the area of the sea has diminished by one-third and its water volume has decreased 60 percent.

The Aral Sea disaster was the product of the "self-sufficiency" policy mentioned above. During the 1970s cotton, a strategic crop, totally replaced fruits and vegetables in the agricultural sector of the Central Asian Soviet republics. The priority given to producing this high water-consumption crop led to ecological catastrophe.

The RBMK-type nuclear reactor "came" to the civil service from the military sector. This type of reactor has some basic defects in its construction, and these evidently caused the Chernobyl catastrophe. It looks as though this disaster did not occur by mere chance. Ecological security was of very little importance for the military sector.

If we exclude economic and social failure and consider ecology alone, the collapse of the central planning system was inevitable. Contrary to the market economy, in the so-called "socialist economy" demand and supply curves do not intersect one another. A rise in supply leads to a rise in demand and to a permanent deficit as a result. So there are no limits except natural (physical) ones to the inefficient use of resources. The end result of this system is ecological collapse. If Western norms for resource use and energy consumption were applied, the country could produce the same amount of final product with half the intermediate product!

Demilitarization of the Economy

The cost of constructing one fighter plane corresponds to the money needed to build forty thousand drugstores.[3] But when money has already been invested in a military product, one should expend some additional effort in order to make it pay.

A great number of environmentalists in our country place great hopes on the reconversion process, although it is evident that nowadays reconversion takes more than it gives back.

The involvement of the Commonwealth in the market system, and the liberalization of prices and their stabilization at the world level, call for belt-tightening *and* a decrease in the level of consumption for the average citizen. But there is a positive element in the process. Reconversion has now become an irreversible process. In the past, before *perestroika* began, the Communist authorities were allowed to spend from 10 to 30 percent of the GNP on the arms race. At today's new prices this would mean the tremendous sum of $300 to $350 billion.[4] Clearly, there is no going back to militarization!

But the path to reconversion is a very difficult one as well. The financial costs and energy expenditures on the reconversion of chemical weapons are likely to surpass all the expense of their creation. All the reserves of mustard gas must be destroyed. There is no clear solution under current economic conditions to the problem of reconverting phosphororganic substances. Even if we manage to transfer all these dangerous substances to the civilian sector of the economy after significant processing, we would increase the total output of chemical goods by only a few percentage points.

As we have seen, there are a great number of technological, economic, and environmental considerations we must take into account. In the author's opinion, there are also two basic decisions that must be made if we want to accelerate the process of reconversion in the former Soviet Union.

First, we must remove from the military sector control of the military plants that could most usefully be reconverted. These need real economic freedom. Instead of such a rational course, the Military Commission on the Invention of New Military Weapons of the CIS Defense Ministry has assumed leadership of the reconversion policy! Again, attempts to provide reforms are made mostly from above, and do not depart from the old framework.

Second, there are many military enterprises (with a strict work ethic) that are just impossible to convert because of great economic cost. They must be closed. The government refuses to make this inevitable decision. Salaries account for just 20 percent of total military costs. We could keep paying the salaries and social benefits of the released personnel. Then, as experts estimate, the tremendous amounts of ferrous and nonferrous metal, plastic, and cloth, to the total cost of 100 to 120 billion rubles per year,* could be transferred to the civilian sector of the economy.[5] This transfer would also bring a tremendous ecological advantage, since the military is responsible for the major environmental threats, as I have already mentioned.

For a better understanding of the scale of the changes we have to make in reconversion in the former Soviet Union, just imagine a separate military state with its own secret cities, economic laws, and moral principles, but located in the same ecological space with the civilian state, consuming the same natural resources and polluting the common environment.

Today the situation is beginning to change. We have more information about past ecological crimes like the nuclear explosions in Kystim (Ural region) before the Chernobyl accident and radioactive waste graves in the aquatoria of the Baltic Sea and the Barents Sea. Reforms begin with access to information. In addition, we are starting to see the beginning of

---

*In 1989 rubles.

cooperation between managers of military plants and local nature protection committees regarding pollution control and pollution penalties policy.

The Conservation of Natural Resources

There has been a reduction in GNP in each of the independent states of the former Soviet Union. Extraction of natural resources has also decreased. Total industrial output according to the latest estimates has dropped 15 percent.[6] In the author's view, extraction of oil and coal has diminished an average of 10 to 12 percent. Only gas production has stabilized. From the ecological point of view, these developments have had a positive effect (for example, the level of pollution in Moscow has decreased). However, the difference in percentage of decline between industrial output and mining already shows the accelerated effect that further decreases in natural resource extraction might have on total industrial output. There is nothing strange in this tendency, as the economy has a very rigid structure mostly oriented toward domestic sources of supply (viz. the above-mentioned policy of "self-sufficiency"). It is not flexible in terms of possibilities for swift replacement of natural resources by artificial materials or changes in the structure of the raw materials it consumes. Imports from the former socialist countries of Eastern Europe have decreased by more than half and have ceased to be important. This fall in production cannot continue any longer.

There is no doubt that this process is a very negative one. Decline in production necessarily going hand in hand with the restructuring of the economy is a fairy tale interpretation of the current situation of the former USSR. Decline in production only extends the disproportions of the economy. Retail trade is the sector of the economy that suffers most. Turnover for the first three months of 1992 was 63 percent of the same period in 1991, largely because of the barter system that the enterprises prefer to use with one another.[7]

Stimulation of economic growth is needed now. It is rather naive to expect radical changes in the processing industries resulting in savings of energy and natural resources. These industries have come only a very little part of the way toward a market economy. The most effective, environmentally sound strategy is one of creating market conditions: privatization and decentralization.

Mining is the main sector in the former Soviet economy where radical changes are most needed. The economy is pressed for time.

Lack of advanced technologies is one of the main reasons that the former USSR will totally drain its reservoirs of oil by the middle of the twenty-first century. Privatization of oil extraction fields may be a premature act. As an intermediary step, they could become worker's collectives or be assigned as private property.

The Russian draft law "On the State Privatization Program for 1991" correctly, in the author's opinion, identifies subsoil resources located in Russia as appropriate objects of privatization, whereas enterprises of the energy complex may be privatized but remain under state control. The main indicator of the effectiveness of fuel resources extraction should be the coefficient of the percentage of the reserve pumped from the well head. In some cases this indicator stands in contradiction to the short-term maximization of profits. The coefficient still equals 60 percent, as it did in 1970. So, one can increase extraction more than one-third "simply" using advanced technology without further depleting natural resources.

It is clear to me that this number one priority in national development strategy cannot be carried out independently by the former *nomenklatura* directors who have gotten the chance to become owners of the oil fields.

A change in forms of ownership is not enough. There must also be a nationwide policy of close cooperation with the transnational corporations and Western governments. The so-called "Russian national patriots" and fundamentalists from the other independent states have to understand that a self-isolation policy is a way toward ecological collapse. There is a strong wish from the other side to cooperate, and CIS officials need to face the truth that the exploitation of fuel resources is the main sector of the economy that can attract significant investment from abroad.

As Robert E. Ebel states:

> Why do we continually speculate about the ability of the Soviet Union to export oil? First, we care about the level of Soviet oil exports because further declines in such exports will give OPEC more direct control over the world oil market. . . . Second, the Soviet Union must be able to earn hard currency if it is to meet its foreign debt obligations, and to present some semblance of credit worthiness to bankers and governments. . . . Third, and of equal importance, the development of oil outside the U.S. and away from the Persian Gulf would be responsive to one of the major elements of our National Energy Strategy.[8]

A policy of conservation of natural resources and the maximization of the extraction time period must become the basic criteria in the search for Western contractors on a competitive basis. Unfortunately, the mass media in the Commonwealth pay major attention to the profit issues.

Introducing these criteria means a complete rejection of the traditional acceleration policy in favor of a more balanced type of development. There are shifts in this direction. The Russian Ministry of Ecology and Natural Resource Use together with the Ministry of Fuel and Energy of Russia are realizing a joint project of minimizing the losses of oil and gas in the pipeline.

Innovation in Social Protection from Radiation and Other Environmental Hazards

Significant changes are taking place in the Commonwealth concerning the protection of human health from harmful influences in the environment. Because of the deep economic crisis the different forms of compensation are not very substantial in monetary terms, but there has been a fundamental change in the way of thinking about and approaching this problem. These changes are the concrete results of *glasnost* (openness) and the participation of ordinary people in the working commissions for solving nature protection problems.

In 1988, hard-line critics came out against the standard of 35 rem, defined as "the limit of the individual dose during the life span established for the control areas of the RSFSR, Byelorussia, and the Ukraine affected by radioactive cotamination as a result of the accident at the Chernobyl nuclear power plant," and adopted that year by the USSR Ministry of Public Health. This standard represents the lowest threshold of unacceptable risk, i.e., the limit of the dose per life span; if it is exceeded, residence is prohibited and people must be resettled to uncontaminated areas. So the standard was transformed into a special decision according to which a population receiving under 35 rem during its life span would not have to be resettled.[9]

Specialists, representatives from different public organizations, writers, and journalists then began an unprecedented antinuclear campaign. Deputies at all levels refused to adopt these standards and called for additional protection measures and compensation activities. As a result, different programs based on local conditions of radioactive pollution appeared in the hardest hit republics (now independent states).

These programs were a first step against the centralized command system. The second step was a moratorium on constructing nuclear power plants in some of the republics and finally the closing of the Chernobyl nuclear power plant by independent Ukraine.

The reader should not underestimate the radical nature of these political and social changes. Before Chernobyl there was Kystim, an unknown accident, and cancer diseases in Semipalatinsk (Kazakhstan) caused by underground tests of nuclear weapons. This proving ground has now been closed by a decision of Kazakhstan's president at the demand of the local inhabitants.

In the compensation policy for victims of Chernobyl the stress was placed on the differentiative approach. The compensation policy combined both money payments and natural benefits, including a provision for compensation of damage caused to the health of the population residing in the contaminated areas.

The victims of Chernobyl have priority in obtaining improved housing, such as a cottage in the countryside. Among the new forms of compensation is the construction or repair of dentures free of charge.

The author does not want to present a cheerful picture. All the negative elements of a poor society could be found in the Chernobyl case: bureaucratic formalism, corruption. . . . The point that gives hope is that the people of the Commonwealth are beginning to solve their social problems themselves on a cooperative basis.

Cooperation and initiative are ways to solve problems of social welfare on a local level. Slow progress in this sphere has been achieved through the joint efforts of working personnel, local inhabitants, representatives of the trade unions, and local deputies. All existing forms of compensation and benefits that are used now have been summarized by the author and presented in Table 1. They concern the personnel working in a hazardous environment as well as a local population living near a harmful production enterprise.

The benefits of this system lie in its complex approach to the health care problem. Usually a combination of these forms is used. The defects lie mainly in the lack of an adequate differentiation of benefits relative to heightened risk groups based on sex, age, social status, regional geophysical and climatic conditions, and other factors. Social policy must be more tightly tied to the level of risk.

The terms *level of risk, risk assessment,* and *risk management* are newcomers in the lexicon of top officials. Up until recently, although

Table 1

Different Forms of Benefits and Compensation Dealing with Health Restoration or Prevention of Risk of an Occupational Disease

Nutrition	Relaxation	Medical treatment	Money compensation	Other benefits
Milk distribution free of charge	Additional vacation from 12 up to 24 days	Additional vacation from 12 to 24 days	Salary raise or tariff	Improved housing conditions
Fruit juices & drinks free of charge	Providing vouchers to a sanatorium	Providing medicine free of charge	Change regional coefficients & bonus to basic wage vouchers for vacation free of charge	Providing privilege order for cottage in countryside
Carbonated water free of charge	Shortened workday (by 4–6 hrs) and work week	Periodic prophylactic treatment in an after-work sanatorium		Providing local preventive actions: maintenance of conditioners, coal filters
	Special break during workday		Transportation fare for vacation free of charge	
	Earlier retirement			

the level of traumas, work-related diseases, and mortality cases was high, the aim of the Soviet type of production was held to be the total guarantee of the worker's safety. The demagogic character of this appeal was typical of many useless slogans of the era of so-called "developed socialism." Most forms of compensation do not deal with risk level, because that can be treated as an indicator of the result of the implementation of different compensation and benefits. A decreasing risk level means the diminishing probability of damage to human health.

The author carried out one of the first studies in the area of compensation policy for heightened risk among coal miners in the Kuzbass region in 1985, but he could publish the results only at the beginning of 1991.[10] The studies were made at the production association dealing with coal extraction called Severokuzbassugol, which consists of 14 shafts with 17,000 underground workers who mine an average of 11 million tons of coal per year. The average annual level of risk of death in the association was found to be 12.8×10^4. On average, 12 to 13 out of 10,000 workers die each year. This level is higher than the level of risk in an atomic plant at normal exploitation, which ranges between 2×10^4 and 3×10^4, and it is six times higher than so-called ordinary risks (2×10^4) associated with conditions in everyday life: death as a result of traffic accidents, mishaps in homes, etc. If incidence of death is combined with severe trauma such as spine fracture or loss of limbs, then the risk rises to 17×10^4 per year. The level of death risk roughly corresponds to the U.S. coal industry average at the end of the 1970s (14×10^4). For all practical purposes, every half-million tons of extracted coal "costs" one human life. According to information available to the author on coal fields in the state of Kentucky, each million tons of extracted coal is the "price of life" of one miner.

On the basis of this data, a marginal level of risk (R_{mar}) for mortality cases may be established as a common social standard for different types of activities approved by the national legislature. It does not cover classes of volunteers accepting high-risk activities, like mountain climbing. But it addresses problems associated with the closing of those types of production most dangerous for human health. Compensation and benefit activities (mentioned in Table 1) can be used only when the risk level is between R_{mar} and 2×10^4.

A commission of experts began a study at the request of the Russian Parliament with a view to adopting a legislative act regulating protection policy for high-risk professions. One of the commission's tasks was to generalize the results obtained in different branches of industry.

Studying Severokuzbassugol the author estimated the "risk price" of an average coal miner, or as it is sometimes called, the "price of life," α, is as follows:

$$d = \frac{\Delta C}{\Delta R}$$

Where ΔC is the monetary assessment of all types of compensations and benefits (see Table 1) associated with high-risk working conditions;

ΔR is the loss of a full-value life: premature death (as a result of a death case, disability, a trauma received) as compared to the number of years "due" on average to a given birth cohort;

α may be interpreted as the physical loss of all functions of an individual, and loss of man-years associated with the partial loss of creative, intellectual, and muscular functions of the individual; these functions are brought—with the aid of expertly determined coefficients—to a linear form. This integral parameter for injury to health helps solve the problem under discussion as it takes account of the difference in age and sex and expresses the final effect that results when various harmful factors act upon human health.

Given fluctuations in the various variables, α in our example equals 19 to 42 rubles per day of lost life. This represents minimal social protection. Moreover, if a day of life of a coal miner "costs" 40 rubles, then a day of life of a nuclear power plant worker "costs" 100 rubles. Generally, variation in α over different branches of the economy ranges from 40 to 200 rubles per day. Surely, even a compensation of 200 rubles for a day of "underlived" life looks very, very modest.

Studies such as mine in the area of risk analysis constituted significant progress in the field of social policy. First, they demonstrated that there were no absolutely safe technologies and that each worker must understand the possible threats awaiting him. Consequently, the choice of profession becomes more rational. Second, governmental bodies, managers of enterprises, and trade union representatives can propose realistic and purposeful policies ensuring increased compensation for heightened risk. Third, nature protection and safety activities need real, not "paper," results regarding decreasing the level of risk of injury to human health. Fourth, we need to reach a common standard on an acceptable level of risk $R_{acc} < R_{mar}$ and to uphold this standard in realizing the principle of social justice, "equal compensation for equal level of risk."*

Economic and Institutional Innovations in Nature Protection

The most radical innovation of 1991 was the introduction of pollution charges in the former Soviet Union, including fees for the emission of hazardous substances into the atmosphere, discharges into the water, and solid waste. The pollution charge took the form of a charge per unit of *each* hazardous substance polluting the environment.

The author had the honor to be a leader of the scientific part of the pollution charges program in Russia. He can conclude that other independent states of the former USSR shared the same approach.

The tax collection principle was taken as basic. Pollution charges were differentiated by regions according to local ecological programs.

*acc = average cost of compensation.

They were estimated at a level that ensured accumulation of the necessary amounts of money for pollution abatement. Attention was paid to establishing appropriate fee levels that did not drain enterprise resources.

This approach, which has some analogies in Western Europe, seems to be the most reasonable in modern Russian conditions. First, the proposals to use economic damage caused by pollution as a base are not appropriate because (a) one cannot calculate the value of the damage very precisely, and this leads to endless debates between polluters and environmentalists, (b) current estimates of damage in Russia are so high that there can be no argument for total compensation of damage, (c) damage is usually calculated on the basis of losses to the national economy (this point was very popular in the 1970s), but when this practice is transferred to the market economy, one cannot identify any one institution representing the interests of the national economy.

Proposal number two was to maintain the pollution charge at the marginal cost of pollution control. It is similar to the American system. Within the context of such a system, it pays firms to invest to reduce pollution up to the point where the marginal cost of control is equal to the pollution tax rate.[11] Again, this approach seems to be inappropriate because of the underdeveloped market conditions and the yet unsolved problems of privatization. It is impossible to minimize the aggregate costs of pollution control using this model of pollution charges in the modern Russian economy when the state enterprises are still under the care of the state and still rely on state aid and financing.

Consequently, it was decided to use pollution charges to construct a new financial mechanism that invested in nature protection and was independent from the state budget. Because of differences in local ecological policy it was also decided to eliminate unified standards of pollution charges as fixed and compulsory for all Russian areas, although recommendations for calculating procedures and average estimates were kept. It was recommended that coefficients of potential threat to human health (toxicity, bad odor, etc.) be used for each substance during calculation of a pollution charge. The local nature protection committees have the right to increase the average pollution charge (if they find it possible to use it as an initial value) based on the location of a polluter (center of a city, countryside, etc.), climatic and landscape characteristics, possible synergetic effect, and so on.

This procedure allows for the more direct linking of money and resources with the goals of the regional environmental plans. New market mechanisms are present in the order of fund distribution. The practice of direct capital investments that existed earlier proved to be very ineffective, as investments for environmental purposes in the form of direct state donations were usually utilized only 40 to 50 percent or were wasted on different goals having nothing to do with environmental protection.

The total sum of pollution charges accumulating in a special regional environmental fund are distributed among the contractors on a competitive basis and on a credit order. That is why the regional environmental fund is usually under the sponsorship of the local nature protection committee and the local bank. Some enterprises may receive more money back than they paid in, in the form of pollution charges, but the level of responsibility increases.

Thus from 1991 on, economic methods in environmental policy have been given priority over administration ones. In the last six years ecological issues became the focus of public concern. In public opinion polls they rank fourth after such urgent social needs as nutrition, improved housing conditions, and health care. The peak of the green movement in the former USSR was in 1989–90. Now we can observe a certain decline in its activity for two major reasons: (1) The environmental, or green, movement in 1989–90 was part of a widespread movement for independence and national sovereignty in each of the former republics. After the dissolution of the USSR, the activists became involved in the political and social management systems in their own republics. (2) In 1990 the economic crisis deepened sharply. Some harmful enterprises and plant shops were reopened, after having been closed because of environmental alarm, to produce the necessary products. The lack of drugs may be partially explained by the drop in production resulting from the closing of pharmaceutical factories. The ambitious retooling plans of their managers came to naught because of the lack of foreign investment.

In general, despite the sometimes nationalistic and even chauvinistic character of slogans and speeches, the most well-known and outstanding public environmental organizations have performed their functions in a democratic manner, strengthening the new principles of the market economy.

The strengthening of state power in environmental protection is now well under way. The Russian Ministry of Ecology and Natural Resource Use has been given the control function in the field of rational use and protection of mineral resources, forests, land, and water. Duplication of air quality control inspections has been eliminated, and staff and equipment have been transferred from the former All-Union Committee for Hydrometeorology and Environmental Control to the new ministry.

These radical institutional changes provide the opportunity to treat the environment in a holistic manner, as a single object of management. The main point now is to improve the work of the ministry itself and to escape the danger of total bureaucratization and formality.

Similar to the American Council on Environmental Quality, the position of State Counselor for Ecology and Public Health has been established. He and his staff are subordinated directly to the Russian president. Their functions are to provide advice and long-term forecasts as well as to coordinate policy concerning ecological breaches and possible threats to human health.

We have made great strides in improving the economic and institutional mechanisms of environmental management. But radical changes can occur only after there has been significant progress in economic, social, and political life. The continuation of radical reforms is the way to sustainable, environmentally sound development.

Notes

1. *Moscow News*, no. 44 (November 3, 1991), 11.
2. *Izvestiia*, October 30, 1991.
3. The Hunger Project, *Ending Hunger: An Idea Whose Time Has Come* (New York: Praeger Publishers, 1985), p. 271.
4. *Nezavisimaia gazeta*, June 11, 1991, 4.
5. Ibid.
6. *New York Times International*, February 14, 1992, A6.
7. Ibid.
8. Statement of Mr. Robert E. Ebel, Vice President, International Affairs, Ensearch Corporation, "On Oil and the Former Soviet Union," before the Subcommittee on Energy and Power of the Committee on Energy and Commerce, U.S. House of Representatives, December 11, 1991, pp. 4–5.
9. *Environmental Management in the USSR*, (VINITI, 1991), 40.
10. *Gornyi Zhurnal*, January 1, 1991.
11. Robert N. Stavins, "Economic-Incentive Mechanism for Environmental Protection." Workshop in Application of Methods to Integrate Environmental Considerations in Economic Planning, 1–12 October 1990, UNEP–Center of International Projects of the USSR, p. 11.

6

New Directions in Environmental Protection Management in the Baltic States

Evaldas Vebra

For far too long a time, totalitarian socialism trumpeted its concern for the welfare of its people, but events proved it to be a system totally incapable of solving essential environmental problems. The over-centralized, monopolistic style of Soviet economic management must be considered the root cause of the steadily deteriorating ecological situation in the Baltic states.

Although this paper discusses environmental conditions in all the Baltic republics, its focus is on Lithuania. The situation in Latvia and Estonia is dealt with in less detail. Climatic conditions and the scarcity of species make Lithuania's ecosystems particularly sensitive to pollution damage. Pollution damage has had a great impact on Lithuania's environment because human economic activity is closely linked with natural and seminatural ecosystems, in particular, streams, lakes, and forests.

Annual airborne emissions in Lithuania are estimated at about 1 million tons (of pollutants), among them 443,000 tons of carbon dioxide, 188,000 tons of sulfur dioxide, and 112,000 tons of hydrocarbons. The

The author is director general of the Department of Environmental Protection, Republic of Lithuania.

proportion of traffic pollutants in the sum total of anthropogenic emissions exceeds 50 percent, the rest being from stationary sources. The largest share of emissions from stationary sources are those from power and heat generation; these constitute 34.6 percent of all emissions. Emissions from the construction materials industry comprise 21 percent, and those from the petrochemical industry constitute 13 percent. Among these latter are volatile organic compounds such as acetone, toluene, and methylene chloride.

A twenty-year-old ongoing study of air quality, together with meteorological data from the republic's six largest cities and industrial centers, provides the following picture of the status of air pollution in Lithuania. The main air pollutants originate from traffic emissions: the highest annual concentrations of dust, carbon dioxide and nitrogen oxide exceed by two to five times the legal amounts prescribed by law. The maximum concentrations of specific organic compounds (formaldehyde, phenol, benzopyrene) are two times higher than the legal limits. The volume of direct sewage and wastewater discharge into surface waters in Lithuania amounts to 450 million m/a,[1] of which 124 million m/a (27.6 percent) are nontreated, 114 million m/a (25–34 percent) are treated. Most of the polluted wastewater (396 million m/a, (or 88.1 percent), is discharged from 49 towns. Only 19.6 percent of all wastewater is treated. The total input to surface waters of Lithuania during 1989 was estimated at about 64,000 m/a of organic matter as BOD,[2] 48,000 m/a of suspended solids, 540 m/a of oil products, 7800 m/a of total mineral nitrogen, 880 m/a of mineral phosphorus, and 1000 m/a of metals (iron, lead, zinc, nickel, chrome). The wastewater of Vilnius and Kaunas, the two largest cities in Lithuania, is the main source of waste, comprising 58 percent of the total load.

Data collected from systematic monitoring procedures (covering the 54 main rivers, 5 biggest lakes, and 2 reservoirs) is used to quantify the state of Lithuanian surface waters. The State Geological Service has been performing groundwater monitoring in Lithuania since 1946. The natural hydraulic regime is studied at 49 key sites. The basic observation network has 168 observation points and the special observation network 125 points. Special hydrogeological[3] investigations of groundwater quality are based on regional and local data. On the regional level, groundwater is being studied at 50 different sites, distributed among 700 observation points, representing different geologic-hydrogeologic conditions and characterizing the impact of different polluting agents on groundwater quality. Information about underground resources is stored in data banks at the State Geological Service of Lithuania.

The state of Lithuanian surface waters reflects the interaction between atmospheric loading, catchment sensitivity, and the load of organic material as well as nutrients originating from wastewater. Fortunately, in Lithuania rivers and lakes with normal oxygen conditions predominate, and 4 percent of the rivers have a mean annual concentration of 13 parts per million.

Organic pollution is the main kind of pollution in the surface waters of Lithuania. The share of rivers with a low quantity of organic matter (BOD 5,[4] one or two times less oxygen than allowed by legal standards) is about 60 percent. Only about 3 percent of Lithuania's rivers are estimated as highly polluted: BOD 5, 35 to 50 times less oxygen than allowed by legal standards.

The state of the coastal sea areas of the Baltic republics is the result of both the state of the Baltic Sea as a whole and the effect of local pollution sources. In closed and shallow bays and wherever it is close to pollution sources, land-based pollution is the major factor. By contrast, in the open sea (the southern coast of the Gulf of Finland, the Gulf of Riga, Kursiu Bay, the western coast of Saaremaa and Hiiumaa), pollution conditions depend on the general pollution level of the whole Baltic Sea area. The organic substances carried to sea by municipal sewage have caused microbiological pollution in the coastal waters and have led to the closure of swimming beaches.

The substances most harmful to the ecosystem of the Baltic Sea today are nutrients, particularly phosphorus, nitrogen, and silicate compounds. The aforementioned compounds are carried to the sea by municipal and industrial wastewater via rivers as diffuse pollution from agriculture, and are also deposited from the atmosphere. The increase of nutrient concentration in sea water causes eutrophication or mass development of phytoplankton. Decomposition of algae consumes dissolved oxygen in water, and the oxygen concentration decreases to zero. During the period of zero oxygen concentration, hydrogen sulfide is formed. Since hydrogen sulfide is a poisonous gas, it destroys the bottom fauna.

Since both phosphorus and nitrogen concentrations in the whole Baltic Sea area indicate a growing tendency, our major task is to reduce the amount of nutrients discharged into the sea and to create no new pollution sources.

The monitoring of harmful substances in the Baltic republics' coastal waters is not yet satisfactory. Still, occasional observations suggest that their level is less high than that of the waters of the Baltic proper.

Lithuania's Environmental Protection System

Shortly after the restoration of Lithuania's statehood on March 11, 1990, the republic's entire environmental protection system was radically rearranged. Lithuania was the first among the European republics of the former USSR to reorganize the State (USSR) Environmental Protection Committee into the Department of Environmental Protection of the Republic of Lithuania, accountable to the Supreme Council of Lithuania. Latvia shortly followed suit. The old State Environmental Protection Committee was reorganized into the Environmental Protection Committee of Latvia, accountable to the Supreme Council of Latvia. These decisions were adopted with the specific aim of providing an effective way of eliminating the fundamental causes of environmental deterioration, stopping abuses of power on the part of the executive authorities, and solving deep-rooted environmental protection problems.

Regulations of the Department of Environmental Protection of the Republic of Lithuania have the force of law. The relevant legislation stipulates that the Department of Environmental Protection is the responsible state organ for all questions pertaining to natural resource management and environmental protection. Decisions adopted by the department that fall within its area of jurisdiction are binding on all ministries, local authorities, military units, and other legal entities and individuals. The department coordinates the elaboration of all normative legal acts pertaining to natural resources and environmental protection that may be proposed by ministries, departments, and local authorities. The department is further authorized to ensure the management of natural resource use and environmental protection throughout the republic, its coastal waters, continental shelf, and economic zone. It must preserve scenic and natural areas typical to Lithuania, including different types of terrain, ecosystems with unique environmental value, and natural monuments of scientific, educational, historic, and cultural significance. In the performance of these tasks, the Department of Environmental Protection of Lithuania implements a single unified policy embracing both natural resource use and environmental protection. It performs the following functions: It provides continuous monitoring of all natural resource use and environmental protection. When authorized by the Supreme Council of Lithuania and on its own initiative, it may prepare draft legislation, adopt normative acts on matters that fall within its jurisdiction, and approve standards for natural resource use and environmental protection. It also regulates and supervises the evaluation and exploitation of natural resources and determines the parameters of natural resource use. In addition, the Department of Environmental Protection regulates and supervises activities in all protected areas including the protected zones around natural monuments. It further manages state reserves, compiles and specifies entries of species that should be protected in the Red Book, determines requirements for ecological expertise and project coordination and performs those activities upon request. It organizes republican theme programs that relate to natural resource use and environmental protection and supervises their realization. It organizes, coordinates, and conducts complex ecological monitoring and research on natural resource use and environmental protection. It sets up a nature protection fund and administers the proceeds in compliance with the regulations of the state nature protection fund. It cooperates with foreign countries and represents the Republic of Lithuania in international organizations as well as meetings on natural resource use and environmental protection. Other functions include supervising the implementation of international agreements on environmental protection, systematically and publicly informing the republic's inhabitants about the state of the environment, and coordinating environmental education. When necessary, the department may implement other environmental protection measures.

The Department of Environmental Protection of the Republic of Lithuania is authorized to submit assessments and proposals to the appropriate bodies responsible for approving all projects involving construction, reconstruction, and prospective development and to hold up construction as well as reconstruction of projects in the event they fail to meet environmental protection regulations; and to restrict or hold up operations of enterprises, offices, and organizations if these violate environmental regulations, if environmental protection measures are not implemented, or if these operations do not meet legal environmental protection standards. The Department is authorized to submit to the Supreme Council of the Republic of Lithuania projects for state reserves, protected areas, and plans for the establishment of national nature parks. It may declare objects natural monuments and request damage compensation resulting from pollution and irrational use of resources. The department prepares and approves methods of damage assessment and environmental taxation. It reviews materials regarding civil violations of environmental laws and holds the guilty parties accountable according to legally established procedures. It issues permits for the exploration and exploitation of natural resources and for municipal and industrial waste storage, dumping, and the emission of hazardous substances into the environment. It sets national standards for the discharge of pollutants and issues permits for blasting and hydrotechnical activities. It is empowered to detain and inspect any ships and navigable vessels in Lithuania's interior and territorial waters and in the waters of the economic zone, regardless of the department or nation to which these vessels belong. The department conducts state monitoring of environmental protection, reviews all projects prepared by the government and all information from public agencies regarding natural resource use and environmental protection, and may appeal to the Supreme Council of the Republic of Lithuania to invalidate governmental acts if they violate environmental laws. Finally, it is authorized to obtain from the heads of enterprises, offices, and organizations as well as other individuals all necessary oral and verbal statements of intent, certificates, and copies of documents regarding natural resource use and environmental protection.

The Environmental Protection Committee of the Republic of Latvia performs virtually the same functions. In Estonia, there has been no real change in the management of environmental protection, as the Environmental Protection Ministry accountable to the government was in existence for some time prior to independence. At the present time, the Nature Protection Commission of the Supreme Council is discussing the possibility of the Environmental Protection Ministry being made accountable to the Supreme Council of the Republic, as it is in Latvia and Lithuania.

The Department of Environmental Protection of the Republic of Lithuania, in cooperation with the country's scientists, has developed a new approach to environmental protection. It follows from the obvious fact that environmental protection and natural resource use are integral parts of the evolution of the biosphere and human social development as well as being necessary to human economic and cultural activity. Each nation has a right not only to freedom but to existence in the natural and social environment that is most conducive to its physical and mental development. These rights determine the priority of environmental demands over commercial attitudes toward natural resource use. Present and future generations have an equal right to a clean environment and to natural resources. These must not be destroyed.

The restoration of Lithuanian statehood with its new political and environmental realities requires a new perception of environmental protection and natural resource use. From what has been said above, the natural and anthropogenic systems should function so as to provide the necessary background not only for social development and the rational use of natural resources, but also for the conservation and rehabilitation of nature. To achieve these objectives we must develop state policies for nature protection and natural resource use, based on legal, economic, cultural, technological, and administrative measures that will monitor national economic processes and assign priorities to development trends in accordance with the amount of available resources, environmental conditions, resistance of both geo- and ecosystems to anthropogenic influence, and possibilities for their rehabilitation. The policy must further restore and expand traditional attitudes toward nature by instilling a conscientious awareness of the necessity of environmental protection.

Environmental management principles should proceed from the fact that both environmental protection and natural resources use constitute an integral process which must be supported by legal and economic regulation, by efficient territorial management embodied into law that assigns specific environmental responsibilities to designated state administrative bodies and local authorities, and by social regulation that guarantees social justice in the exploitation of natural resources. In this connection, the promotion of ecologically oriented ways of thinking in all spheres of human activity is of primary importance, as is the concept of integrated land use management that promotes a comprehensive approach to land use planning and regional development. The state should take the initiative in developing a comprehensive system of environmental monitoring and in coordinating scientific and practical approaches to environmental protection and natural resources use. The state should further take the lead in promoting international cooperation and in publicizing information on environmental conditions and the measures that the state has taken to remedy them.

If we wish to optimize national economic development, it is absolutely essential to root all management strategies for environmental protection and natural resource use on the environmental and geological parameters present in any given piece of land. Second, we must implement the basic regulations and requirements of such international agreements as the international convention on long-range transboundary air pollution, the Montreal Protocol, and the Baltic Sea Living Resources Conservation Agreement. Third, we must create and implement Lithuania's state system of environmental standards if we wish to stabilize and gradually diminish the negative anthropogenic effect on the environment. Fourth, we must use industrial products and raw materials that are low in toxicity, and we must introduce low-waste technologies and those that require little energy or natural resources. Finally, we must set up automated environmental pollution control and monitoring systems in areas where there are major potential environmental hazards.

To achieve these goals, a comprehensive Environmental Protection Law (EPL) was adopted on January 21, 1992. It will serve as the basis for the creation of a uniform legal environmental protection system. The EPL recognizes commonly accepted international environmental protection principles, including environmental impact assessment and the "polluter pays" principle. The law sets forth guidelines for the implementation of these principles. The following legislation based on the EPL is currently being drafted: a law on protected areas, a waste management law, a law on forest protection and forest use, a soil protection and use law, a law on the protection and exploitation of mineral resources, a water resources law, a clean air law, and a law on protecting the Baltic Sea from pollution.

In the area of land use, we endorse basic land use management principles that require the functional integration of regional/local interests and foster an ecosystem approach within geo-ecological regions. To achieve this goal we must provide the requisite economic and social incentives, and target environmental regulations to localities on the basis of differences in environmental and socioeconomic conditions. We must also promote environmental management strategies that take into consideration and build on land use management practices of the past, in the interests of historical continuity. Finally, we must develop a land use plan which will serve as a framework for Lithuania's development, within which will be elaborated a network of specially protected conservation and cultural areas.

In order to optimize national economic practices, it is useful to evaluate Lithuania's national economic structure from both the economic and environmental points of view. We must limit nuclear energy and promote the use of alternative energy sources as far as possible, and create an economic system that integrates natural resource protection and utilization.

In the transition of the Lithuanian economy from the old administrative command system to an economy managed by market principles there is no automatic presumption that natural resources will be used rationally, that the environment will be efficiently and effectively protected, or that many years of backwardness will be eliminated. On the contrary, pollution is typically considered an externality in market economies, and it is the task of the state to apply appropriate measures for abolishing or at least reducing its effect. Thus, the main goal of reforming environmental protection management is to implement a system of economic regulations that would compensate for the imperfections of a market economy and ensure the effective realization of the state's environmental protection policy.

The basic components of such an environmental protection management system are as follows:

• taxes on natural resources and pollution;
• a price system;
• state subsidies and credits;
• the creation of a system of economic stimulation, sanctions, and compensation.

The main task of the new market-based system of management of environmental protection and natural resource use is to change the centralized management and distribution system, by involving those enterprises concerned with environmental protection and the rational use of natural resources in the process.

The first stage in the implementation of the new system of environmental management is the introduction of taxes for environmental pollution and prices for natural resources. These were introduced in 1991. The appropriate laws are now being put into place. To get the system of taxes for environmental pollution started at this time, when not a single enterprise can meet the health standards or predicted pollutants discharge standards set by international agreement, temporary standards for pollutants and emissions into water and the atmosphere were introduced for every enterprise beginning in 1991. At the same time, standards corresponding to health norms as well as specific time limits were set. The temporary standards are programmed to become stricter with each coming year until the health standards are reached. Taxes are determined on the discharge of every pollutant into the water or atmosphere that exceeds the legal standard. The taxes depend on toxicity and amount of pollutants. Depending on the manner in which the discharge deviates from the norm, taxes are divided into two types: basic and increased. The basic taxes are paid for emissions of pollutants within the set allowable limits. They are determined according to the damage done to the environment and included in production costs. That way the "polluter pays" principle is implemented. The inclusion of this tax into production costs reduces the competitiveness of goods produced by production processes with a clearly negative impact on the environment. The increased cost is a direct reflection of the increase in production costs. A fall in demand for the product will encourage the producer to decrease the pollutant discharge.

When the allowable limit is exceeded, the tax increases. The new tax is determined by multiplying the basic tax by a coefficient, which, in its turn, is determined by the degree to which the limit is exceeded. This tax exceeds the capital necessary to achieve the health standards for environmental quality and is made on the income that is left to the enterprise after the income tax is paid. This tax encourages the polluter to choose either to implement environmental protection measures or to see the temporarily compatible limit become stricter with every passing year. The taxes for water pollution increased in this way exceed the cost of construction for a municipal sewage treatment plant; those for atmospheric pollution exceed the cost of construction of a fuel oil desulphurization plant as well as filters in power plants.

When the maximum allowable limit of emissions is achieved, a progressive income tax on preferential terms will be applied or totally eliminated.

Charges for emergency hazardous emissions as a rule exceed the basic tax several times over.

Taxes for environmental pollution constitute the source of the state's means to subsidize environmental protection. Certain specific environmental protection activities that cannot be stimulated by other economic means are subsidized. These include enterprises that are unable financially to diminish their negative impact on the environment but that are indispensable for Lithuania's national economy today. Also subsidized are interest rates and depreciation levels. At present, the funds obtained from basic taxes are almost equal to the state budget for environmental protection. As this constitutes a very small amount (0.6 percent of the national income or 1.2 percent of budget expenditures), the system of increased taxes forces enterprises to finance environmental protection measures from their own funds.

These taxes, introduced along with prices on natural resources, will enable us to manage recycling and waste utilization. The mistakes made by the developed countries in subsidizing primary raw material production can be avoided. Since Lithuania does not boast an abundance of primary raw materials, waste utilization should be subsidized to avoid pollution in processing primary raw materials and landfills and to extend the amount of material resources.

The measures outlined above have to reflect actual socioecological costs as well as stimulate the implementation of pollutant-control measures, nonwaste and clean-waste production technologies, waste utilization, and recycling. Taxes on natural resources in Lithuania should stimulate a more economic use of scarce natural resources.

The gradual implementation of the new system of economic/environmental management will allow Lithuania's national economy to reform and rebuild in conformance with the country's environmental needs. The implementation of all the above-mentioned trends in environmental protection and natural resource utilization should be based on a unified system of environmental protection legislation and an all-round scientific approach. Of first priority is the development of the fundamental and applied environmental sciences as well as a unified system of environmental protection in education that would make the population more aware of the traditional national approach to environmental problems and public activity.

The Role of the Environmental Movement

The movement of the Greens in the Baltic states began at the same time as Lithuania's national revival, when outstanding Lithuanian writers and artists for the first time openly described the catastrophic environmental situation and met severe opposition from the authorities. When in 1988 the Zemyna club appeared in Vilnius, hundreds of Vilnius inhabitants immediately joined it. The main task of the club was to bring the ecological problems of Vilnius to public attention. Its first successful protest action was against the proposed construction of a highway through several residential districts of Vilnius. The next important step by Zemyna and the Sajudis movement was putting an end to the construction of the third block at the Ignalina Nuclear Power Plant. At that time the task seemed unrealistic. But a million signatures on a petition and a rally at the Nuclear Power Plant, where thousands formed a "life ring" around the plant, forced the authorities to halt construction.

In 1988, the Atgaja Club in Kaunas organized another big protest action. In a ten-day trip down the two biggest rivers in Lithuania, the Nemunas and Neris, the demonstrators stopped in villages to participate in rallies, which not only expressed ecological protest but served as focal points for national revival as well. A rally in Kaunas gathered over seventy thousand people. A group of one hundred cyclists traveled around Lithuania to publicize ecological ideas.

On September 1, 1989, thousands of people gathered on the shore of the Baltic Sea. By joining hands they expressed their protest against the pollution of the Baltic Sea and showed their determination to do their utmost to save it.

A constituent conference of the Greens took place in the autumn of 1988. On July 15, 1989, the Green Party was established in Lithuania. At that time, it was the first Green Party in the Soviet Union. Later, counterparts appeared in Estonia and Latvia. Zigmas Vaigvila, one of the founders of the Greens' movement, became the leader of the Green Party. The Green Party of Lithuania has actively joined the political life of the republic. The Greens set forth their main principles in their election program and ran candidates for elections. Four of their members were elected to the Supreme Council of the Republic of Lithuania.

The Green Party of Lithuania stands for humankind's sacred right to live in a healthy environment, the right to live in a free society capable of preserving ecological balance, the right to a system of values, based on a way of life formed through centuries of common life, that also respects the customs and traditions of other nations living in harmony with nature. They consider independence the natural right of every nation. They stand for the demilitarization of Lithuania as an integral part of the global process of the disarmament and peace and urge the abolition of military activities, which they see as the heaviest ecological threat in the world today. They believe in the need for ecological security. In government, they insist on the priority of a policy of nature protection, on the publicizing of the ecological situation and strict control in nature protection, and on the state's full responsibility for violations of civil rights. The Green Party of Lithuania and the Sajudis movement both stand for new trends in environmental protection and management, namely, for the accountability of the Department of Environmental Protection of the Republic of Lithuania to the Supreme Council of the Republic of Lithuania. They nominated E. Vebra as a candidate for the position of Director General of the Department of Environmental Protection and won the election.

Notes

1. m/a = metric tons per annum (year).
2. BOD = biochemical oxygen demand. BOD is a measurement of how much oxygen it takes to break down organic waste introduced into water. The higher the BOD, the more oxygen demanded.
3. Hydrogeology is the study of the movement or distribution of underground water through rock.
4. BOD 5 means measuring the BOD in the water for a period of five days.

PART II

The Influence of Environmental Movements

7

The Emergence of the Environmental Movement in Eastern Europe and Its Role in the Revolutions of 1989

Duncan Fisher

Introduction

Very little analysis exists on independent environmental organizations in Eastern Europe. Considerable work was undertaken on the Soviet Union in the 1970s, but as this predates the emergence of independent environmental organizations, the conclusion is invariably that such organizations play no role.[1] The aim of this analysis is to go beyond the notion that the emergence of the environmental movement can be explained by a series of isolated events converging at a particular moment in time, for example, environmental pollution, Gorbachev, and Chernobyl. These factors have shaped the growth of the environmental movement; they do not explain it. An attempt is made to place the emergence of environmental politics within the political context of Eastern Europe from the 1950s onward.

This paper is not about the causes of environmental pollution in communist systems,[2] although the approach adopted suggests some

---

The author is associated with the Ecological Studies Institute in London.

important reasons, most significantly the lack of public participation, feedback, and pressure. The paper takes the story as far as the beginning of the post-communist period, that is, summer 1990. More analysis is needed of what has happened since the revolutions, and this paper identifies some possible next steps in this process.

The Origins of Environmental Concern

The characteristic feature of the system that Stalin imposed on Eastern Europe in the early 1950s was the ideology of perfection. There was a single truth, and criticism was impossible. The death of Stalin removed the symbol of unity and perfection, and opened up the possibility of change. Through the 1960s, official ideology was presented in terms of reform from above, rather than revolution. Instead of a salvationist promise of terrestrial paradise, there was an incrementalist view— building socialism, methodically and scientifically. Economic growth and the improvement of living standards became the main source of political legitimacy. It is in this context that the increased interest in environmental management can be understood, both in terms of its effect on economic growth and on living standards. Environmental legislation was drawn up in ever-increasing quantities,[3] and new state institutions were created.[4]

During the latter part of the 1960s and the 1970s, a process of political decay became apparent, as the state was no longer able to maintain the promises on which it had based its legitimacy. Economic growth was slowing and public services declining in quality. This process was particularly acute in Poland in the 1970s, where the policy of borrowing from the West backfired, and the state proved unwilling or unable to provide society with the most basic services. The health system, education, retail trade, local transport, housing construction, and environmental regulation were all rapidly deteriorating.[5] The convergence of these events contributed to the growing alienation between the state and society, and between the state and intellectuals, that are described below.

The State and Scientists

As other chapters have noted, environmental protest emerged first from within the scientific establishment.[6] On the one hand, scientists were needed in order to provide the objective assessments necessary for the regime to maintain its legitimacy; access to data was a privilege that could be denied at the state's discretion. But at the same time scientists became increasingly disenchanted with their off-stage consultative role, with no power to determine and implement solutions.[7] The disbursement of information as a privilege could not forever buy the support of the intellectuals. Increasingly, they tended to "abuse" this privilege by allowing information to get into the hands of oppositional groups, or speaking out themselves in a manner critical of the state.

In Serbia considerable tension developed in the 1970s between the Academy of Sciences and the state over an environmental study.[8] In Romania, where there was very much less room for open disagreement, there were seminars on ecology at the Free University of Bucharest, where criticism of the regime was carefully formulated by implication only.[9] In 1983 the Hungarian Academy of Sciences produced a critical report of the Gabčikovo-Nagymaros Dam project, although the Academy was subsequently forced into silence on this issue until 1988.[10] In the 1980s, the Ecological Section of the Society of Biologists within the Czechoslovak Academy of Sciences produced two documents describing the environment in Czechoslovakia. The first, in 1983, based on an even earlier document, was suppressed and then published by Charter 77.[11] The second, in 1989, became the basis of the postrevolutionary Czech government's statement on the environment, as some of its authors took ministerial posts. Slovak scientists provided the environmental information for *Bratislava nahlas* (Bratislava Outloud), a report published by the Slovak Union of Nature and Landscape Protectors in 1987.

The State and Society

Two key features of the political arrangements of the 1960s and 1970s were the exclusion of society from the decision-making process and the necessary corollary of this, the restriction of information flows. The state imposed a paternalistic form of political legitimacy: it would guarantee basic security in return for quiescence and obedience.

Deteriorating environmental conditions in the 1960s and 1970s were one among many areas where the lack of participation and the lack of information emphasized the powerlessness of society to correct the mistakes of the ruling bureaucracy.[12] Demands for the correction of these imbalances were an essential part of the program of many independent East European environmental organizations in the 1980s. In some cases organizations emerged as a direct consequence of increased restrictions on information, as in the case of the Danube Blues in 1985, who responded with a public leafletting campaign.[13] *Ecoglasnost* in Bulgaria specifically demanded open information (hence its name). On the subject of participation, its program stated:

> A basic fact about our social and economic life is that different social groups participate unequally in the process of taking the decisions that set the path of the overall development of society. Those who make the strategic decisions are not the same people as those who have to face the consequences. This basic social fact unquestionably applies to policy in the ecological sphere. Here we have privileged chiefs and unprivileged consumers. Moreover, the degree of an individual's responsibility in decision making is in inverse proportion to the actual suffering caused him by . . . environmental pollution.[14]

Autonomous social activity, however, was one of the fundamental tenets of socialism and was part of the more consensual relationship the regimes were seeking with society as part of the post-Stalinist approach. The regimes, therefore, had to remain formally committed to the creation and support of autonomous social activity. As part of the de-Stalinization process, Khrushchev advocated a "people's state" and supported a greater role for social organizations in nonsensitive areas, including nature conservation.[15] At the same time, it was necessary to deny any real autonomy to the so-called autonomous organizations. The official policy of "controlled autonomous organizations" is expressed clearly in a report to the national conference of the Bulgarian Communist Party in January 1988:

> It would be wrong for us to oppose the creation of autonomous groups, autonomous associations, and other forms of popular self-expression. We are, however, an organized society and cannot accept the creation of conditions that will breed anarchy, chaos, and demagogy. . . . Therefore, it is totally normal and proper to require such autonomous organizations to set themselves up within self-managing public bodies as an inseparable part of them and not as closed and dissociated castes. In this way the autonomous groups will be able to receive the necessary help, to enrich the life of the self-managing organizations, and to be under their control.[16]

The state feared the emergence of independent activity around the environment. The roots of this fear can be understood by returning to the system of legitimacy that the state was attempting to promote.

The Facade of Order and the Impact of Disorder

With political decay came another shift in official ideology. Khrushchev's reform from above had led to the Prague Spring of 1968, and so in the 1970s it was abandoned. Reform was replaced by prudent scientific management of an already established order. The key concepts became consolidation and qualitative growth.[17] The widening gap between reality and the ideology on which the regimes were basing their legitimacy necessitated the creation of a facade of order. This facade was carefully constructed through the use of censorship, as is illustrated graphically in the *Polish Black Book*, a reference manual for Polish censors in the 1970s.[18] All reference to disorder had to be eliminated, including information on environmental degradation: "Information on direct threats to life or health caused by industry or chemical agents used in agriculture, or threats to the natural environment in Poland, should be eliminated from works on environmental protection."[19]

The main function of the promotion of this facade was to confuse. Reliable information is essential for confident criticism and to indicate to society where the boundaries of criticism lie. In this context, the significance of criticism of the environment becomes clear. Environmental degradation could not be entirely hidden from public view, and so it disrupted the carefully constructed facade of order.[20] At the same time it both undermined the regimes' promises of a good life and questioned the ideology of unlimited growth in an indirect manner that was difficult to repress.[21]

The Environmental Movement in the 1980s

The process of political decay, manifested in increasing environmental deterioration and in a growing alienation among the state, scientists, and society, was one of the primary reasons for the emergence of politically active environmental groups in the 1980s. The influence of the growing environmental movement in the West was also an important factor, partly through hidden contacts between environmentalists in the two halves of Europe.[22]

The Configuration of the Environmental Movement in the 1980s

Much less research has been done on the composition of environmental organizations in Eastern Europe than in Western Europe. It appears from personal observation that the make-up was similar. There is a strong correlation between educational level and level of activity within organizations. This correlation appeared particularly strong in countries with a generally low level of social activity (e.g., Serbia), and in groups that were politically active. It was less so with locally based and state-sponsored nature conservation activity. Mass protest, of which there are numerous examples, only tended to occur when populations felt themselves immediately threatened.

There were two categories of environmental organizations: those created "from above" and those created "from below." The exact nature of groups within these two categories and the balance and interaction between the two varied from country to country and over time, and was a function of the degree of tolerance by the regime of uncontrolled social activity. In countries where tolerance of independent activity was high, activities could take place within officially approved social organizations, particularly at the grass-roots level where central control was weakest. Where tolerance was low, independent activity was precipitated into illegal opposition or dissidence. Under these conditions it was normal for the state to begin creating more institutions of its own in an attempt to remove the necessity for independent organizations. Where an alternative locus of independent activity existed, such as the Evangelical Church in the German Democratic Republic and the Catholic Church in Poland, environmental activity tended to gravitate toward it. The church played a particularly important role as safe haven in the GDR, where there were fewer opportunities to operate outside this locus.

At one end of the spectrum lay Albania and Romania, where independent groups were not tolerated, and state-sponsored social organizations were totally controlled. In both countries there were scientists working on ecological issues at the universities and academies, and in Romania some of the data got into the hands of a loose association of intellectuals under the name of Romanian Democratic Action, which produced an extensive report in 1986.

The situation in Bulgaria was slightly less severe, and the dynamics of protest and suppression were more lively. Ecology had become a focus of protest in 1987 in response to intense pollution floating across the Danube from Romania into the town of Ruse.[23] Increasing press openness at the time elevated the Ruse affair to a national issue. In February 1988 the discussion group "Man, Ecology, Space" started in Sofia and declared its support for the Committee for the Ecological Defense of Ruse. The committee was quickly and effectively suppressed by the Bulgarian authorities, but the problems at Ruse did not disappear.

In 1989 several independent groups emerged,[24] among them Ecoglasnost, which was founded on March 2, 1989. In response to this kind of activity, the Bulgarian state itself became active in creating environmental organizations, most notably the National Committee for Nature Protection.[25] In 1986 the Ecological Youth Club was set up in Sofia, and in 1988, the National Movement for the Protection and Regeneration of the Environment was set up within the Fatherland Front, in response to the social unrest in Ruse.[26] When Ecoglasnost emerged, it was declared unnecessary by the authorities. In October 1989 the Ecology National Youth Club was set up under the guidance of the Komsomol Central Committee.[27]

Next in the spectrum was Czechoslovakia. Control of the constituent parts of state-sponsored social organizations was less total, and the articulation of political alternatives within these sometimes passed without repression. The extent of toleration differed between the Czech Republic and the Slovak Republic; opposition was less tolerated in the former, where the legacy of 1968 was stronger.

In Slovakia the Bratislava city branch of the Slovak Union of Nature and Landscape Protectors became increasingly radical in its criticism of the Gabcikovo-Nagymaros Dam project.[28] Its journal criticized the scheme in 1981 and as a result was suppressed for six months and censorship subsequently tightened. In October 1987 there was further trouble after the publication of *Bratislava nahlas*, a detailed report on environmental conditions in Bratislava.[29] But by 1988 a whole issue of the journal of the Bratislava city branch could be devoted to criticism of the Gabčikovo-Nagymaros Dam scheme, without penalties.

In Prague, on the other hand, opposition was precipitated into unofficial groups. Charter 77 established a working group on the environment in 1978 and published a number of documents on the subject, some of which contained data obtained from scientists working in state research institutions.[30] The most important of these was the report commissioned by the state from the Czechoslovak Academy of Sciences in 1981, which Charter 77 published in December 1983. Only one samizdat journal was published in Czechoslovakia, *Ecological Bulletin*. During the 1980s, it reprinted several texts on the environment, and kept readers informed of environmental activity in Czechoslovakia and the rest of Eastern Europe. In 1989 various loose environmental circles emerged, including the Independent Ecological Society and Children of the Earth. These circles undertook demonstrations in Prague during 1989. One such took place in Stromovka Park, in protest against the proposed construction of a road through it.

Meanwhile, open environmental criticism was emerging from within the Czechoslovak Academy of Sciences. There were a number of criticisms of the Gabčikovo-Nagymaros Dam project. The focus of this activity became the Ecological Section of the Society of Biologists within the academy. As its name suggests, the section lay fairly low in the hierarchical structure of the academy. Primarily due to the political skill of its head, Josef Vavrousek, the section managed to keep the delicate balance of staying in existence within the academy (thereby insuring access to data) at the same time as it maintained a critical distance and informal, hidden contacts with oppositional circles. In November 1988 it produced the first full critique of the Gabčikovo-Nagymaros Dam project to appear in Czechoslovakia. Later, in January 1989, this was published in *Nika*, the journal of the Czech Union of Defenders of Nature, the Czech equivalent of the Slovak Union of Nature and Landscape Protectors. Publication drew an attack on the organization from the party daily, *Rude pravo*, a few months later.[31] Although the Czech Union enjoyed less toleration than the Slovak Union, it too had been gradually expanding the limits of criticism since 1987, mainly through its journal, *Nika*.[32]

The German Democratic Republic provides the prime example of how opposition groups used an already existing resource: the space for independent activity and criticism provided by the Evangelical Church. As a result of this space and the exposure to the environmental politics of West Germany, the environmental movement in the GDR was one of the earliest of those in Eastern Europe to emerge in the 1970s,[33] and was more widespread than might be expected from the low level of toleration of independent social activity. Paradoxically the state-sponsored Society for Nature and Environment, founded in 1980 within the Cultural Union of the GDR, was more restricted than the independent organizations sheltering within the Evangelical Church.[34]

There were two kinds of environmental activity within the church. On the one hand there were initiatives sponsored by the church and its pastors—declarations, an information center, research, local group activities, fund raising, and public discussions.[35] On the other hand, environmental groups, many of which were not religious in the traditional sense of the term, found refuge in the church. These groups created the Arche network in 1988. Tensions arose between the groups and the congregations of the local churches, but the church leadership not only managed to maintain a place within the church for the groups, but often defended individuals who got into trouble with the authorities. The environmental groups did not leave the church until 1989 during the revolutionary period.

Yugoslavia serves as an example of relatively open social structures—a function of the self-management system—although the degree of organization of the environmental movement has varied widely between the republics. Environmental debate in all the republics during the 1980s revolved around the question of nuclear power, culminating in a federal moratorium in 1988 on the building of further power stations. In Slovenia in 1983, student environmental activists joined Yugoslavia's first ecological group to the official mass youth organization, the Socialist Youth Alliance.[36] As the 1980s wore on, alternative values (environmental, peace, and feminist) found full expression within the Alliance.[37] In Croatia in 1986, a group of intellectuals formed an independent group called *Svarun*, which one year later also entered the Socialist Youth Alliance.[38] Very little organized activity beyond the local level took place in Serbia or the other republics. A Serbian environmental movement emerged only in May 1990.[39] In 1986 a group of intellectuals in Belgrade formed the Committee for the Protection of Man and the Environment,[40] and a research institute named the Center for Socio-Eco Research is now playing an important role as a focal point for the emerging environmental movement in Serbia.[41]

Similar features were apparent in Hungary in the 1980s. There were a wide range of local activities,[42] a number of active conservation clubs,[43] and university groups.[44] Independent environmental activity was not permitted until 1988, when legislation was put in place allowing independent organizations to obtain legal status outside state-sponsored social organizations. In the localities, at a distance from central control exercised in Budapest, state-sponsored mass organizations such as the National Patriotic Front, with local offices throughout the country, did not act to suppress local initiatives from below. Indeed, newly emerging groups made use of state-sponsored structures to improve communication and coordination.[45] Similarly, the Communist Youth League provided the framework for independently minded university groups.[46] Meanwhile, from 1984 onwards, environmental activity in Budapest was dominated by the issue of the Gabčikovo-Nagymaros Dam system[47] and was much more explicitly political. In April 1988, in response to increasing environmental activism in Budapest, the National Patriotic Front set up the Hungarian Society for Nature Conservationists. Its reception was very different in the localities, where it took over the role of the National Patriotic Front, and in Budapest, where it was seen as an extension of Stalinist methods.[48]

Circumstances in Poland were rather exceptional in the early 1980s. Several independent environmental organizations emerged: one within Solidarity, one within Rural Solidarity, and the most well known, the Polish Ecological Club, closely associated with Solidarity. Founded in September 1980, the club was officially registered as an independent group in May 1981 with 17 branches across the country. Its national reach made it unique at the time in Eastern Europe. After December 1981, however, the situation reverted to that pertaining in other East European countries: There was no room for the Polish Ecological Club in state-sponsored institutions and so it went underground. As conditions became more tolerant through the 1980s, the Polish Ecological Club re-emerged with renewed vigor as part of a rapidly expanding environmental movement. The club held two national conventions in 1983 and 1987. The independent group Freedom and Peace (WiP), founded in 1985, was particularly active in open campaigning during the 1980s.[49]

At the same time the state-sponsored League for the Protection of Nature grew in size, and local groups began to take increasingly independent stands. Formally the league had been a typical state-sponsored organization, boasting large membership and emphasizing education rather than independent participation.[50] The church too responded to environmental issues, focusing on spiritual and moral aspects of environmental concern. A Franciscan Ecology Movement was founded in 1986.

In response to these developments, the Polish state began creating its own social institutions. In 1986 it tried to gather all the various movements into one within the League for the Protection of Nature.[51] But the constituent elements of the league itself quickly became more independent.[52] In 1988 the National Foundation for the Protection of the Environment was created, sponsored by the Social Ecological Movement, an earlier creation of the Patriotic Movement of National Rebirth.[53]

By 1988 there was open and genuine interaction between the authorities and environmental experts in Poland. In October about thirty experts met with Wojciech Jaruzelski to discuss and launch the National Program for the Protection of the Environment until 2010.[54] The environmental experts recommended, among other things, the removal of restrictions on access to information on the environment. In 1989 Solidarity and the government held a round table on ecology, at which the Polish Ecological Club played a leading role.

The Environment and the Revolutions

The only countries where environmental issues played a significant role in precipitating political change were Czechoslovakia, Hungary, and Bulgaria, and in all cases it was not the environmental issues themselves that were crucial, but the fact that they provided a focus for social discontent at the right moment in time.

Czechoslovakia

In Czechoslovakia environmental demonstrations were becoming commonplace, particularly in Prague.[55] The weekend before the revolution occurred, environmental protests took place in Teplice. The authorities promised a public meeting with the inhabitants of the town on Monday, November 20. The meeting turned into a massive celebration of the revolution, which had begun in Prague the preceding Friday, November 17. All the demonstrations in Prague in the days prior to the revolution were focused on the environment.

Hungary

The issue of the Gabčikovo-Nagymaros Dam system provided a focus for political controversy in the process of political change in Hungary.[56] Opposition to the scheme was revitalized in 1988. There were numerous demonstrations, petitions and other actions. New groups emerged. An international conference of environmental groups was organized, the Academy of Sciences stated its opposition to the project openly, and debate within the administration became open. The issue provided a rallying point for the disparate opposition forces. The parliamentary debate in October 1988 turned into a test of the credibility of the Communist Party under Karoly Grosz. When Parliament voted in favor of continuing the project,[57] the dam scheme became the symbol of the old way of government. Reformers, especially Prime Minister Miklos Nemeth, accused the Communist Party, and Karoly Grosz as it leader, of going ahead with the project in an "undemocratic manner." In a speech before Parliament on June 2, 1989, Nemeth attacked the dam scheme, using it as an argument for democratization and greater independence in the fields of economics, culture, and science. A few months later, in October 1989, Parliament voted for the withdrawal of Hungary from the project.

Bulgaria

International environmental conferences were a favorite activity of the Bulgarian state. This policy proved to be the regime's downfall, with the environmental Conference on Security and Cooperation in Europe (CSCE) in October–November 1989. The subjects of the ongoing series of CSCE conferences are divided into three baskets. Basket III concerns human and social rights, and Western countries tended to focus on these. Basket II concerned technical cooperation in various fields, including the environment, and was of particular interest to East European governments. The dynamic that drove the process was the pressure of Western governments for human rights concessions in exchange for technical assistance to the East European regimes. A conference specifically devoted to the environment was proposed by the East European governments. The Western governments were unenthusiastic but agreed on condition that human rights be discussed in the context of the environment (the so-called "interdependence" of all CSCE subjects). At the conference in Sofia in October–November 1989, differences in perspective persisted. The U.S. delegation stated: "How can we take seriously the word of some CSCE partners on the environment when, in other contexts, their deeds contradict their public pronouncements?" The Soviet delegation said the opposite: "It is unacceptable to conclude ecological agreements conditional on other political negotiations, to use ecology as a tool for applying pressure in solving other problems, including political ones."

Delegations in Sofia emphasized the extent of public participation in their own countries. Hungary, Poland, the United Kingdom, France, and the United State invited representatives of environmental nongovernmental organizations (NGOs) onto their delegations.[58] The Hungarian Duna Kor, Danube Circle, was largely responsible for drafting the Hungarian proposals on transboundary water pollution, one of the official subjects of the conference.

The other East European delegations were forced to play the same diplomatic game, displaying a commitment in their proposals and speeches to social participation in environmental regulation. Bulgaria's delegation even included Petar Beron, a leading member of Ecoglasnost, but not as a representative of that "illegal" organization. By avoiding the distinction between official and unofficial environmental NGOs, the East European states could wax lyrical about the role of social organizations. The issue of rights, the antithesis of a paternalistic relation between state and society, was studiously avoided. Discussion of rights was replaced with an emphasis on the need for education of society.

Ecoglasnost rose to prominence in Bulgaria in the months preceding the conference, carefully developing a strategy to use the conference to promote its cause.[59] A number of attempts had been made from 1988 onwards to organize oppositional groups, all of which had been met with varying degrees of repression. However, Ecoglasnost did not experience the same degree of repression as did other groups, and as a result became an umbrella for the opposition. It produced two kinds of documents: those solely devoted to environmental and conservation issues (such as "Charter 89"),[60] and those putting forward demands for freedom of information, the right of association, and the need for radical social change, in the language of the forthcoming conference.[61] The conference itself was the scene of intense activity, with extensive interaction between Western delegations and members of Ecoglasnost and other independent NGOs.[62] Ecoglasnost organized two petitions and a series of open meetings. Mass demonstrations began the day after the close of the conference on November 3. On November 10, Todor Zhivkov resigned. Although this change was the result of longer term power struggles within the power elite, only catalyzed, not caused, by the CSCE conference, Ecoglasnost benefited greatly from the public's association of it with the fall of the former regime.

The Environmental Movement after the Revolutions

With the rapid disintegration of the Communist regimes in 1989, the situation for environmental NGOs changed completely. The distinction between officially sponsored and independent NGOs evaporated. Formerly unofficial groups came out into the open and were joined by a multitude of new groups. National networks were quickly established.[63] Organizations formerly sponsored by the state either disappeared (in Bulgaria, the GDR, Romania and Serbia) or quickly asserted their independence and began presenting a new image.[64]

Conditions in all the countries favored the creation of green parties.[65] First, and perhaps most obviously, is the example of the West, which was exerting a powerful influence in all sectors, not just the environment. Secondly, the urge to participate in elections was very strong: not only were elections seen as the symbol of the new-found political freedom, but the parliaments were considered the only place where environmental priorities could be advocated effectively at a time of extensive redrafting of legislation. These tendencies coexisted with a strong public distrust of politics per se, a result of the former political system.[66] Along with the articulation of alternative values, the green parties offered a more immediate form of participation, an attractive feature of social movements in general.[67]

Arguments in favor of participating in elections drew some nonparty groups into party political activity, especially where the nonparty group had such a strong reputation that it was guaranteed some electoral success. In Bulgaria the Green Party emerged from Ecoglasnost in late November 1989,[68] causing some confusion and conflict at the time. The manner in which the Green Party came into being excluded people within Ecoglasnost who wanted to participate in electoral politics, and who thus felt out-maneuvered. In the end, both groups took part. Public confusion was reduced by the fact that both were members of the United Democratic Forum (UDF), and as such the electorate was not asked to choose between them directly.

The Ecological Movement of Romania (MER) used similar arguments to explain its participation in the elections.[69] This time, confusion between the MER and the Green Party at the ballot box was not avoided (see below). Tension developed within the movement over the question of participation, with a split largely along generational differences. The leadership of the Romanian movement is much older than any other environmental NGO in Eastern Europe. In March 1990, MER announced that the movement would have a special political commission, the members of which could enter Parliament. However, as a guarantee of the movement's nonparty political character, the movement's president would not be able to enter Parliament. At the local level, MER groups were allowed to decide for themselves whether or not to participate in the elections. This rather complex message was not widely understood, and the public generally considered MER just another party.

In both Bulgaria and Romania, the environmental movements were very conscious of the widespread public mistrust of politics, and made moves not to lose support through their partisan political activity. In Bulgaria, members of Ecoglasnost proposed that the organization could go as far as Parliament, but no further; it would remain nongovernmental.[70] This solution was termed a form of "socioecological self-protection of the population and control over management resolutions."[71] To allay suspicions of a political party, the Ecological Movement of Romania propagated a universal, nonexclusive, moral, ethical, and nonpartisan approach.[72]

The Elections

The environment was a symbolically significant but not the most important issue in the elections of 1990. Environmental degradation was seen as the legacy of the former regimes, and regeneration of the environment was seen as part of the establishment of a new and more humane order. It was also a subject of internationally recognized legitimacy and popularity. While virtually every party included sections on the environment in its manifesto,[73] in the great majority of cases, the references represented no more than a symbolic indictment of the previous regime.[74]

Environmental disputes converged with election campaigns in several countries. In Hungary, environmental parties took part in various local campaigns.[75] In Bulgaria, the environment played a special role in the election campaign,[76] as a result of the elevation of environmental issues in domestic politics in 1989. The Belene nuclear power station in Shvistov was one focus of controversy.[77] The Ministry of the

Environment was accused on the radio of withholding information like its bureaucratic predecessors,[78] while scientists attacked the former regime for suppressing data after the Chernobyl accident.[79] In addition, transborder chemical pollution in Ruse became an issue once again.[80]

Election Results

Slovenia

The greatest electoral success of a green party was in Slovenia. The Green Party entered the elections within a seven-party coalition, the Democratic United Opposition of Slovenia (DEMOS). DEMOS won the elections on April 8 and 12, 1990, with 53 percent of the seats in the National Assembly (126 out of 240). The Green Party won 9 percent of the votes and gained 8 seats in the Socio-Political Chamber (80 seats), 8 in the Chamber of Municipalities (80 seats), 1 in the Chamber of Associated Labor (80 seats), and 4 positions in the government. The Minister of Energy was supported by the Green Party in the elections, but is a member of the Green Section of the Party of Democratic Renewal (formerly the Communist Party). The prime minister, Lozje Peterle (Christian Democrat), has environmental experience, having worked on such issues for four years in the Institute of Social Planning.[81]

The sources of this success are complex. The environment was not the most important issue in the elections. The future shape of Yugoslavia and national concerns took this place.[82] Yet, the Green Party benefited from a certain congruence between national and environmental concerns. The national symbol of Slovenia is a green leaf, and in Slovenia, as elsewhere in the bloc, the tendency had been growing to relate environmental destruction to insensitive economic management directed from Belgrade. During the 1980s, the green movement had established a reputation for favoring political change in Slovenia as part of a broader opposition within the Socialist Youth Alliance. The fact that the movement remained united and decisive through the political upheavals in 1989 allowed it to reap the benefits of its reputation. In contrast, the Liberal Party, another successor of the Socialist Youth Alliance, remained weak and divided in the period preceding the elections and fared poorly at the polls. A final and one of the most important elements of the Green Party's success was its strong position within the coalition. Because DEMOS needed the Green Party to assure a ruling majority, the party was able to stipulate its conditions for entrance, allowing it to keep its program intact. Coalition politics were necessitated by the nonproportional voting system for two of the chambers and by the two-thirds majority voting rule in the new constituent assembly.

Croatia

The failure of the greens in Croatia contrasts dramatically with their success in Slovenia. No seats at all were gained in the elections. The green movement had not been especially visible during the preceding years. The time period between the announcement and the holding of elections was only two months, and the movement lacked both resources and an organizational base from which to prepare a proper campaign. Even more important, the campaign itself was dominated by national and constitutional concerns to a much greater extent than in Slovenia. The "first past the post" voting system did not encourage the formation of an opposition coalition like DEMOS, and none was formed.[83] The new Croatian government is now unique in Europe for having no environmental ministry. Such is the low priority accorded to environmental issues there.

Romania

In Romania the Green Party (PER) and Green Movement (MER) obtained a few seats in the elections. An opinion poll carried out by the German INFAS Institute before the elections predicted the results fairly accurately, except in the case of MER and PER. It predicted about 5 percent for MER, and almost 0 percent for PER. This would have reflected the relative degree of organization and public profile of the two groups. In the event, however, the electorate, confused by the multitude of parties, voted for the Green Party as well as the Green Movement, because the former's name appeared near the top of the ballot booklet, while the Movement was buried in the middle. The total green vote added up to the 5 percent predicted by the German opinion poll.

MER and PER entered coalitions in the Parliament and the Senate. MER, PER, and two Social Democratic parties have created an ecology oriented parliamentary group. Because of the requirement of a minimum of ten members in a parliamentary group, the single MER representative in the Senate has been forced into an unlikely alliance with the National Liberal Party.

Bulgaria

In Bulgaria, the Socialist Party (BSP) obtained 211 out of 400 seats, and the UDF 164 seats. The support for UDF, Ecoglasnost, and the Green Party was concentrated in Sofia, where UDF obtained 53 percent of the votes and BSP only 39 percent.[84] Ecoglasnost obtained 25 seats and the Green Party 14 seats. These two groups obtained between them, therefore, just under 10 percent of the seats, the highest proportion anywhere in Eastern Europe. The fact that UDF remains in opposition, however, prevents the environmentalists' strong showing from being translated into the sort of success seen in Slovenia.

GDR

The Green Party in the GDR entered into a coalition with the Women's League and obtained 1.96 percent of the votes and 8 out of 400 seats. The winning Alliance for Germany 90 obtained 48.14 percent of the votes and 193 seats. Once in Parliament the Green Party and the Women's League split over a disagreement over how to share the 8 seats between the two parties.[85] These two groups then formed a joint parliamentary group of 12 with Alliance 90. Wider coalitions were agreed in response to the all-German elections, where parties were required to get more than 5 percent of the total German vote.[86]

Czechoslovakia

In Czechoslovakia the "green vote" went to Civic Forum, which was backing the country's leading environmentalists for the posts of Czech and federal ministers of the environment. A proportional system with a minimum of 5 percent excluded all green party candidates in the Czech and federal parliaments. In Slovakia, Civic Forum's counterpart, Public Against Violence, did not attract much of the green vote, which went to the Slovak Green Party. Because the minimum required to obtain a seat in the Parliament was only 3 percent, the Green Party won 6 out of 150 seats in the Slovak National Council.

Hungary

In Hungary, because of the divisions discussed earlier, the Green Party was very weak, and was not even able to participate in the elections in Budapest. In addition, public interest in green affairs had fallen off dramatically after controversy had ceased over the environmental cause célèbre, the Danube dams.

Conclusion: The Future

The situation in Central and Eastern Europe[87] is changing rapidly. With the shift from idealism to pragmatism since the revolutions, the environmental issue has lost much of its former significance as a symbol of the commitment to repairing the damage of the old order and to building a new. Indeed, measures to protect the environment are now often seen as a break in the process of introducing free-market economies, as powerful economic lobbies argue that cleaning the environment is an unacceptable curb on economic recovery.

The apparent decreasing importance of environmental considerations on the political agenda may be ascribed in part to the lack of a politically powerful advocate of environmental priorities. In the West, environmental NGOs have mobilized and channeled public opinion to the extent that these organizations cannot be ignored. In Central and Eastern Europe, while public opinion is strong, the mechanisms for channeling it into a political lobby are not yet developed. Until strong environmental advocates are established within the countries of Central and Eastern Europe,[88] the political importance of environmental considerations in the corridors of power is likely to be low relative to other issues.

A number of factors will determine the process of development of the environmental movement in Central and Eastern Europe. One factor that will militate against the rapid development of a strong environmental movement is the long tradition throughout the region of state dominance and weak society, reinforced by the experience of the past 40 years. Cultural differences between countries will create big variations. Nowhere is this already more apparent than in Yugoslavia, where the fractured political system has produced extreme differences in the extent and scope of development among the republican environmental movements.

Another important factor that will hamper the development of a strong environmental movement is the lack of resources. Political and economic instability will heighten this weakness. New NGOs in the West almost always make extensive use of the resources provided by already existing organizations.[89] No such basis yet exists in Central and Eastern Europe. A characteristic feature of Central and East European

NGOs is likely to be financial crisis for some years to come. Furthermore, there is little tradition of raising money through membership subscriptions, and a lack of knowledge of the techniques Western NGOs have developed to mobilize public opinion and maintain public support.

This rather gloomy picture should be balanced by some of the advantages enjoyed by Central and East European environmental NGOs that Western organizations did not enjoy in the 1970s. Most important is the fact that public concern for the environment is already strong. In the 1970s, Western environmental NGOs had not only to mobilize public opinion but to a large extent had to create it first. Secondly, there is the possibility of the international transfer of resources, from the wealthy environmental NGOs in Western Europe and North America. This transfer is taking place in a wide variety of ways—provision of capital equipment, joint conferences, internships, provision of documentation, and the execution of joint projects (such as a coordinated response to Western investment). The usual phenomenon of using existing NGO resources is therefore repeating itself, but on an international scale. It is too early to determine how effective this international assistance is.

Lastly, an important factor will be the political priority attached to the environment on the part of Western institutions currently involved in assisting Central and East European countries. Western governments and multilateral banks active in the region are coming under considerable pressure from environmental lobbies within Western Europe, in particular the World Bank and the European Bank for Reconstruction and Development. Western companies investing in Central and Eastern Europe also have an incentive to "impose" environmental standards if and when they do not exist, given that much of the product of such investment is intended for Western markets.

Observers of the environmental movement in Central and Eastern Europe in the 1990s will want to see how these different factors interact and balance each other.

Notes

1. See, for example, D. E. Powell, "The Social Cost of Modernization: Ecological Problems in the USSR," *World Politics*, 23 (1971); P. Pryde, *Conservation in the Soviet Union* (Cambridge: Cambridge University Press, 1972); Marshall I.

Goldman, *The Spoils of Progress* (Cambridge, MA: MIT Press, 1972); K. Bush, "The Soviet Response to Environmental Disruption," *Problems of Communism*, 21 July–August 1972, pp. 21–31; C. Zum Brunnen, "The Lake Baikal Controversy," in I. Volgyes, ed., *Environmental Deterioration in the Soviet Union and Eastern Europe* (New York: Praeger, 1974), pp. 80–122; D. R. Kelley, "Environmental Policy-Making in the USSR: The Role of Industrial and Environmental Interest Groups," *Soviet Studies* 24, no. 4 (1976): 570–89; W. A. Jackson, *Soviet Resource Management and the Environment* (Columbus, OH: American Association for the Advancement of Slavic Studies, 1978).

2. The two most complete analyses are I. Oldberg, "Planned Economy and Environmental Problems: Eastern Europe from a Comparative Perspective," *Bidgrag till Oststatsforskningen* 11, no. 2 (Nordic Committee for Soviet and East European Research, 1983) and J. M. Kramer, "The Environmental Crisis in Eastern Europe: The Price for Progress," *Slavic Review* 42 (1983): 204–20.

3. The best study is of the Soviet Union and Yugoslavia by Barbara Jancar, which sets out in table form all environmental laws passed in this period: B. Jancar, *Environmental Management in the Soviet Union and Yugoslavia: Structure and Regulation in Communist Federal States* (Durham, NC: Duke University Press, 1987), appendices 1 & 2.

4. V. Sobell, "The Ecological Crisis in Eastern Europe," RFE, BR/5 (20 January 1988), pp. 9–10; J. Fullenbach, *European Environmental Policy: East and West*, trans. F. Carter and J. Manton (London: Butterworths, 1981), p. 33; G. Enyedi, A. J. Gijswijt, and B. Rhode, *Environmental Polities in East and West* (London: Taylor Graham, 1987), pp. 216–17; M. Persanyi, "Gongos, Quangos, Blues and Greens (A comprehensive description of nongovernmental organizations in environmental protection in Hungary)," paper prepared for presentation at the Conference on Environmental Constraints and Opportunities in the Social Organizations of Space, Udine, Italy, 7–10 June 1989, p. 4.

5. This decay is graphically described in two reports by the Experience and Future Discussion Group (DiP) in Warsaw in 1978. The environment is included as one among many elements of overall collapse, although in a list of problems, ranked according to seriousness, it comes last. The Experience and Future Discussion Group, *Poland Today: The State of the Republic* (White Plains, NY: M.E. Sharpe, 1981), pp. 76, 89–90 and 163.

6. The most thorough analysis of this development is in the Soviet Union, e.g., T. Gustafson, *Reform in the Soviet Politics: Lessons of Recent Policies on Land and Water* (Cambridge: Cambridge University Press, 1981), pp. 231–38; J. DeBardeleben, *The Environment and Marxism-Leninism: The Soviet and East European Experience* (Boulder, CO: Westview Press, 1985), p. 60. Waller notes that specialist debate also became a legitimate part of the political process in Eastern Europe (M. Waller, "The Ecology Issue in Eastern Europe: Protest and Movements," *Journal of Communist Studies* 5, no. 3 [September 1989]: 309).

7. In the case of the Soviet Union, this frustration is described by C. E. Ziegler, *Environmental Policy in the USSR* (London: Pinter, 1987), p. 66.

8. D. Fisher, *Report on a Visit to Yugoslavia* (London: Ecological Studies Institute, May 1990), p. 7.

9. D. Fisher, *Report on Two Visits to Romania* (London: Ecological Studies Institute, March/April 1990), p. 2.

10. D. Fisher, *Public Intervention in Pollution Aspects of Transboundary Wastercourses and International Lakes: European Experience* (London: Ecological Studies Institute, August 1989), pp. 17 and 19.

11. Given in *East European Reporter* 1, no. 1 (Spring 1985): 9–10.

12. The situation in Eastern Europe in this respect was different only in degree from the West. It occurs wherever incentives for bureaucrats cause their own interests and social interests to diverge (J. Baden and R. L. Stroup, *Bureaucracy versus Environment: The Environmental Costs of Bureaucratic Governance* [Ann Arbor, MI: University of Michigan Press, 1981], pp. 217–18).

13. *East European Reporter* 2, no. 2 (1986): 5–7.

14. Quoted in RFE *Bulgarian SR* 7, no. 3 (7 August 1989).

15. Ziegler (1987), pp. 51–52.

16. Quoted in RFE *Bulgarian SR* 1, no. 1 (3 February 1989). The state's ideological commitment to participation in the environmental sphere is also evident in the chapter on the GDR in Enyedi et al. (1987), pp. 160–61. *The Hungarian National Concept and Requirements for National Policy* (1980) stated: "The active and permanent cooperation of the widest strata of society is an essential condition for a successful environment. It is promoted by the social and mass organizations" (Persanyi [1989], p. 3).

17. L. Sochor, *Contribution to an Analysis of the Conservative Features of the Ideology of "Real Socialism"* (Vienna: Crises in Soviet-Type Systems, Study No. 4, 1984), pp. 21–22.

18. J. L. Curry, *The Black Book of Polish Censorship* (New York: Random House, 1984).

19. *Ibid.*, p. 212; specific regulations on control of environmental information are given on pp. 218–27.

20. This is the main argument of Václav Havel in his celebrated essay, "The Power of the Powerless." The power of the powerless is their ability to strike at the foundations of the facade of order by not playing the game and thus revealing the hollowness of the real state of society (see Václav Havel et al., *The Power of the Powerless* [London: Palach Press, 1985]).

21. Persanyi (1989), p. 17.

22. For example, the British Jan Hus Foundation, which supported the Czechoslovak opposition, sent Tom Burke of the Green Alliance in London to make contacts with Czech and Slovak environmentalists from 1986 onward.

23. RFE *Bulgarian SR* 10, no. 2 (4 November 1987); *Bulgarian SR* 13, no. 1 (25 November 1987); *Romanian SR* 5, no. 1 (29 March 1988); *East European Newsletter* 3, no. 1 (11 January 1989): 2.

24. *East European Newsletter* 3, no. 1 (11 January 1989): 1–3; 3, no. 11 (31 May 1989): 1–3; 3, no. 17 (28 August 1989): 4–6; 3, no. 18 (11 September 1989): 5–6; 3, no. 19 (October 1989): 6–7; RFE *Bulgarian SR* 2, no. 3 (9 March 1989); *Bulgarian SR* 4, no. 3 (22 May 1989); *East European Reporter*, 3, no. 4 (Spring/Summer 1989): 26–28; 4, no. 1 (Winter 1989/90): 83–85.

25. Enyedi et al. (1987), pp. 66–67.

26. RFE BR/42 (20 March 1987).

27. RFE *Bulgarian SR* 10, no. 5 (5 December 1989).

28. The following three paragraphs are based on Fisher (August 1989), pp.

15–17; and D. Fisher, *Report on a Visit to Czechoslovakia* (London: Ecological Studies Institute, December 1989), annex 1.

29. The report is reproduced in *East European Reporter* 3, no. 3 (Autumn 1988): 26–30.

30. These are listed in Waller (1989), pp. 314–15.

31. RFE *Czechoslovak SR* 17, no. 6 (18 August 1989).

32. RFE *Czechoslovak SR* 4, no. 5 (12 March 1988); *Bulgarian SR* 13, no. 10 (1 September 1988).

33. DeBardeleben (1985), p. 79.

34. G. Kallenbach, "The Part of the Church in the Environmental Movement of the GDR," paper given at SEED Popular Forum, Bergen, Norway, 14 May 1990, p. 3.

35. Kallenbach (1990); DeBardeleben (1985), p. 89.

36. Fisher (May 1990), pp. 8, 12.

37. Helsinki Watch, *From Below: Independent Peace and Environmental Movements in Eastern Europe and the USSR* (New York: Helsinki Watch Report, October 1987), pp. 193–95.

38. Fisher (May 1990), p. 13.

39. *Ibid.*, pp. 5–6.

40. Helsinki Watch (1987), p. 192.

41. Fisher (May 1990), p. 7.

42. Persanyi (1989), pp. 13–14; Waller (1989), p. 321; T. Fleischer, "The Blue Danube," *East European Reporter* 4, no. 2 (Spring/Summer 1990): 78.

43. Persanyi (1989), p. 14.

44. *Ibid.*, pp. 15–16.

45. *Ibid.*, p. 6.

46. *Ibid.*, p. 9; L. Solyom, "Hungary: Citizens; Participation in the Environmental Movement," *IFDA Dossier* 64 (March/April 1988): 28–29.

47. The response to the Gabcikovo-Nagymaros Dam system is discussed in various documents: Fisher (August 1989), pp. 12–26; Solyom (1988), pp. 24–28.

48. See, for example, the comments of Persanyi (1989), p. 6.

49. This activity is described in Helsinki Watch (1987), pp. 79–80, 92–95.

50. Swedish-Polish Association for Environmental Protection, "Proceedings from SPM Seminar on Swedish-Polish Environmental Cooperation, February 23–24, 1988" (Upsala: Swedish Polish Association for Environmental Protection, 1989), pp. 69–73.

51. RFE *BR/42* (20 March 1987).

52. Sobell (1988), pp. 12–13.

53. RFE *Poland SR* 1 (11 January 1989).

54. M. Sobelman, "New Objectives in the Area of Environmental Protection in Poland," *Environmental Policy Review: The Soviet Union and Eastern Europe* 3, no. 1 (January 1989): 22–27.

55. *Bloc* (November-December 1989), p. 14; Palach Press, *Uncensored Czechoslovakia:* December 13, 1989, p. 18; December 17, 1989, p. 13; December 19, 1989, p. 17; RFE *Czechoslovak SR* 19, no. 8 (20 September 1989).

56. Fisher (August 1989), pp. 19–20; Y. Golan, "Suspension of the Work on the Bos-Nagymaros Dam," *Environmental Policy Review: The Soviet Union and Eastern Europe* 3, no. 2 (July 1989); Persanyi (1989), pp. 8–9.

57. RFE *Hungarian SR* 16, no. 3 (28 October 1988).

58. From now on the established Western terminology will be used. The rather vague term, nongovernmental organization (NGO), here represents the equivalent of more exact terms such as social movement or organization preferred by some social scientists, for example, J. D. McCarthy and M. N. Zald, "Resource Mobilization and Social Movements: A Partial Theory," in M. N. Zald and J. D. McCarthy, eds., *Social Movements in an Organizational Society* (New Brunswick, NJ: Transaction Books, 1987), pp. 15–42.

59. D. Fisher, *Report on a Visit to Bulgaria* (London: Ecological Studies Institute, February 1990), pp. 3–4.

60. The text may be found in Fisher (February 1990), annex 3.

61. Fisher (February 1990), annex 2.

62. *East European Newsletter* 3, no. 21 (October 1989): 6; RFE *Bulgarian SR* 10, no. 5 (5 December 1989); personal observation.

63. Ecoglasnost in Bulgaria, made up of about 90 local groups (Fisher [February 1990], p. 5); the Green Alliance in Croatia (Fisher [May 1990], p. 15); the Green Movement in Serbia (*Ibid.*, p. 5); the Green League in the GDR; the Green Circle in Czechoslovakia (Fisher [December 1989], p. 3); the Ecological Movement of Romania (Fisher [March/April 1990], p. 3).

64. In Czechoslovakia, the old leaderships of the Czech and Slovak Unions of Nature Protectors were dismissed, the Brontosaurus youth organization came out of the Socialist Youth Movement, and the Ecological Section of the Biological Society came out of the Academy of Sciences (Fisher [December 1989], pp. 2–3; *East European Newsletter* 4, no. 1 [January 1990], p. 4 [written by D. Fisher]); in Hungary the National Society of Nature Protectors began reforming itself and developing the already existing network of local groups around the country.

65. Bulgaria: The Bulgarian Green Party founded in December 1989 (Fisher [February 1990], p. 6; BBC Summary of World Broadcasts: EE/0654 B/2 [5 January 1990]); GDR: Founded in November 1989, with a founding congress in Halle in February 1990; Czechoslovakia: Numerous local parties formed in December 1989, which formed a federated Czech and Slovak Green Party in February 1990 (Fisher [December 1989], pp. 3–4; BBC Summary of World Broadcasts: EE/0662 B/8 [15 January 1990]; EE/0677 B/4 [1 February 1990]; EE/0692 B/5 [19 February 1990]; EE/0681 B/3 [6 February 1990]); Hungary: Green Party founded in November 1989 (*Manchester Guardian*, 20 November 1989); Poland: The first green party was founded in Cracow in December 1988. This has since split into a number of warring factions (A. Delorme, "Green Parties in Poland" [Cracow, December, 1989]); Romania: There are several parties around the country, the most important of which was the Green Party of Romania (PER), founded in 1990 (Fisher [March/April 1990], p. 8); Yugoslavia: Bosnian-Hercegovinan Green Party founded in 1989 (*East European Newsletter* 4, no. 3 [February 1990], p. 6); Serbian Green Party founded in February 1990 (Fisher [May 1990]: 4); Slovenian Green Party founded in January 1990 (Fisher [May 1990]: 9).

66. White et al. observe the large nonvoting proportions of the electorate in Poland, Hungary and Czechoslovakia in a highly politicized situation (S. White, J. Gardner, G. Schopflin, and T. Saich, *Communist and Postcommunist Political Systems: An Introduction* [London: Macmillan, 1990], pp. 63–68).

67. V. Melucci, "Social Movements and the Democratization of Everyday

Life," in J. Keane, ed., *Civil Society and the State* (London: Verso, 1988), p. 222; V. Melucci, *Nomads of the Present*, trans. and ed. by J. Keane and P. Mier (London: Verso, 1989), pp. 7–8.

68. Fisher (February 1990), p. 4.

69. Fisher (March/April 1990), pp. 5–6.

70. Fisher (February 1990), pp. 4–5.

71. BBC Summary of World Broadcasts: EE/0731 B/2–3 (5 April 1990).

72. Fisher (March/April 1990), p. 5.

73. Bulgarian manifestos are discussed in Fisher (February 1990): 8–10; the Romanian parties' views on ecology are discussed in Fisher (March/April 1990): 8. GDR election manifestos are reproduced in *East European Reporter* 4, no. 1 (Winter 1989/90): 22–26; the manifesto of GDR's "Democracy Now" is reproduced *Across Frontiers* (Fall–Winter 1989–90): 5–6.

74. According to Persanyi (1989), p. 9, this was the case in Hungary.

75. Persanyi (1989), p. 10.

76. There is a lengthy survey of this activity in V. Gavrilov, "Environmental Damage Creates Serious Problem for Government," *Report on Eastern Europe* 1, no. 21 (Radio Free Europe, 25 May 1990): 4–12.

77. BBC Summary of World Broadcasts: EE/0691 B/1 (17 February 1990), EE/0695 B/2 (22 February 1990), EE/W0118 A/11 (8 March 1990), EE/0782 B/3–4 (5 June 1990).

78. BBC Summary of World Broadcasts: EE/0752 B/3 (1 May 1990).

79. BBC Summary of World Broadcasts: EE/W0109i (4 January 1990), EE/W0116 A/3–4 (22 February 1990), EE/0731 B/2–3 (5 April 1990).

80. BBC Summary of World Broadcasts: EE/W0117 A/5 (1 March 1990), EE/0772i (24 May 1990), EE/W0130 A/5 (31 May 1990), EE/0783 B/2–3 (6 June 1990), EE/0785 A2/2 (8 June 1990), EE/0786i (9 June 1990), EE/0787i (11 June 1990), EE/0792 A2/1 (16 June 1990), EE/0809i (6 July 1990), EE/0825 A2/1 (25 July 1990), EE/0828–9 A2/1 (28 July 1990), EE/0831 A2/3 (1 August 1990).

81. Fisher (May 1990), p. 9; *East European Newsletter* 4, no. 13 (June 1990): 7–8 (written by D. Fisher).

82. *East European Newsletter* 4, no. 9 (April 1990): 5.

83. Each candidate needed to win more than 50 percent of the seats in his/her constituency; if a second round was necessary, all candidates achieving less than 7 percent of the votes were disqualified (Fisher [May 1990], p. 13).

84. *East European Newsletter* 4, no. 13 (June 1990): 5.

85. BBC Summary of World Broadcasts: EE/0732 B/3 (27 March 1990).

86. BBC Summary of World Broadcasts: EE/0836 B/9 (7 August 1990).

87. Since the revolutions, the term "Eastern Europe" is being replaced by the term "Central and Eastern Europe."

88. The Ecological Studies Institute in London is currently undertaking a broad analysis of this issue.

89. A. Oberschall as cited in C. Tilly, *From Mobilization to Revolution* (Reading, MA: Addison-Wesley, 1978), p. 81; P. Lowe and J. Goyder, *Environmental Groups in Politics* (London: George Allen & Unwin, 1983), p. 47; McCarthy and Zald (1987), p. 34.

8

The History of Environmental Protection in Poland and the Growth of Awareness and Activism

Stanley J. Kabala

Over the centuries, from the times of royal prerogative to those of socialist industrialization, the concept and practice of environmental protection in Poland has manifested uniquely Polish features as well as exhibiting characteristics typical of differing historical periods. In the turbulent political climate of the 1980s in Poland, ecological issues were found at the center of acute social concern and political debate more than at any other time in the country's history. Protection of the natural environment became both an element of contention between regime and opposition and a ground for hoped-for accommodation between government and people.

Royal Poland, The Time of the Pacifications, and the Interwar Era

The characteristic feature of the protection of nature in royal Poland from the sixteenth through eighteenth centuries—that is, until the historic partitions that removed the Polish state from the political map of

---

The author is affiliated with the Center for Hazardous Materials Research in Pittsburgh.

Europe and the protection of nature from the jurisdiction of specifically Polish authorities—was the royal protection of particular species and reserves typical of that practiced by monarchs in Europe over those centuries. Particularly noteworthy is the long preservation in Poland by royal decree of the European bison.[1] Beginning in the eighth century with the protection of the beaver during the reign of Boleslaw the Brave, traditional conservation of natural resources took shape in the fourteenth century (under Wladyslaw Jagiello, the king of the joined commonwealth of Poland and Lithuania) with the prohibition of excessive cutting and export of pine and the promulgation of severe restrictions on the hunting of deer, boar, tarpon, and moose. Succeeding kings, Zygmunt I the Old in the fifteenth century, and Stefan Batory and Zygmunt III Wasa in the sixteenth century, issued further decrees on the protection of threatened species.[2]

In the era of the partitions (1797–1918) the idea of nature protection took shape as a manifestation of Polish patriotism. In the Prussian partition (the west and north of today's Poland) an inventory of natural monuments was undertaken. In 1906 in the Russian partition (today's Poland eastward from Warsaw and parts of today's Belarus and Ukraine) the Polish Association of Nature Lovers was founded. In the Austrian partition, today's southern Poland, the provincial assembly passed a law in 1869 on protection of indigenous alpine fauna of the Tatra Mountains. In the same region in 1886 a reserve was established in the Pieniny range along today's Polish-Czechoslovak border, and in 1902 an organization for the protection of the Tatras was founded.[3]

Trench warfare on the Eastern Front took its toll on the Bialowieza, one of Europe's last stands of primeval forest, as both the German and the Russian armies cut its massive ancient trees to provide the vast supply of beams required for construction of trenches. This was the first of two times in this century when Poland's nature would pay the price of hosting the battles of modern armies.

In 1918 Poland reasserted its independence and undertook the establishment of Polish administration over its territory. Nature conservation took its place in this effort. The brief twenty-year period of Polish independence saw remarkable national efforts in economic development and the overdue creation of an economic infrastructure.[4] Activity on all fronts in what was a heady time for Poles was paralleled by achievements in conservation as well, as the new state turned its attention to the protection of its age-old but newly reclaimed natural patrimony. In 1919, a poacher killed the last female bison in the ancient Bialowieza Forest in eastern Poland, then one of the last remaining habitats of this indigenous European species on the continent. Polish naturalists, among them Wladyslaw Szafer, the father of Polish nature conservation, began efforts to return the bison to Bialowieza, an event that took place in 1929. Poland's Bialowieza National Park and the adjoining park across the border in the USSR are today the only location on the continent where the European bison roams free in its natural habitat.

Activity in the interwar years showed the influence of Walery Goetel, another of the forefathers of nature protection in Poland, whose work expanded the concept of protection of natural resources from its then narrow meaning as the careful use of mineral wealth to comprise the preservation of the whole of nature, including man. Goetel is also responsible for introducing into Polish discussion the idea of the synonymity of the concepts of the protection of natural resources and their rational use.[5]

In 1920 a National Council on the Protection of Nature was established and in 1922 the Sejm (Parliament) passed the country's first water resource management law.[6] In 1928 the League for the Protection of Nature was founded. The year 1932 saw one of the few instances of Polish-Czechoslovak cooperation of the entire interwar period—a time marked by continual diplomatic quarreling—as the two new states established two national parks to create a transboundary reserve in the Tatra Mountains that formed their border. The 1930s witnessed the establishment of Poland's first national parks, Great Poland in the west in 1931, Bialowieza in the east in 1932, and Tatra Mountains in the south in 1938, and over one hundred nature preserves. A 1934 law on the protection of nature established the basis of national environmental regulation. Like much else begun by the new Poland between the wars, these efforts barely had time to take effect before they were obviated by the Second World War.

The fact that the formal war that began in Poland in September 1939 lasted only a short time and caused only limited destruction of the countryside indicated nothing about the ultimate environmental effect of the war on Poland. During the Nazi occupation (1939–1944) Poland's nature bore the brunt of violence in two ways. For nearly five years the German occupiers ruthlessly exploited their invincible position and scoured Poland for any and all natural resources that could be shipped to Germany for the war effort. Then in 1944, the westward movement of the Russian front caused devastation across the length and breadth of the country.

People's Poland

Establishment of communist rule in Poland in the postwar era had little impact on nature conservation in a country whose every effort was directed to physical and psychological recovery from the vast devastation of the war. Poland's postwar reconstruction did include incorporation of nature protection into the legal basis of the new Polish People's Republic. Like most communist states and many other countries with contemporary, that is, post–World War II, constitutions, Poland placed the legal foundation for environmental protection in that document. Establishment of a new framework of law reflected two worldwide trends: that of moving from the essentially passive mode of conservation to the active mode of protection in the official attitude toward nature, and that of incorporating the right of citizens to a sound environment in new national constitutions. Article 13 of the new Constitution stated that "The Polish People's Republic ensures the protection and rational development of the natural environment, constituting the nationwide wealth," while Article 71 asserted that citizens "have the right to benefit from the values of the natural environment and the obligation to protect it."

Legislative elaboration of these fundamental provisions principally took the form of a 1949 Statute on the Protection of Nature, a 1974 Statute on Water Resource Management, and the 1980 Statute on the Protection and Shaping of the Environment that currently governs environmental protection and administration in Poland. Legal reference to the protection of nature (comprising its resources, living and nonliving elements, and the "landscape") began with the 1949 law, which set up a Ministry of Forestry and Forest Industries and created a National Council for the Protection of Nature.[7] In 1970 the Polish Committee for Environmental Protection was formed with the Vice Premier as chairman. In 1972 the Ministry of Territorial Management and Environmental Protection was established. The maintenance and expansion of the country's system of national parks, protected areas and species, and "landscape parks," constituting continuation of programs begun in the interwar period, is perhaps the most notable conservation achievement of this era. In Poland, as throughout most of the world during the quarter century following the Second World War, economic growth dominated the imaginations of countries and governments, with environment rarely given a second thought. The idea that natural processes possessed carrying capacities that could be exceeded to the detriment of both nature and man was unknown or not regarded as pertinent. In this context Poland undertook the industrialization policies that in two decades transformed it from the primarily agricultural country it had been into a substantial industrialized country that became, together with Czechoslovakia and the GDR, one of Eastern Europe's major industrial powers. When Poland undertook its development program in the early 1950s it followed the model formulated and applied in the Soviet Union two decades before: the so-called "extensive pattern of development" that saw the creation of heavy industry and the achievement of import substitution as the road to socialism. Under this pattern, rates of growth in national product derive from increases in the quantity of labor, capital, and resource inputs into the productive process. The social aspects of this pattern involved draining the traditional farm labor force for industrial employment, bringing women into the work force, and forcing heavy direct investment in industrial capacity at the expense of both consumption and social and economic infrastructure.

The objective of the planners of Poland's industrialization drive in the 1950s was to create an industrial structure regarded at the time as the most conducive to growth.[8] Doing so amounted to an imitation of the Soviet pattern of the 1930s—a pattern, it must be noted, that was developed in a country of considerably different culture, historical position, and economic conditions, and which moreover is virtually unique in the world in size and resource endowment. In Poland massive and concentrated investment was made in the coal mining, ferrous and nonferrous metallurgical, heavy machinery, chemical, and shipbuilding industries and included the creation of gigantic new facilities that symbolized Poland's conversion into an industrial country, such as the Lenin Steelworks near Cracow (known, together with the new city that was built with it, as Nowa Huta, or "New Mill").

When the environmental effects of this decades-long industrialization drive began to come to light, they were referred to as the price that the nation had to pay for progress or dismissed with statements to the effect that once the country had achieved prosperity its booming economy could direct attention to environmental protection. This situation lasted until the period of economic collapse and political dissension at the beginning of the 1980s: the time of Solidarity.

The Environmental Significance of Solidarity

The significance of Solidarity in the history of environmental affairs in Poland is paramount. Events during the brief era of Solidarity moved as rapidly in matters of ecology as in all other areas of Polish life, and an environmental movement was born that outlived its outlawed parent union. With its long tradition of nature protection, beginning in modern times in the mid-nineteenth century, as can be seen from a review of the country's environmental literature, the science of ecology was able to establish itself as a discipline over the 1970s in a pattern that resembled the one taking place in other parts of the world. Ecological awareness and parallel social activism were, however, things that had yet to appear. This was due to several factors. First was the dearth of information in Poland on the subject of environmental degradation in the country. In contrast to the relatively free flow of information on many topics in Poland, the government had retained its virtual monopoly on the development and dissemination of technical data. What information there was on environmental problems did not make its way to the public at large or even to a significant scientific readership. Second was the very limited amount of research being done on the subject, clearly not one of high priority with the government in a system where the government controlled allocations—hence topics—for research. Third was the relative newness of the issue of ecological degradation in a country that had begun only thirty years before to industrialize and where the equation in the popular mind of belching smokestacks with progress was still strong. This general mindset was certainly receptive—at least for a while—to the government's repeated assertions to the effect that pollution was the price Poland had to pay for prosperity and a rising standard of living and that, in any case, what technology damaged, technology would repair.* Voiced in the 1970s, ecological misgivings about the country's development and the risks posed by industrial technologies appeared misplaced at a time when bustling investment, rising wages, and full shops seemed to prove the government right.

This situation was in contrast to that in Hungary, for example, where by the late 1970s a high level of ecological awareness was evident. The impetus to environmental protection that seemed to come

---

*Phrased this way, the assertion is a subtle but significant reworking of Prof. Szaler's dictum that "what technology damages, technology *must* repair."

evident. The impetus to environmental protection that seemed to come in Hungary from a strong and committed scientific community had no equivalent in Poland. State environmental programs in Poland appeared to be "principally a matter of rhetoric rather than action," commented one Western observer comparing the two countries at the time.[9] To be sure, 1978 saw the publication of Professor Jan Juda's study of air quality conditions and the extent of the problem of air pollution nationwide. This work would receive great attention in just a few years and come to serve as the basis for much further research as well, but at the time its impact on both social awareness and official policy was minimal.[10]

The government was thoroughly committed to its industrialization policies and there was no sign of the emergence of a popular environmental movement. It must be remembered that this was during the time when the "New Investment Policy" of the 1970s still promised to bring prosperity to the country and increased legitimacy to its communist government.

The only public organization with an environmental agenda was the official League for the Protection of Nature (*Liga Ochrony Przyrody*, or LOP), Poland's oldest environmental group. Under the country's communist regime the LOP had become a mouthpiece for official positions on ecological matters. Its functions were limited to largely traditional activities in nature education and nature conservation, and it was not looked upon by Polish citizens as a body to which to turn for aggressive action. A survey of Warsaw's populace in 1976 and 1977 found that only 13.6 percent of those questioned would turn to the LOP to solve environmental problems. This was less than the 14.8 percent who would try to solve a problem by themselves and far less than the 54.7 percent who would look to government councils and ministries.[11]

Precisely what course environmental affairs would have taken in Poland through times of continued prosperity or economic decline in the absence of political upheaval is something we cannot know. What did take place is nothing less than remarkable. In 1980, Solidarity, Eastern Europe's first independent self-governing trade union, was born—and with it a new force in Poland's polity. Despite the eventual suppression of Solidarity, the time of social and political openness it made possible transformed Poland in ways that martial law could not eradicate and left behind a Polish ecological movement as part of its legacy.

As Solidarity opened up Poland's civic life, the truth about every facet of Polish society, economy, politics, and recent history burst forth. Information was like rainfall after a drought in this society long starved for truth and too well educated to accept in its place the "facts" supplied by the regime. (A vivid example of the Polish people's desire for authentic history was their reaction to historical exhibits and reports on the officially suppressed events in Szczecin in 1970 during which shipyard workers involved in demonstrations were killed.) Virtually no area of affairs was safe from leaks by Poles willing to contribute knowledge in their fields to the general flow. The environment was no exception as heretofore concealed information on the condition of the country under ecological assault flowed from every source. When the government lifted its ban on the subject in 1980, a flood of discussion of environmental matters swept through popular as well as scientific journals. Government data and industrial records were made public by administrators, officials, and scientists throughout the country sympathetic to the aims of Solidarity.

Local chapters of Solidarity took on the function of investigating, compiling, and reporting instances of environmental abuse. Among its famous theses issued in 1981, the national organization included environmental protection as number 16, demanding social control of open decision-making processes, the introduction of business accounting into industrial management so as to assure proper costing of environmental losses, the establishment of specific environmental protection funds to be placed at the disposal of local government, the conversion of ecologically harmful industries and the construction of adequate waste treatment systems, the overhaul of environmental protection regulations, and the provision of full information to the public and the union.

Most striking, but entirely normal for the times, was the publication by *Przyroda Polska* (Polish Nature) of its special mid-1981 edition entitled "The State of the Natural Environment in Poland and the Threat to Human Health."[12] The report compiled the best information existing in Poland on the extent of the ecological threat to the country and its people, presented an estimate of the toll in economic and social welfare that was being exacted, and proposed ways out of the crisis. The document, the organ of an official, government-sponsored organization, the LOP, forcefully brought to the attention of the Polish people the dimensions of the natural disaster they were facing, knowledge of which the government had seen fit to keep from them. The data in the special supplement—itself sanctified by publication in a quasi-official publication—went on to be incorporated into other scientific and official reports and, perhaps more important, found its way into the country's large and effective system of underground publications, such as the 1984 item "Poland in the Eighties" put out by the *Przedswit* (Dawn) publishing house, an operation with strong ties to Solidarity.[13]

The case of the Skawina aluminum plant is illustrative of the impact of the times on environmental affairs. The thirty-year-old plant, fourteen kilometers to the southwest of Cracow, had an annual production capacity of 50,000 tons and produced half the aluminum smelted in Poland.[14] Although by 1980 its value to the economy was 1.5 billion zlotys a year, it also generated over 2000 tons of fluoride pollutant, the extremely toxic residue of the smelting process. In the late 1970s, scientific data showed that the plant posed a serious health hazard to its workers and to residents in an area of some 230 square kilometers surrounding it. According to one source, the majority of the 2500 employees working in the plant at the time qualified for medical disability pensions as a result of prolonged exposure to the chemical.

The fluorine content in tested plant species around Skawina was one hundred times that found in unpolluted areas and was found to be the cause of cattle poisoning on farms in the area. The high incidence of arthritis and skeletal ailments in young and middle-aged people in the Cracow region had been linked to prolonged exposure to fluoride pollution.[15]

It is unlikely that the situation would ever have been remedied had it not been for the rise of Solidarity and the opportunities made possible by the renewal of public political life in Poland. In late 1980, a coalition of the new trade union, scientists, local environmentalists, and the press demanded that the aluminum plant be closed down. More than one observer has noted that during this time Poland's public life resembled that of Western liberal states.

> The *Gazeta Krakowska* showed what an ungagged press might do. Under a new editor, it took up an environmentalist campaign against the nearby Huta Skawina aluminum works. Within a month, the aluminum works was closed.[16]

A partial shutdown of the plant's electrolyzer at the end of 1980 resulted in a 30 percent reduction of fluoride emissions.[17] Continued pressure by Cracow city authorities, the press, and the newly formed Polish Ecological Club (PKE) caused the State Ministry of Metallurgy to close the remainder of the Skawina works in January 1981. The plant has never been reopened.

The Skawina episode represented the apex of political activism on environmental matters in the first half of 1980 and a significant political development. Acting from purely ecological motives, a public coalition in a communist country forced the closing and virtual abandonment of a major industrial facility that produced half its nation's supply of aluminum. Despite the reestablishment of the regime's political monopoly, that shutdown was maintained. At the time of the imposition of martial law and suppression of Solidarity in December 1981, the fate of its organizational offspring, the Polish Ecological Club, was not clear. In fact the Polish environmental lobby was tolerated by the Polish government and grew into a nationwide network of club chapters active on regional and national environmental questions.[18]

Government Response to Environmental Disaster

By the middle of the 1980s the extent of the environmental crisis facing Poland had been assessed by institutions no less significant than the Academy of Sciences and the National Planning Commission. Official documents cited data from the landmark 1985 study by Kassenberg and Rolewicz, *The Spatial Diagnosis of Environmental Protection in Poland.* Twenty-seven regions, comprising 11.3 percent of the country's land area and 35.5 percent of its population, were designated as areas of "ecological hazard." Five of them were designated areas of "ecological disaster" because of the extreme severity of the pollution to which they were subjected. These were Upper Silesia and Rybnik in the mining and steel region of southern Poland, the industrialized area around Cracow, the Legnica-Głogow copper mining region in west-central Poland, and Gdansk on the Baltic.[19] Calculations of the economic losses resulting from the degradation of the environment and waste of natural resources were staggering—equivalent to 10 percent of the country's GNP each year.[20] The issue became the cause of grave concern in the country, receiving steadily greater attention from the scientific community, the public, and the government, coming to be referred to in official discussions as nothing less than the "ecological barrier to the development of the country."

A convergence of circumstances at mid-decade indicated that Poland might begin to give greater care to what was still at the time a relatively closed topic in Eastern Europe. Elements identified at the time were the growing recognition by other Central European governments of the need for an international response to industrially induced environmental decay; the apparent acceptance by the Polish scientific community of a public-interest role in the ecological discussion; the continued existence, activity, and acceptability of public environmental groups; and a government that, although still committed to industrial growth, was open to advice on environmental matters.[21] The outcome of the 1984 Munich Conference on Transboundary Air Pollution and the (then) uncharacteristically open and positive participation of Eastern Bloc countries in the conference was seen as an example of the sort of external force for environmental improvement to which the Warsaw government might acquiesce. While Poland did not join the "30 Percent Club," those industrial nations who agreed in 1984 to reduce national emissions of sulfur dioxide in 1990 to 30 percent of 1980 levels, claiming economic inability to do so, its actions on other international fronts were positive.

The Polish scientists who responded to the need for their technical abilities during the Solidarity era showed no sign of abandoning this style of involvement, especially insofar as it formed a part of their regular professional scientific work. At the time it was speculated that Polish scientists, as a community, might come to play a role in environmental affairs not unlike that played by their counterparts in Hungary.[22] While it seemed that Polish scientists became the harshest critics of their own inadequate action on this matter, indications were that their role in environmental policy making was growing.[23]

The involvement of social organizations became a fixture in the environmental policy process, even though the extent of their influence was not clear. The Polish Ecological Club spread across the country and constituted a network of active local action groups composed of citizens, scientists, and local municipal officials whose voice was regularly heard on matters of local and national environmental policy.

In a significant move in 1985, the government elevated environmental affairs to cabinet-level status by establishing the Ministry of Environmental Protection and Natural Resources. While the ministry was to remain the stepchild among ministries, operating at continual disadvantage vis-à-vis the industrial ministries whose polluting activities it was to regulate and control, it nevertheless steadily gained ground even within the political context of the communist government in Poland.

By 1988 environmental issues had come to play such a large role in public discussion that the government felt itself obliged to create an officially based environmental organization, *Ekologiczny Ruch Spoleczny*, or the Social Movement for Ecology (ERS), to serve as an umbrella organization for environmental activity in the country. As the last official environmental organization to take shape in People's Poland, the ERS was to have been an organization of organizations with a program of public education, coordination of ecological groups at the local and national levels, and research and technical assistance. The ERS had links to the Patriotic Movement for National Salvation (PRON) and to the Polish Academy of Sciences, whose president was its chair. While it was not clear with what degree of freedom the ERS would move nor how successful it would be in mobilizing the participation of Polish society in an official movement, the fact that it was created—and with rather prestigious connections—indicated how important the government found it to appear to be moving positively on ecological matters.[24]

The Environment as a Test of Legitimacy

Efforts such as the creation of the ERS were indications that the Polish regime realized how wide was the divide that separated it from the populace. It is difficult to determine how well informed ordinary Poles were on environmental issues. But it is clear that the Polish citizen who chose to become informed on ecological issues at a nontechnical level could certainly do so, thanks to a number of factors: the severity of environmental problems that simply had pushed them into the open; the frequency and relative candor with which they had come to appear in the standard media; the wide circulation and avid readership granted the "alternative" press, such as the Catholic periodicals; and the ready availability of often highly accurate, unofficial, underground publications. An informal survey in 1985 of press coverage of ecological issues by the country's daily newspapers conducted by the staff of *Aura*, Poland's leading environmental magazine, found that 5 to 10 percent of the contents dealt with the subject.[25]

Unfortunately, after so many years of obfuscation, withholding of information, and outright misrepresentation on so many subjects, the Polish regime suffered from the same syndrome as the boy who cried wolf. Even when the government told the truth, the people were inclined not to believe it. In the environmental arena, as in virtually all spheres of civil life in Poland, the "opposition" had the ear and the trust of the populace. A combination of well-developed reflexes and calculated self-defense caused people to believe the PKE, the authors published in *Tygodnik Powszechny*, the respected Catholic weekly, or some other unofficial source and to discount the government's reports. Ironically, there seemed to be one exception where government information was not discounted but rather magnified: when the government reported that a given situation was bad, Poles were inclined to conclude that it was even worse than reported.

To be sure, this was not a recipe for successful social mobilization in a context in which addressing the pressing needs of environmental protection might mean diverting economic resources and thereby further infringing on the standard of living in a country where economic austerity had followed economic crisis to encroach on the average citizen's financial means. In such a situation political good faith—if not full trust—is crucial.

From where was the first move to come? Some Polish observers maintained that the technical work of many years of such groups as the PKE would be matched in the near future by general social discontent with the state of the environment sufficiently acute to mobilize powerful public opinion on the issue. They held, as has been noted, that the Polish public knew the degree of ecological degradation that the country endured from both personal experience and media sources, and that their tolerance would not hold for long. Speculation in 1988 predicted a political crisis with ecological content as early as the first years of the next decade.

The highly competent technical work of the PKE and similar organizations placed ideas in the country's environmental discussion and occasionally shaped the terms of that discussion. The task for activist groups like the PKE was to challenge the country's dominant paradigm of development. Before the events of 1989 this meant challenging Poland's heavy industry lobby—a task made difficult by the fact that this was where Poland's political authorities believed their economic bread was buttered. They were loath to revise its status without strong new pressure to do so. This pressure could come only from an angry public that felt threatened by environmental deterioration.

The decentralizing thrust of the 1988 Second Stage of Economic Reform was clearly an attempt to introduce elements of initiative and flexibility into Poland's calcified economic system. It was based on the assumption that broadening responsibility for economic decisions would engender parallel responsibility for the economic system as a whole. Seen this way, the reforms had as their long-term object that ever-elusive goal of the country's communist regime, the achievement of legitimacy in the eyes of the people. Now, while it certainly had been possible for communist regimes to achieve a degree of legitimacy without popular participation in politics, Poland's elite had been reduced to striving for the former by means of the latter.

There was the danger, when viewed from the Party headquarters at the corner of Jerozolimskie and Nowy Swiat in Warsaw, that participation in economic decision making would carry over into participation in political decision making of a sort—as Poles are wont to make it—unacceptable to a Party ever jealous of its "leading role" in political affairs. Poland's recurrent political crises regularly took on forms quite different from the specific events that triggered them, often exceeding the expectations of both sympathizers and antagonists. It was entirely possible that restive Poles, ostensibly moved to action by an intolerable ecological threat, might be found giving vent to a decade of internalized dissatisfaction with matters social and economic and once again actively calling into question their country's entire political and economic system. As reality in 1989 surpassed speculation, events in Poland moved along remarkably similar lines.

Environment in the Transition to Noncommunist Rule

At the end of the 1980s Polish authorities seemed to be aware of the fact that the country was approaching a day of reckoning with its environment that had the potential to be as politically disruptive as the country's economic problems had been. No less prestigious a body than the Polish Academy of Sciences had cautioned in 1987 that continued decline of quality of life in Poland brought about by acute ecological stress could lead to increasing and unmanageable social discontent. Even the government's Second Stage of Economic Reform held little promise for environmental improvement as a result of its continuing "technocratic" emphasis on resource-intensive industry. The academy averred that for Poland to continue this wrongheaded policy would lead to social catastrophe.

> If in the 1990s there emerges ecological catastrophe of the type described here, it may well result in increasing social tension. The problem of environmental protection is such that it can lead to a stratification of society into those threatened and those in authority.[26]

This was a reasoned and scholarly way of putting the problem that had been described, less circumspectly, as follows.

> It is hard to imagine environmental degradation not playing a role in the next Polish crisis or to imagine that this crisis is very far off. People are aware of the degree of ecological degradation and the threat it poses to them and their tolerance will not hold for long.[27]

As these remarks indicate, despite increasing activity in all quarters, the field of environmental affairs in Poland was not without the potential for conflict and tension. To a great degree this tension mirrored conflicts in society as a whole that went far beyond the obvious antagonisms between those whose first interest is the environment and those who continue to place other interests, such as industrial investment, first.

The relationship that began to develop between the PKE and the newer ERS evokes the tone of environmental affairs in Poland just before the end of communist rule. Even though it was an officially registered organization, the PKE was, all the same, a creation of the Solidarity era, and it regularly found itself in opposition to official policies and projects. The ERS was a child of PRON, a fact which by itself led many Poles to consider it misbegotten. To fulfill its image as Poland's environmental umbrella organization, the ERS wanted the PKE to become a member organization. The latter refused, indicating that it welcomed cooperation with the ERS on issues of mutual concern, but preferred to maintain its autonomy.[28] Some members of PKE suspected that the ERS would be little more than a front for official development and environmental policies, the very policies that had brought Poland into its crisis. Others, perhaps representative of the PKE as a whole, were essentially angry at the monopoly on innovative activity that had been granted the ERS. If such a program was good for the ERS, why, they ask, could not other organizations be empowered to act in the same ways? Why was this promising avenue to be restricted to only one organization when several others, at least, had comparable competence and perhaps greater experience?

The government remained the most crucial variable in the Polish environmental equation, but its increasingly open recognition of the problem continued to be accompanied by insufficient constructive action to alleviate it. Much that happened on the environmental scene in Poland in the last half of the 1980s can only be assessed as positive. The whole country, from top to bottom, came to understand the ecological threat it faced. Both a comprehensive diagnosis and a comprehensive response had been prepared. What remained to be seen was whether there existed the political will in the government to implement it or the political power in the public to force it to do so, over the loud objections of those economic actors who still found it profitable and convenient to pollute.

Events at the end of the decade offered some indication that the country's leaders were willing to take a stance that placed environmental issues on a par with the country's other serious problems. One of the first actions of the government of Prime Minister Mieczyslaw Rakowski after it assumed power in mid-1988 was to announce that environmental protection was to be one of the three elements of its program of economic recovery, along with the development of agriculture and the expansion of the housing construction industry. Those who know Poland's economic failings will note the significance of including environment with the dual Achilles' heels of postwar Polish economic history.

By the beginning of 1989 political events in Poland had moved so far and so fast that the regime formally offered to legalize Solidarity as a first step in the process of beginning a dialogue on national reconstruction. This regained legal status led Solidarity to become the organizing force behind the opposition victory over the PZPR in the midyear parliamentary elections that gave Poland the first noncommunist government in Eastern Europe in forty years. The significance of environmental concerns in Poland's public life can be seen in the text of Solidarity's formal response in January 1989 to the government's offer of legalization. The union's proposal for the 1989 government–opposition roundtable talks placed environmental protection in a central position among the issues it placed on the agenda. Solidarity's response to the government offer contained five points addressing the issues of union freedom, the rule of law, and in point three "the dramatic economic, ecological, and material situation in Poland" that demanded reform.[29]

From an ecological point of view the most famous and significant step in the process that led to the end of communist rule in Poland was the activity of the Sub-Unit on Ecology of the Government–Opposition Roundtable Talks of early 1989. The participants in the work of the Ecology Sub-Unit amounted to a "who's who" of environmental affairs in Poland, bringing together on opposite sides of the discussion individuals who were personal friends and professional colleagues in other walks of life. One example is appropriate. Roman Andrzejewski, coordinating director of the well-known and well-regarded Central Project of Basic Research on Ecological Issues in Poland (and eventually, in 1990, a Vice Minister of Environmental Protection, Natural Resources, and Forestry under the noncommunist government) was a government signatory of the protocol arrived at by the Sub-Unit. His colleagues Stefan Kozlowski and Andrzej Kassenberg (in 1990 respectively Vice-Chair of the Sejm Committee on Environmental Protection, Natural Resources, and Forestry, and Director of the National Planning Commission's "Green Lungs of Poland" Project) were signatories for the opposition–Solidarity side.

Together the three had authored the 1987 study *Ekologiczne podstawy rozwoju spolecznego-gospodarczego kraju* [Ecological Elements of the Socioeconomic Development of the Country].[30] The study explored three variants of development for Poland referred to as the "resource and energy intensive, or regressive," model; the basic needs (stabilizing) model, and the "ecodevelopment" (corrective) model. These provisional theses parallel to a great degree the tenets of the *ekorozwoj* [ecodevelopment] program for Poland adopted by the Polish Ecological Club in 1987.[31]

Disagreement between the coalition–government and opposition–Solidarity sides centered principally on one issue: the status of the fuel-power sector in the national economy. Because consensus was reached on the fact that ecological disaster in Poland could be avoided only by limiting the use of coal, the coalition–government side asserted that there was no "rational basis for eliminating (a priori) the role of nuclear power in the national balance of fuels and energy."[32] Taking into account an assessment of risks posed by coal-based and coal-plus-nuclear-energy variants, this side strongly questioned the wisdom of a national energy policy that abandoned Poland's first two planned nuclear facilities at Zarnowiec and Klempicz, saying that to do so would pose a real danger to the availability of energy in the 1990s.

The opposition–Solidarity side stated that nuclear power in Poland was overly expensive, excessively capital-consuming, and as a result, seriously inflationary. The share of total national investment proposed for the nuclear power program would acutely hinder modernization of other branches of the economy, in particular the pursuit of efficiency in the fossil fuels branch. The debate formed itself into a discussion very much like that taking place in the industrialized West: a contest of nuclear energy versus energy efficiency.

The significance of the Roundtable Protocol on Ecology is that it comprised (disagreements and all) the next generation of environmental issues and policymakers in Poland. These issues and people from both parties to the talks were, in 1990, to enter the country's policymaking arena. The conclusions and recommendations of the protocol are a shorthand guide to Polish environmental policy currently being designed in Warsaw by the noncommunist government. The Mazowiecki government that assumed power in mid-1989 retained concern for environmental protection in its program, despite the fact that it is only one of a series of major problems that the country must address.[33]

For environmental protection to figure prominently in the programs of two successive new governments from opposite ends of the political spectrum is significant in Poland's current political context, in which the country's leaders are faced with the unenviable task of redeeming the country's economy to the satisfaction of both the international financial system and their own people. Poland must chart an economic course that addresses the interwoven problems of economic stagnation, environmental havoc, and economic reorientation simultaneously.

Notes

1. Grazyna Borys, *"Pojecie i organizacja ochrony srodowiska"* [The Concept and Organization of Environmental Protection] (Jelenia Gora: Karkonosze Scientific Society, 1987).

2. Walery Goetel, *"Tradycje ruchu ochrony przyrody w Polsce"* [Traditions of

the Nature Protection Movement in Poland], in Leon Lustacz, ed., *Prawo a Ochrona Srodowiska* [Law and Environmental Protection] (Krakow, 1975).

3. Borys, 1987.

4. M. K. Dziewanowski, *Poland in the Twentieth Century* (New York: Columbia University Press, 1977, 1980).

5. Pawel Zukowski, *Podstawowe problemy wspolczesnej techniki i ochrony srodowiska* [Fundamental Problems of Contemporary Technology and Environmental Protection] (Warsaw: National Scientific Publishers, 1987).

6. Jerzy Kurbiel, presentation at the conference on "Environmental Problems and Policies in Eastern Europe," held at the Wilson Center of the Smithsonian Institution, Washington, DC, June, 1987.

7. *Dziennik Ustaw* [Statutory Register], no. 25.

8. Zbigniew M. Fallenbuchl, "Some Structural Aspects of the Soviet-Type Investment Policy," *Soviet Studies* 16, no. 4 (1965), pp. 432–47.

9. Edward J. Kormondy, "Environmental Protection in Hungary and Poland," *Environment*, December 1980, p.31.

10. Jan Juda et al., *Ocena stanu zagrozenia srodowiska emisja zanieczyszczen powietrza, wynikajaca z procesu spalania paliw* [An Estimate of the Threat to the Environment by Air Pollution Resulting from the Combustion of Fossil Fuels] (Warsaw: Polish Academy of Sciences Committee on Man and the Environment, 1978).

11. Christine M. Sadowski, "Citizens, Voluntary Associations, and the Policy Process," in Maurice D. Simon and Roger E. Kanet, eds., *Background to Crisis: Policy and Politics in Gierek's Poland* (Boulder, CO: Westview Press, 1981), pp. 207, 209.

12. League for the Preservation of Nature, "Raport Ligi ochrony przyrody o stanie srodowiska przyrodniczego w Polsce i zagrozeni zdrowia ludzkiego" [The Report of the League for the Protection of Nature on the State of the Natural Environment in Poland and the Threat to Human Health], *Przyroda Polska* [Polish Nature], nos. 5–6 (May-June 1981).

13. *"Polska Lat Osiemdziesatych"* [Poland in the Eighties], *National Education Notebooks* (Warsaw: Przedswit, 1984).

14. Eugeniusz Pudlis, "Life Without Fluoride: The Continuing Story of Polish Pollution," *Ambio*, no. 6 (1981), p. 349.

15. Sarah M. Terry, "Poland's Environmental Crisis," report prepared for the National Academy of Sciences, unpub., 1988.

16. Timothy Garton Ash, *The Polish Revolution* (New York: Scribner's Sons, 1983).

17. Pudlis, 1981.

18. Zbigniew Fura, "The Polish Ecological Club," *Environment*, November 1985, pp. 4–5, 43, and personal conversation, April 1988.

19. Andrzej Kassenberg and Czeslawa Rolewicz, *Przestrzanna diagnoza ochrony srodowiska w Polsce* [The Spatial Diagnosis of Environmental Protection in Poland] (Warsaw: Polish Academy of Sciences Committee on the Spatial Development of the Country, 1985).

20. Andrzej Kassenberg, "Diagnosis of Environmental Protection Problems in Poland," in Wladyslaw Grodzinski, Ellis B. Cowling, and Alicia Breymeyer, eds., *Ecological Risks: Perspectives from Poland and the United States* (Washington, DC: National Academy Press, 1990); and Antoni Symonowicz, "Straty z tytulu

degradacji srodowiska: ich charakterystyka i probu szacunku" [Losses from the Degradation of the Environment: Their Character and an Attempt at Estimation], in Adam Ginsberg-Gebert and Zbigniew Bochniarz, eds., *Ekonomiczne problemy ochrony srodowiska* [Economic Problems of Environmental Protection] (Wroclaw: Ossolineum, 1988).

21. Stanley J. Kabala, "Poland: Facing the Hidden Costs of Development," *Environment*, November 1985, pp. 6–13, 37–42.

22. Stanley J. Kabala, "The State of Environmental Affairs in Poland: Regulation, Activism, and Public Concern in a Centrally Planned System," unpub., 1988.

23. Zdzislaw Kaczmarek et al., "Ksztaltowanie i ochrona srodowiska przyrodniczego oraz racjonalne wykorzystanie zasobow naturalnych" [The Development and Protection of the Environment and the Rational Use of Natural Resources], *Nauka Polska*, nos. 3–4 (1986).

24. Stanley J. Kabala, "Environmental Protection as an Element of International Economic Cooperation in Poland," in Wladyslaw Grodzinski, Ellis B. Cowling, and Alicia Breymeyer, eds., *Ecological Risks: Perspectives from Poland and the United States* (Washington, DC: National Academy Press, 1990).

25. Janusz Zareba, Assistant Editor, *Aura*, remarks, April 1988.

26. Polish Academy of Sciences, Committee on Man and the Environment, *Ocena skutecznosci i kierunkow dzialania w dziedzinie ochrony i ksztaltowania srodowiska: ekspertyza koncowa* [Assessment of the Effectiveness and Direction of Measures in the Field of Environmental Protection: Summary and Conclusions] (Warsaw: Polish Academy of Sciences, 1987).

27. Professor Stanislaw Sitnicki, Central School of Planning and Statistics, Warsaw, remarks, 1988.

28. Roman Andrzejewski, Central School of Rural Economics/Academy of Agriculture, remarks, 1988.

29. "Protokol Podzespolu d/s ekologii Okraglego stolu" [Report of the Roundtable Sub-Unit on Ecology], Warsaw, March 1989.

30. Roman Andrzejewski, Stefan Kozlowski, and Andrzej Kassenberg, *Ekologiczne podstawy rozwoju spolecznego-gospodarczego kraju* [Ecological Elements of the Socio-Economic Development of the Country] (Warsaw: National Planning Commission, 1987).

31. "Tezy programowe" [Program Theses], Polish Ecological Club, February 1987.

32. *Protokol*, 1989.

33. "Blueprint: Environment and Development for Poland: Declaration of Sustainable Development, Blueprint for International Workshop on Institutional Design for Environmental Protection in Poland" (St. Paul: University of Minnesota, 1990).

9

Red Pollution, Green Evolution, Revolution in Hungary

Environmentalists and Societal Transition

Miklos Persanyi

The real history of the Hungarian environmental movement is much more complex than it appears in some Western newspapers, or as it has been interpreted to the international public by some of its participants, who sometimes mix their individual experience with the entire process. There are also some misunderstandings about the role of the environmental challenges in the politico-economic development of Eastern Europe. Some basic arguments, which will be detailed in this paper, are as follows:

1. Although environmental degradation is an increasingly severe problem and environmental factors played a unique role in the great Hungarian and East European historical changes of 1988–89, the current social basis of environmentalism is quite limited. Rumors about a strong environmental movement in Hungary are false.

2. The apparent strength of the Hungarian and the East European environmental movements of the late 1980s came from their intercon-

The author is affiliated with the Hungarian Ministry of the Environment in Budapest.

nection to the democratic opposition. The experience of this region teaches a much broader lesson: At the end of the twentieth century, in the middle-industrialized countries, environmental issues have become the standard targets for every kind of political movement in opposing existing authoritarian structures.

3. Environmental groups, which were in the forefront of the political breakthrough of the anticommunist revolution one or two years ago, have only moderate opportunities to influence economic processes after the change in system, and their role is much less than that of the well-organized, experienced professional Western environmental NGOs that enjoy broad social support.

4. Despite these facts, the roots of the Hungarian environmental movement are relatively deep. They come from different sources and reflect several different theories of environmentalism. Although the main factions of the movement generally work independently of one another, in some particular cases they have networked. The few internationally active groups and personalities represent only a small percentage of environmental activists.

The country is now facing great challenges. Among the most serious problems are the difficult and often frustrating task of rebuilding a market-oriented economy, the simultaneous decentralization and privatization of the means of production, coping with the huge foreign debt, and developing and operating a democratic political system. At the same time, Hungary must deal with the international and national ramifications of pollution, stemming in part from an outmoded industrial infrastructure.

Early Environmentalists

Some of the environmental problems confronting the country, such as alkalized agricultural land, were inherited from times past. However, most of the problems arose during the period following the Second World War, known euphemistically as the period of "socialist reconstruction." In Hungary, as elsewhere in Eastern Europe, this Stalinist policy consisted of reliance on heavy industry to build a strong military-industrial complex without regard to efficiency in the utilization of energy, material, and human resources. Environmental protection measures remained in the background as the country struggled to build up its industrial and agricultural base. Production, consumption, and life-style patterns that were friendly to nature and on a human scale almost disappeared in a feverish haste to mechanize, chemicalize, plasticize, and centralize production—all inspired by a political ideology that claimed superiority over the global industrialization process.[1]

Grass-roots or professional organizations, which could have criticized these developments, disappeared or became politically controlled during the violent centralization of the 1950s. Virtually every social organization that did not come from the ideologists of the Communist Party was dissolved. Not only were religious or cultural organizations disbanded, but also conservation and animal rights societies that had been established at the turn of the century, at roughly the same time as the oldest American conservation organizations.

The first signs of a modern environmental movement in Hungary appeared in the early 1970s. The movement was, however, restrained, buffered, and later absorbed by the country's one-party political structure. The transformation of the entire socio-economic system coincided with a general strengthening of the environmental movement in a very important period of East European history. The subsequent "information revolution" in Hungary helped increase public awareness of the issues.

The year 1956 left a deep impression on Hungarian society regarding possibilities for political activity. Despite slogans about "collectivism" and "socialist democracy," many social networks fell apart, individuals became more isolated, more unable to express and represent their real interests and confront a power that seemed invincible.

By the early 1960s, signs of environmental deterioration were obvious. At the end of the sixties and in the early seventies more and more intellectuals, beginning with scientists, journalists, and writers, made their concern public. The intellectual enthusiasm of this early, premature environmental movement partly came from abroad through the mediation of scientists. It was soon chilled by the Communist Party that had just replaced the reform-minded leaders of the Hungarian new economic method (NEM) with orthodox ones because of the rigid suspicion of the Brezhnev apparatus. It was a time when the party was expelling the best Hungarian philosophers and sociologists for their criticisms of the communist system. It was also the time when Hungary, like other Soviet satellites, remained far from the 1972 United Nations Conference on the Human Environment, and when the first report of the Club of Rome was solidly rejected as a new imperialist trick to hinder the socialist community in overtaking capitalism.

Still, there were inconclusive studies prepared by party and government experts that suggested there was a crisis but that it could be contained and dealt with locally. In 1976, the Act on the Human Environment was passed with many constraints and compromises, and a quasi-autonomous governmental body was set up. When environmental degradation worsened, Hungary—along with its neighbors—was unable to handle the consequences of decades of environmental neglect. By the beginning of the 1980s the country was faced with a plethora of environmental woes.

Public Opinion

Falling living standards sharpened public awareness of pollution as the weakening economy spent less and less on environmental protection. By the end of the 1980s, environmental awareness had considerably increased. Polls conducted in 1988 showed that almost no one thought environmental protection was, on the whole, satisfactory in Hungary. The great majority (79 percent) expressed a wish that society ensure that natural resources be maintained to benefit future generations. Many (62 per cent) said that they believed that environmental protection had priority over production. An overwhelming majority would accept lower living standards if health hazards could be reduced. Environmental protection was seen by 36 percent as a major concern. About a third (34 percent) said information on environmental protection was insufficient. Increasing numbers of people called for more forceful action to promote environmental protection.[2]

The majority of the population (54 per cent) perceived environmental problems in their own neighborhood in 1988. The six environmental problems that received the highest ranking in a 1990 public opinion survey were: vehicular traffic (39 per cent), industry, industrial facility (28 per cent), air pollution (17 per cent), waste storage, waste disposal (15 per cent), use of chemicals (12 per cent), water pollution, bad drinking water (10 per cent).[3] In 1990, 57 percent responded that they perceived environmental problems hazardous to health in their own neighborhood. The ratio was 83 percent in Budapest, while in rural settlements only 41 percent.[4]

There is much direct evidence that environmental concerns are higher in urban areas than in the countryside, and this is confirmed by opinion survey data. It is easy to understand, because the urban population experiences a greater incidence of environmental problems. Tension was nevertheless detectable between the concerns of "urban greens" and the immediate interests of the rural population in several conflicts over nature conservation issues. Two other important findings of the public opinion polls are that the perception of environmental problems increases with level of education and decreases in older age groups.

The Hungarian public's attitude towards environmental problem-solving options is also important. The basic fact is that people do not trust government measures any more and are insisting on the right to know and to influence decisions. They generally agree with the idea of higher public spending on environmental programs or of more fines or taxes for polluters, but most refuse proposals affecting their personal budget.[5]

The majority of the population (71 percent) cannot see any place for personal involvement in solving environmental problems, and less than a third of those questioned could provide at least one example of a possible environmental activity of their own. The actions suggested related to the household and individual behavior during leisure time. The most frequent example was no littering. The involvement of Hungarian citizens in organized environmental actions, protests, or membership in environmental groups is generally rare; its significance level is below the statistical error level.[6] Membership in the permanently active groups comes only from a narrow stratum of society consisting mostly of young, highly educated intellectuals and students. The role of other social groups in environmental activities is marginal. Most are involved only in single-issue environmental protests.

Judit Vesarhelyi, one of the central personalities of the Hungarian environmental movement, recently wrote,

> Ironically enough, many parts of the Hungarian environmental movement lacked even environmental awareness! . . . When the state withholds access to the basic structures of democracy—the free spread of information, for example, or the right to express an opinion—any focus of popular discontent becomes a means of challenging the regime. Even if people did not fully understand the functioning of bank-filtered wells or variations in ground water, they knew very well that they wanted to conserve their landscape, towns, forests and waterways. And they knew that the government wanted to destroy all of this.[7]

Her statement bears out the statistical evidence that there is much less mass popular support for environmental issues and movements in a middle-developed (or redeveloping) country like Hungary than in the highly developed industrialized countries. But her statement also raises the question as to what proportion of the Hungarian population can be considered bona fide participants in the environmental movement. Several tens of thousands of people participated in the successful demonstration against the Danube dams in 1988, but participation in one protest does not mean that the environmental movement increased by several tens of thousands of new members. On the contrary, the reality is completely different. Kildow, Moomow, and Lazar offer a more sober assessment:

> The absence of effectively organized social and political groups to articulate environmental concerns and counterbalance the overwhelming pressure for economic growth has left a serious vacuum in new policy making processes. Though groups like the Danube Circle in Hungary served to polarize anti-governmental sentiments under the old regime, the sad fact is that NGOs, environmentally related or not, are woefully disorganized, confused as to what to do, and competing against each other at this time in Hungary.[8]

Three types of fundamental preconditions for environmentalism may be said to influence the role and strength of environmental movements in a given society. In first place are what might be called the environmental preconditions: If the environment is sufficiently deteriorated or if pollution becomes the immediate cause of loss of health or material damage, then people will become environmentalists. The first precondition generates many popularly supported initiatives, protests, and demonstrations. Most of these are at the local level and focus on one very specific issue. But environmental degradation is not enough. If it were, the strongest environmental movements would be in Third World countries, where environmental decay is now among the worst in the world. The second precondition is economic: Basic needs must be met, such as food, housing, and health care, and the elements of a leisure society must be in place. Finally, there are the "built-up" preconditions. These include factors that promote public awareness, such as the level of general culture, the level of political culture, science, and technology, and most important, the nature of the political system. Is it public enough? Democratic enough? Innovative enough? If all these qualities exist in a society, then the society has opportunities for efficient environmental protection, public awareness is high, and public participation is strong. If they do not, then a country must go through a long process to achieve these conditions, a process we are now undergoing in Eastern Europe.[9]

Local Protests

In recent years, local environmental awareness has been increasing significantly and has been expressed in a number of protests, mostly against waste dumping or processing sites. Initially, these protests were about residential land values and other local economic concerns and did not stem from environmental interests of the participants. Most of them are single-issue actions that end in failure or success and are very similar to protests in Western countries.[10] The East European peculiarity of such protests is that they reflect the great social changes sweeping the country in which local autonomy has increased and the relationship between power and the citizenry has moved toward new forms of democracy.

Consequently, after the democratic transition, people are not simply spectators or passive recipients of these wider changes but increasingly have the possibility and the courage to act on their own behalf. Moreover, with the increasing illegitimacy of the communist regime both at the central and local level, especially in the late 1980s, almost all organized local protests were successful. The government and its technocrats were unable to persuade citizens that their projects had benefits and not only costs and risks for them.

The first local environmental protest in Hungary burst out against lead pollution in a metallurgical factory at Nagyteteny in the outskirts of Budapest in 1977. Another major scandal and panic situation took place in 1981 at Vac, where inappropriate hazardous waste dumping polluted the drinking water of the city. During the 1980s a series of protests obstructed the establishment of hazardous waste dumping sites and incinerators. The first really organized action against the central government took place in Zsambek, 20 miles from Budapest, in 1981.[11] More recently, such local protests have become quite common, almost a permanent feature of life. In just one year, 1988, the following local environmental protests had national reverberations: protest against the location of a dumping site for low-level radioactive wastes from the Paks nuclear power plant at Ofalu; demonstration against enlargement of an isotope dump in Puspokszilagy; protest against the illegal dumping of hazardous wastes at Monorierdo and Apajpuszta; protest against the establishment of hazardous waste dumping sites at Kuncsorba, Kapolnasnyeak, and Aszod; demonstration against the construction of a lead-battery reprocessing plant at Gyongyosoroszi; and protest against bauxite mining that threatened the thermal lake at Heviz. At the same time car-parks have proliferated, and depots for toxics, pesticides, and other chemicals have operated for decades without any reaction from local residents, even though they pose a greater risk than many of the projects currently being opposed.[12]

The main reason for these environmental protests is not deep-seated ecological concern. In some cases, concern about health effects is a motivating factor, but whether this reflects an environmental consciousness is questionable. Rather, these demonstrations reflect the grievous economic, political, and cultural injustices that society has suffered and that have made it distrustful of the centers of power and its technocrats. Distrust is the main reason why, during the current period of transformation and democratization, Hungary is witnessing a widespread mushrooming of local protests in many respects similar to the NIMBY syndrome in Western societies. People are at the end of their tether, their patience and self-denial exhausted. Too often in the past, demands have been placed upon them and only rarely have their own needs been recognized. Now they are unwilling to tolerate environmental damage or risk on behalf of others, only on their own.

Hence, the first independent environmental NGOs in Eastern Europe grew out of disaffected groups of students and intellectuals, appalled at the lack of concern for environmental protection shown by the authorities. Later these various individual groups merged as the beginning of an open political opposition.

Environmental Activity under State Socialism

During the long period of one-party rule, environmental matters were handled by official, government-sanctioned organizations. Most groups were controlled or dominated by the Hungarian Socialist Worker's Party (HSWP), which ruled Hungary for 40 years. Although environmental matters crept into party congress documents from 1975 on, the party's highest executive body, the Central Committee, never dealt with an environmental agenda. The Socialist Worker's Party attempted to bottle up environmental issues inside the traditional monolithic political structure. This maneuver worked, up to a point. But during the turbulent 1980s, it failed categorically as nongovernmental "green groups" proliferated.

In the decade of the 1970s, a creature of the HSWP, the National Patriotic Front (NPF), saw emerging environmental concerns as a way of revitalizing the organization by injecting it with "new" and important environmental issues. NPF leaders viewed the environmental movement as one they could direct. Because of its relative distance from the mainstream of power, the neglect of environmental issues by the party leaders, and the absence of any organized opposition in the country, the NPF was the only alternative for those intellectuals who wanted to take part in environmental policy at either the local or national level. The NPF aimed to coordinate the environmental activity of other organizations, movements, and sometimes state institutions. Within the framework of the NPF-sponsored association of Government Organized Nongovernmental Organizations (GONGOs), environmental tasks were spread out among the participating organizations. Youth organizations, for example, formed action groups in schools, and trade unions organized environmental activities in factories.

At the margin of this network, devoted conservationists formed the Hungarian Ornithological Society, which now numbers some 15,000 members. It is the most solid and biggest environmental organization and has stressed its basic distance from any form of politics for a long time.

But the NPF's efforts at directing the groundswell of environmental concern was doomed to failure. By the 1980s the NPF had already lost its lead role, as independent groups were formed, many of them coalescing around one or two issues. Although the NPF, with the approval of the Communist Party in the background, tried to regain its lead role in 1988 with the formation of the first legally accepted environmental citizen organization, the Hungarian Society for Environmental Protection, the entire organization was relegated to the sidelines. The NPF itself lost its role in the political transition and fell apart in 1989.

By then, environmental issues had assumed an increasingly important political complexion. In 1988–89, radical reformers within the Socialist Worker's Party were in league with some of the more strident environmental groups in an effort to force the Parliament to confront ecological issues and gain more credence with the public. After the abolition of the HSWP, some of its previous reformist members set up the working group of "Socialist Greens."

Scientific organizations played important roles in the environmental debate in Hungary from the late 1960s on. For many years they were virtually the only group striving, in an organized way, to preserve the environment and curb the excesses of "Five Year Plans" that paid scant attention to the environmental repercussions of their development goals.

The Hungarian Academy of Sciences was the first scientific body to deal effectively with environmental problems at the end of the 1960s. A major environmental conference held in 1972, following the Stockholm United Nations Conference on the Human Environment, launched the Academy into the forefront of environmental science in Hungary. Over the course of the next two decades, the Academy set up a number of top-notch research programs, including the Lake Balaton clean-up project, which gained it widespread acclaim and support. The Academy established permanent committees to consider environmental questions and regularly issued reports and studies on various environmental problems facing the country. It also played a special role in the long Danube dam controversy, sometimes harshly confronting the official government or party standpoint.

In addition to the Academy, the Association of Technical and Scientific Bodies and the Society for the Dissemination of Knowledge were also active participants in the environmental debate. Their role was similar to that of the Academy; however, their membership was much broader, consisting not only of experts but also of researchers, engineers, teachers, students, and the educated public.

The role of experts in Hungary's environmental affairs should not be underestimated. What progress was made during the last twenty years in environmental protection has been due largely to scientists and other experts bringing their views to the attention of the government. Although the political influence of the scientific professional organizations is decreasing under the new democratic conditions, they nevertheless continue to play important mediating roles between the public and the government, and their arbitration is usually acceptable to both sides. And, of course, the scientific community is relied upon to provide the facts behind environmental problems and discussions.

"Green Wave" in the "Anti-Red" Revolution

Environmental movements played a unique role in the political transition in Eastern Europe. The basic reason was the sheer magnitude of environmental problems. However, compared with other countries of the region, Hungary was far from having the worst environmental degradation.

A second reason was that dissident groups viewed environmental problems as a focal element of their agenda. Environmental problems have difficult roots, most of them stemming from the basic nature of the industrial system, and especially from its Stalinist variant. Solutions are possible, but only in the long term and through structural adjustment in the whole economy. Thus, environmental problems provide a good breeding ground for opposition.

Third, Hungary's "green wave" reflected a general global phenomenon. The signs of environmental crisis are evident all over the world. And almost every opposition to an authoritarian regime that has formed in recent years has used the "green weapon." In the Philippines prior to the downfall of President Marcos, all the opposition parties united against the construction of a nuclear power plant. There are similar examples from Taiwan, South Korea, and Brazil. In Eastern Europe "in the space of a few years, environmental activism came up from underground, forming an integral part of the new political landscape. The successes this young movement can claim are nothing short of remarkable given the obstacles placed in its way."[13]

From the mid-1980s, more and more environmental "green groups" emerged from the breeding ground of Hungarian universities and colleges. The oldest and best known university group in Hungary is the Nature Conservation Group of Budapest's Eotvos University. Established in 1983 by a group of young biologists with the intention of creating a green movement, it gained wide publicity during their national campaign to protect Szarsomlyo Mountain in the southern part of the country from limestone mining. After initial setbacks their campaign was eventually successful. They subsequently became engaged in other conservation, environmental, and education issues and served as a solid meeting point for different groups.

Soon there were other independent university environmental groups. The Green Circle of Budapest's Technical University was one of the main forces behind a popular movement to clean up the capital's dirty air. Other university green groups were established at Budapest's Medical College, Godollo Agrarian University, Sopron Forestry School, and the science universities of Debrecen, Szeged, and others.

Regional environmental organizations (mostly at the county level) started their activity in the early 1980s. The first was in Borsod, which is the most polluted area of Hungary. Although the Communist Party apparatus hindered the formation of these groups in most parts of the country, in the second half of the 1980s six or seven regional groups came into being. These focused on the environmental degradation of specific areas, with great emphasis on nature conservation.

In the very last years of the previous regime, by far the main rallying point for the opposition parties with strong environmental programs was the national debate over the Danube dams project. In reality, the conflict over the dams was a sociopolitical struggle rooted in ecology. It emerged in the mid-1980s as a protest movement against the construction of two hydroelectric power stations on the Danube River, one at Gabčikovo in Slovakia and one at Nagymaros-Visegrad in Hungary, about 24 kilometers north of Budapest, in one of the most scenic historic areas of the country. The debate had many of the same features as a social crisis, particularly the demands of the existing political regime, which, *inter alia*, determined the selection of environmentally risky projects.

Perhaps the best known Hungarian environmental movement was the loose collection of green and political groups known collectively as the Danube Movement. These groups, among which was a smaller faction, the Blues, were spearheaded by the Danube Circle, which received the Right Livelihood Award (known as the alternative Nobel Prize) in 1986 for their conservation work. The group's leader, Janos Vargha, who first published an article against the plan in 1981, was awarded the Goldmann Prize in 1990.

The Danube Movement grew into a very broadly based protest movement involving students, officials, academics, professionals, and the public. By writing scientific reports and utilizing the media effectively, these groups were able to mobilize a large public following. As Vesarhelyi stated, "No government can control all channels of communication indefinitely. Even if the official media are strictly controlled, where the opposition is great enough unofficial channels will be created."[14]

The struggle over the dams brought many disparate groups temporarily together under the same banner: reform-minded communists, socialists, social democrats, liberals, Christian democrats, nationalists, and environmentalists. Although all of the new political parties were united in their opposition to the dam complexes, there were great differences in their approach to environmental issues. Some organizations had few if any environmental components in their platforms. Others had significant environmental platforms. Foremost among these should be mentioned the Hungarian Democratic Forum, the leading party in the first elected government, and the strongest opposition parties in the new parliament, the liberal Free Democrats and the Young Democrats.

Integrative Efforts

There were several integrative aspirations within the independent environmental movement at the end of the 1980s. First, the official old-type communist-governed social organizations tried to absorb the newly born movement, with the model followed during the previous decades. Because of the competition between the two types of organizations, but even more because of the excessive suspicion of the conservative party-leaders, the old-type organizations missed the proper time when most of the new environmental groups would have been willing to cooperate.

In 1986, the National Patriotic Front attempted to form an alliance with many of the groups, but this action was banned by the Political Committee of the Communist Party. As former party officials remember, Janos Kadar, General Secretary of the Central Committee and leader of Hungary for more than thirty years, personally objected to the proposal. He was worried that the NPF, headed at that time by Imre Pozsgay, a radical reform-communist, would become a competing political center. Although the NPF supported the initial organization of the Danube opposition in 1984, their next integrative attempt in 1988 was a complete failure despite the fact that at that time the authorities refused the application of the Danube movement for legal registration. The movement abandoned this aim and built up means and methods of operation outside the traditional political system.

The Young Communist League had more success by integrating the less political environmental groups dealing with outdoor education and some forms of local protests. But the major forces of the green movement kept their distance from this organization as well.

One of the oldest unofficial environmental organizations, the university-based ELTE Club of Conservationists, also tried to form a network of the more radical independent green groups in 1984–86. In these years there were very few groups to cooperate with. By and large all wanted to keep their absolute independence from everybody and everything, even from one another, allying only on specific issues when necessity demanded it. The ELTE Club served as an informal information center and contact point. The club was also active in starting to network with green groups in other East European countries. In 1986, the club launched the *Greenway* newsletter in English, to publish environmental news of the network and of the region.

An integrative effort by members of the Danube movement in March 1988 to form a network called "Tuleles" [Survival] proved similarly unsuccessful. Although at that time there were many more environmental groups than there were a few years earlier, significant elements of the movement were not yet willing to confront the existing political system by publicly joining the political opposition.

Just a few months later, in the summer of 1988, the political atmosphere in Hungary changed radically. The argument over the Danube dams unified the forces of the political opposition, the reform-minded communists within the party, and the whole environmental movement. In July, the Nagymaros Committee developed a temporary but very fruitful cooperation between almost all the green groups and the political opposition. A very powerful agenda, coupled with massive popular support and the specific historical situation, was able to unify the Hungarian environmental movement for a short period of time.[15]

In December 1988, leaders of the Danube Circle organized the Green Wave conference to keep the coalition permanently together, but they could not succeed. In early 1989, the Association of Young Environmentalists, an alliance of university green groups, launched a proclamation for integration in the form of a Green Front, with the same failure.

The ongoing work of Hungary's established conservation groups should not be overlooked. With the largest membership among the Hungarian environmental associations, the Hungarian Ornithological Society was well placed in 1989 to set up a National Conservation League with the help of the former leaders of the Youth Council for the Environment, a group previously connected to the Young Communists' League. Both promoted conservation values and educated young people in conservation ethics. They also encouraged the setting aside of more parks and wildlife reserves, and assisted the government in managing them and in surveying new areas.

There are several reasons for the failure of the integration efforts.

Szabo[16] points to the absence of an antinuclear protest movement as the basic reason, because it had been the integrating factor in the German green movement. However, if we want to understand the reasons for the failure, we must first grasp the motives for the integrative efforts. In my opinion, these efforts may be divided into two types, based on their different goals and expectations.

One effort derives from the political-cultural attitude developed during the long decades of the monolithic political structure: the longing for a strong center. People were accustomed to centralization, to unification, to being integrated. It is not simply a kind of "flock behavior"; it derives from a theory of community distorted by Stalinism, that deprived communities of their real independence. Liberty, tolerance, and respect for different opinions are not typical features of emerging democracies, and—for a while at least—common people as well as the environmentalists made an attempt to create a good and wise integrative center which could operate in a much more appropriate manner than the previous one. Democracy is a learning process spanning many generations. A change in political power does not automatically change a person's thinking, expectations, or behavior.

The basis of the second effort was the desire for a politically powerful green party. In the second half of 1989, the whole political situation seemed very promising. The old leadership of the Communist Party was being replaced by reform-minded cadres. Hungary had opened its borders for the East Germans, and the multiparty system had openly replaced the communists' monopoly of politics. There were new agreements on elections. Political parties mushroomed, and more and more members of the green movement thought that there was a big opportunity to win a seat in Parliament. They had experienced massive political support in 1988 against the Danube dams, and they anticipated similar results in the elections as well. During 1989, several green parties were formed locally, each with some dozens of members. Then well-known representatives of environmental organizations with very different political backgrounds began preparations in the summer. In October they formally established and registered the Party of Hungarian Greens with more than one hundred members. The party's membership grew to several hundreds in some months, but important green groups and personalities did not join. The party's performance in the 1989 elections was a complete failure. It did not gain one seat in the Parliament.[17]

The last major integrative effort took place before the elections in March 1990. At that time most of the major competing parties had their environmental sections, and former Danube Circle activists tried to gather them and some other politically interested organizations under the same umbrella. Most of the persons involved in this grouping had been activists together in the Danube protest, but in 1990 they could not find a common language. Competing political interests destroyed the possibilities for cooperation, and after the elections, the victorious governing parties lost their willingness to participate. This failure was the end of a period and the beginning of a new one. In a democratic political system, social interests, including environmental interests, tend to articulate themselves predominantly within the legal structures (such as the Parliament) rather than through the informal networks to which the greens had been accustomed.

After the Transition: Era of the Environmental Low Tide

By the beginning of 1989, many of the country's green groups had lost supporters to the newly emerging alternative political parties. The growing strength of these parties was one reason why the government finally decided to stop construction on Nagymaros until further environmental impact studies could be carried out. The government at that time was headed by reform-minded communists. In order for the government to forge a workable coalition with its radical green wing, a compromise was necessary. Sacrificing the project to green demands was seen as one way toward building a better, more broadly based and responsive government. The government thought that giving up the project was the price it had to pay for continued legitimacy and staying in power. But the decision was not enough.

The political landslide pushed apart not only the communist forces supporting the project, but the political left generally, regardless of the fact that they were not keen on the Danube dams. The new, anti-communist government whose leaders had been allied in opposition with the Danube movement, incorporated many green demands into its program. But within months of taking office, it had come into conflict with the greens over many specific issues. As Kabala writes, "Environmentalism is only one of the many areas of endeavor in Hungarian society and politics undergoing rapid change as Hungary pushes its way through the myriad tasks necessary for the renewal of civil society."[18]

The revolution has had a paradoxical effect on the environmental movement. Its mass basis of support eroded as people who had opposed the communist regime turned their attention toward other pressing social concerns. A good example is the Danube Circle. The circle was allowed to register as a legal, independent organization in December 1988. Its new platform was much more comprehensive than the old, incorporating a wide range of environmental issues, not just the two Danube dams. But its membership and influence on the domestic political process rapidly decreased. Former members of the Danube Circle dispersed. A majority of them became involved in party struggles; others dedicated themselves to their original profession. Only the hard-core people remained in the environmental arena. Because of personality conflicts, most of them work independently from each other, operating smaller offspring groups or, in two cases, institutions with support from abroad. A few of the previous central personalities run the Danube Circle, which is more nostalgia than a living organization.

The Hungarian environmental movement is both heterogeneous and divided. According to the list from the Independent Ecological Center, the number of existing and more or less registered groups is no more than 40, including the green sections of the political parties. Only two or three of them have memberships over one thousand. Six to eight have more than one hundred members, but most of them have only some dozen, sometimes only a couple of members. In a few very extreme cases, only one or two persons have shown up at a group meeting. Although these "Potemkin movements" are not typical, the groups' access to the media and to international contacts is very different, so the visible role of a group may differ entirely from its real support or membership.

There are environmentalists of different philosophical persuasions, from the deep-ecologists to the technocentrists.[19] All kinds of attitudes can be found in Hungary too. This factor, coupled with the very different political curriculum vitae of the activists, puts a premium on divisiveness. The label of "cryptocommunist" is quite frequent in the conflicts between different groups,[20] to which "political adventurist" comes as the accusing response.

The heterogeneity also means that there are groups at the national and regional level as well as in local communities or neighborhoods. Several organizations have the typical green agenda and deal with a broad range of social and political issues, like the West European green parties. There are two cooperating green parties: the Biosphere Party, focusing on global issues, especially on the global value of forest wilderness, and the bigger Hungarian Party of Greens, that is more interested in domestic policy. The Blue List, the Fourth Basic Principle Initiative, and some others, including religious groups, have intellectual, alternative urban life-style programs. The Association for Organic Agriculture is close to other emerging health groups with its antichemicals stance. Some groups specialize in a concrete environmental area, such as the Hungarian Section of the European Youth Forest Action. The remains of the Danube Circle are concerned mainly with water management issues.

University green groups are also flourishing. Although nationally much less visible than four or five years ago, they are a solid part of the movement. The student activists who once ran the groups have graduated, most of them to take up their careers, but they are "on reserve" for green actions at any time. Some of them chose environmental careers in the new government, with varying degrees of success. The new generation of green students are militant as well, but their role is no longer the role of pioneer, and the range of topics is more professionally oriented.

The strongest Hungarian environmental network is the conservation movement. This operates at both the national and local levels, has a broad membership, and is relatively more accepting of common action and cooperation. The eight to ten regional environmental organizations with several hundreds of members also have good connections with this wing of the movement. The major county-based environmental groups are located in Borsod, a big heavy-industrial zone with much natural beauty and a national park, in Gyor, the city in the northwest of Hungary that was most affected by the Danube dam controversy, and in Csongrad and Szabolcs counties in southern and northeastern Hungary, respectively, on the Tisza River. Several organizations focusing mainly on recreation and the protection of natural landmarks are also important. Groups concerned with environmental education are part of this network. Among these is Green Future, whose base is in a polluted industrial district of Budapest, where the first local protest in Hungary took place in 1977.

The picture would not be complete without mention of the continuous activity of scientific, technical, and professional organizations. These organizations have had and will continue to play a political role. Their activity has a strong influence on government decisions. Although they are nearer to political power than the green groups, in the new, multipolar political system, their subordination to the government is much less than it was before. The scientific organizations deal not only with technical and natural science issues, but also with policy issues. A major group is composed of experts in the Association of Technical and Scientific Societies. The Eco-Ratio group, established by dissident bureaucrats under the old regime, focuses on contradictions in, and perspectives for, environmental administration. The role of experts is very likely to increase, as their role is equally important for the further development of Hungarian environmental protection and the NGOs.

Green Intellectual Import and Export: International Assistance

International cooperation, primarily Western support, has played an influential role in the development of several environmental NGOs in Hungary. Western "green ideas" gradually filtered into the thinking of Hungarian intellectuals, as a kind of spiritual import over an extended period of time. Extensive organizational support started in the mid-1980s. Before that, only scientific organizations and the Ornithological Society had international contacts, apart from the very limited cooperation among GONGOs of the communist countries such as national front–like alliances, scientific and cultural associations, or youth organizations.

The Danube protest was the first to be assisted by Western environmental and political forces, and it received great media coverage in the Western press. This coverage helped break the official communication ban and contributed to the success of the movement that eventually led to the revolutionary process of political transition. The Danube movement with its offspring groups and former leading personalities had the broadest international contacts, although its actual membership was not very large.

The ELTE Conservation Club, the Alliance for Nature Conservation, and the Green Party also developed cooperation with their counterparts in the international environmental movement, including the Worldwide Fund for Nature, Friends of the Earth, the European Environmental Bureau, the European Greens, and Esperanto Environmentalists. Several regional Hungarian NGOs have broadened their contacts abroad with groups with similar interests. REFLEX in north-eastern Hungary has joint projects with Austrian and Slovak groups, and Tisza-Kor has projects with its partners in Yugoslavia.

The Western contacts of some Hungarian environmentalists and their better access to financial support in the United States and Western Europe have made possible the establishment of new projects. Among the privately funded groups should be mentioned ISTER, an independent nonprofit group dealing with Eastern European environmental problems, headed by Janos Vargha, and a branch of the PANOS Institute with the same president. The publication of an Eastern European environmental NGO newsletter, *PANOS Feedback,* started in the fall of 1990 with funds coming from the Rockefeller Brothers Fund. In 1989, Judit Vesarhelyi started the Independent Ecological Center with funds from the Soros Foundation, while the German Marshall Fund supports the training of Eastern European NGO leaders in the United States.

Western governments have also financed projects for increasing the efficiency of NGOs in Hungary and throughout Eastern Europe, with the aim of helping countries build up their democratic political system and contributing to environmental problem solving. The best example is the Central and Eastern European Regional Environmental Center in Budapest, with its special focus on the promotion and support of environmental NGOs throughout East Central Europe. Originally proposed by President Bush in 1989, the Center now receives additional support from the European Community, Japan, and other Western governments and organizations. Other instances of government funding include the government of the Netherlands project for cooperation between Dutch and Hungarian NGOs.

Cooperation among the East European environmental NGOs began with the *Greenway* newsletter network started by the ELTE Club. At that time it was a very risky enterprise politically, because international contacts were strictly controlled by the party bureaucracy in all communist countries. Representatives of independent East European green groups would meet each other at Western NGO conferences. In 1986, they held their first meeting on East European soil with Hungarian, Czechoslovak, Polish, and East German participants at Tata in Hungary. This network subsequently declined because participation was random and because better financed networking projects owned by other branches of the movement were growing in competence. The

Youth Council for the Environment and later the National Conservation League also organized international meetings with substantial East European participation.

There are urgent reasons for regional NGO cooperation. After several decades of long neglect, environmental problems are now a major challenge for all of the former communist countries in East Central Europe. However, although the problems of the countries in the region have similar roots, there are few opportunities or regional forums for the development of mutual understanding and the exchange of ideas among these countries. Solutions are impossible, if they are based solely on domestic financial and intellectual resources. The long and painful process can be managed only with the assistance of the more experienced part of the world.

In addition, the environmental NGOs both within one country and within the region are clearly in competition with one another for Western support. Hence they are more willing to cooperate with Western partners than with partners in the region. Hopefully, the importance of the "environmental spiritual import" will lessen as economic and social cooperation redevelops in Eastern Europe.

Conclusions

Environmentalism cannot be viewed as a permanent and constantly expanding movement in Hungary. Its development did not start in the mid-1980s, as several sources suggest, and its perspectives are not as simple as many green activists have imagined. The entire process has been continuous, with ups and downs basically determined by the three major preconditions of environmental social activity (ecological, economic, and built-up preconditions). Environmentalism in any country develops proportionally to the growth of general environmental awareness. As we have seen, it has had different forms and stages in Hungary:

1. Some forms of environmentalism emerged at the end of the last century and have more or less continuously existed in the country to the present day. These are the conservationist groups and organizations for recreational activities.

2. An early and premature, purely intellectual environmental movement emerged in the early 1970s. This activity was constrained and absorbed into the existing power structure by the communist authori-

ties. The official mass organizations of the monolithic political system had defined activities and reached limited success in promoting primitive environmental programs endorsed by the state.

Local environmental protests with no real foundation in or endorsement of environmental values emerged in the late 1970s. Despite their very limited local autonomy, they very successfully confronted the weakened central power during the 1980s.

3. The period of the late 1980s in the Hungarian environmental movement is extremely important. The coalition of a unique set of sociohistorical circumstances made it the period of peak success. Its importance during this period may be compared to the late 1960s and early 1970s in the United States, when the first Earth Day was observed. That time was also a very special historical era of high social and political unrest. The Vietnam war and the citizens' rights and antisegregation movements provided a huge impetus for environmental issues, mobilized masses of people, gave birth to new organizations, and changed the nature of the old environmental and conservation organizations.

4. After the political transition, the role of the environmental groups changed substantially. Most of their supporters or allies turned to areas politically more urgent and profitable. Environmentalists remained alone on their own ground. The birth of the new political system was the era of the green "high tide." New parties adopted relatively strong environmental planks in their programs, and their endorsement of environmental ideas accelerated the erosion of popular support for green groups.

The current and next period is the era of the environmental "low tide," in which environmental issues have secondary importance for the major political forces either in power or in opposition. Being in the government, they have to make compromises, sometimes against all environmental logic. Environmental groups must confront them with their green values, but the inner political conflicts of the movement do not bode well for any major success. The role of the green movement in Hungarian society is not likely to be more influential than in any other middle-developed industrialized country. During this period of low tide, the activity of environmental professionals working in the administration, business, education, research, or the media will be of critical importance.

5. In the long term, the environmental movement in Hungary will

survive to play a role similar to that of the green movements in Western societies. Environmental awareness among the population will steadily increase. Green groups will gain political and professional experience. Many people will become disillusioned by the contradictions inherent in political practice and the free-market economy and will again seek new alternative ways for society.

In the last analysis, Western environmental assistance, both governmental and private, must be seen as the key to Hungary's environmental future. Not only is it critically important in the clean-up of the environmental damage caused by the Stalinist economic policy, but it will play a vital role in helping the country avoid or control the environmental risks or hazards posed by Western investors seeking high profit with low environmental cost in the new East European market.

Notes

1. Miklos Persanyi, "Environmental Protection in Hungary: New Solutions," *US Journal of Environmental and Occupational Health Policy* 1, no. 3 (1991): 72–76.

2. Orszagos Piackutato Intezet, *A lakossag velemenye nehanykornyezatvedelmi kerdesrol* (kezirat) (Budapest: OPI, 1988), p. 42; Laszlo Kulcsar, *Kornyezetgazdalkodas es lakossagi tudatt* (kezirat) (Godollo: GATE, 1988), p. 38.

3. Szocio-Reflex, *Lakossagi velemenyek a kornyezetiproblemak megoldasi lehetosegeirol* (Budapest: Szocio-Reflex, 1990), p. 25.

4. Ibid.

5. Ibid.

6. Ibid.

7. Judit Vesarhelyi, "Hungarian Greens Were Blue," *Gannett Center Journal*, 4, no. 3 (Summer 1990): 143–54.

8. Judith T. Kildow, W. Moomaw, and Arpad von Lazar, "Proposal for Collaborative Research with Hungary and Portugal" (Medford, MA: The Fletcher School of Law and Diplomacy, Tufts University, 1990), p. 11 (unpublished).

9. Persanyi, 1991.

10. Philip D. Lowe and Jane Goyder, *Environmental Groups in Politics* (London: Allen and Unwin, 1983), p. 208.

11. Pal Tamas, "Erdek es kockazatfelismeres," in Anna Vari, ed., *Kockazat es tarsadalom* (Budapest: Akademiai Kiado, 1987).

12. Miklos Persanyi, "The Rural Environment in a Post-Socialist Economy," in P. Lowe, T. Marsden, and S. Whatmore, eds., *Technological Change and the Rural Environment* (London: David Fulton Publishers, 1990), pp. 33–52.

13. Hilary F. French, "Green Revolutions: Environmental Reconstruction in Eastern Europe and the Soviet Union," Worldwatch Paper 99 (Washington, DC: World Watch Institute, 1990), p. 62.

14. Vesarhelyi, 1990.

15. Miklos Persanyi, "GONGOs, QUANGOs, Blues and Greens—NGOs for the Environment in Hungary," paper prepared for the Conference of the International Sociological Society on "Environmental Constraints and Opportunities" (Udine, Italy, 1989), p. 20.

16. Mate Szabo, "Kornyezetvedelem, kornyezetpolitika estarsadalmi mozgalmak," *Kozgazdasagi Szemle*, 36, no. 11 (1989): 1342–54.

17. For details of the 1990 East European elections, see Duncan Fisher's chapter.

18. Stanley J. Kabala, "The Environment: Adjustment to a New Reality," unpublished manuscript, 1991, p. 8.

19. Timothy O'Riordan, *Environmentalism* (London: Pion Limited, 1976), p. 373.

20. For a good example, see Vesarhelyi 1990.

References

Dobossy, Imre, and Kulcsar, Laszlo. "Az okologiai tudattarsadalmi osszetevoi" *Tarsadalomkutatas* 2 (1984).

Knabe, Hubertus. "Glasnost fur die Umwelt," *Osteuropa* 7 (1989): 663–48.

Lanyi, Gabor. "A kuvik eve. - kornyezetvedelmi jelzesek," in Laszlo Vass, ed., *Magyarorszag politikai evkonyve* (Debrecen, 1988).

Muller-Rommel, Friedrich. "Ecology Parties in Western Europe," *West European Politics* 1 (1982): 68–74.

Persanyi, Miklos. "Public Participation and Non-Governmental Organizations: Their Role in Environmental Protection," in Ron Hinrichsen and Gyorgy Enyedi, eds., *State of the Hungarian Environment* (Budapest: Statistical Publishing House, 1990), pp. 40–50.

Persanyi, Miklos. "Danube Dams or Democracy," paper for the World Congress of Sociology (Madrid, 1990): 22.

Solyom, Laszlo. "A tarsadalom reszvetelekornyezetvedelemben," *Medvetanc* 2 (1987): 217–42.

10

Ecology in Slovenia

Leo Seserko

The Ecological Movement, the Greens, and the Effect of the Political Changes on the Main Environmental Problems

The ecological movement in Slovenia has a thirty-year history. At the beginning there was a group of intellectuals—university professors—who around 1960 realized the importance of environmental protection. They founded the first associations and also the Union of Associations for Environmental Protection in Slovenia. They were the early birds during the period of "real-existing socialism." Public opinion and the mass media were mobilized around ecological questions, according to their relative importance. Certain large-scale building plans and development projects led to public debate. Many of the groups' efforts were unsuccessful, especially when they tried to prevent the destruction of prime agricultural land or the construction of polluting industrial plants. Their greatest failure was when they tried to prevent the environmentally damaging and energy-wasteful construction of steel and iron works or aluminum plants. At the same time, the environmental groups were able to register some significant successes. These in-

The author is deputy minister for Environmental Conservation and Regional Development, Republic of Slovenia.

cluded preventing the construction of hydroelectric power stations in the Soča basin in the Alps, halting the damming of the seasonally flowing Cerknica lake, an extraordinary natural phenomenon of the Slovene Karst, and finally, drafting a resolution for a moratorium on nuclear power plant construction that passed in the old Slovene Assembly. Other public demands for environmental protection also penetrated the bureaucratic halls of the old Assembly. One of the most important achievements was a moratorium on water management improvement projects, such as those that would drain swamps and low areas next to rivers and streams, straighten the bends of rivers, and turn the river beds into mountain torrents.

The founding of political parties in 1989 came at the peak of public awareness of the extent of environmental degradation under the communist regime. The favorable political climate encouraged the founding of the Green Party of Slovenia on June 11, 1989. The effort to reach an agreement between the Union of Associations for Environmental Protection and the Greens to run common candidates in the first democratic elections to be held in April 1990 proved unsuccessful. The attempt was frustrated largely because the Greens had already joined the opposition coalition DEMOS, which included all newly established parties. A second reason was that prior to the elections, proportional representation (PR) was introduced into the sociopolitical chamber, which is that chamber of the Slovenian legislature where the representatives of political parties sit. The introduction of PR greatly improved the Greens' chances to win legislative seats running on an independent ticket.

The Assembly of the Republic of Slovenia is composed of three chambers: the sociopolitical chamber, elected by proportional representation and composed of representatives of all citizens eligible to vote; the chamber of communes, elected by majority vote in each commune and composed of representatives of local communities, and the chamber of associated labor. Only employed citizens can vote for this chamber. The Greens along with other political organizations naturally were highly critical of this unequal distribution of voting rights at election time. As a result, under the new Slovene constitution the chamber for associated labor will no longer exist. Typically, the managers of the larger companies were elected to this chamber where they were able to turn the vested interests of the big industrial monopolies into law.

The Parliament of Slovenia deals with every bill in each of the three chambers separately, and if there is no consensus between the three chambers, the issue goes through a coordinating procedure.

As a political party the Slovene Greens ran their own candidates on the political party list in the April 1990 elections and got 8.8 percent of the vote. That translated into 8 deputies in the chamber of political parties. Approximately 18 percent was given to the reformed Communist Party, renamed the Party of Democratic Renewal, followed by the former communist youth organization (ZSMS), now called the Liberal Party (15 percent). The Slovene Farmer's Alliance received 30 percent of the vote, the Slovene Democratic Alliance 10 percent. Following the Green Party of Slovenia came the Social Democratic Party of Slovenia with 8 percent and the Socialist and Trade Party with 4 percent. On the voting list for the chamber of communes the Greens appeared together with other parties of DEMOS and got 8 delegates. In the chamber of associated labor one Green delegate was elected. In all, the Greens obtained 17 representatives out of the total 240 delegates in the Slovene Assembly.

Dr. Dušan Plut, president of the Greens, was elected from the presidential list to serve on the five-member collective Presidency of the Republic of Slovenia.

The vice-president of the Slovene Green Party (ZS), Vane Gosnik, was elected vice-president of the Assembly of the Republic of Slovenia. Since the coalition DEMOS captured the majority in the Assembly (55 percent) in the formation of the government, the Greens got the position of deputy minister in charge of Environmental Conservation and Regional Development, held by the author (Dr. Leo Seserko), the position of Minister of Environmental Conservation and Land Use Management (Miha Jazbinsek), the position of Minister for Research and Technology (Dr. Peter Tancig), and the position of Minister for Power Engineering (Dr. Miha Tomsic).

The Greens also organized committees in 45 out of Slovenia's 60 communes and now have around 3000 members. (The population of Slovenia is 2 million.) At the commune level, the Greens do not always appear in the DEMOS coalition, but sometimes are in the opposition.

All Slovenian parliamentary parties, including the Greens, supported the declaration of Slovene independence, adopted by the Slovene Assembly in July 1990. In December of the same year, 88.5 percent of the citizens approved Slovene independence in a national referendum. In March 1991 the Slovene Assembly endorsed a declaration of separation of Slovenia from Yugoslavia. The Greens were against a large military budget and in favor of a demilitarized state without armed forces with the exception of police and territorial defense units. They supported citizenship for all people living in the republic, with no restriction.

Today's Ecological Movement in Slovenia: Prospects and Perspectives

As a result of the political changes that occurred in both Western and Eastern Europe, the election of four Green ministers to the first postwar democratically elected government in Slovenia reaffirmed environmental protection as an accepted and important European social and cultural interest. The Slovenian government thus was interested in forming a group consisting of like-minded countries whose governments also promoted environmental protection and human rights and in which there could be a political dialogue about economic and regional concerns. However, the political culture of other south Slav countries and of virtually all the former communist countries with the exception of East Germany does not accord such a high status to environmental protection as does Slovenia. In many of these countries there are environmental, human rights, and peace groups, but these have no parliamentary status or even seats in the government.

The role of the Green ministers in the Slovene government, including my position as deputy minister in charge of environmental protection and regional development, is far from being comfortable and pleasant. Day after day we face the economic and political interests of entire economic blocs or various companies that are turning a profit or wish to do so not only on their innovative powers, diligence, and good business, but also through the exploitation of nature in all its forms: vegetation, animals and human beings, underground water, water sources, soil, and air. These economic interests worked well under the communist system because the requisite political mechanisms existed for their enforcement.

When the system fell, they experienced a shock because their political representatives disappeared en masse from their positions of power. Naturally, they were not only interested in their anti-environmental privileges, but they objected to the formation of a legal and social state

in which inviolability of the environment, especially living space, vegetable and animal species, and the health and wealth of people, would
be given its rightful place. Today's difficulty in putting into force the
rights and standards of a healthy living and working environment reflects the historic sacrifice of nature that has occurred in Western
civilization. Since ancient times there has been a sinister shadow lying
over man's material existence and the rights pertaining to it.

But although surprised by the political changes and the decay of
communism, the economic monopolies that had not supported the
changes for ideological reasons but rather for their own self-interest,
immediately started to compensate for what they had lost. Before that
they had been unimaginative and had been lulled into complacence,
heedless of the signs of changing times and the need for the preservation of the planet. They were self-satisfied and blind, defending communism as a guarantee against barbarism, while day after day they
practiced barbarism, mindless of the great damage they were causing
to the natural environment and all living species. This damage, if estimated economically, exceeds their profit a hundred times over. The
economic monopolies can sell cheaper and hence more marketable
products because they destroy and poison the air, underground water,
and soil regardless of people's health and quality of life, or the natural
and cultural inheritance of Slovenia.

The monopolies adapted rapidly to the new political conditions. It
took them only a moment to abandon the internal hierarchy that they
had taken care of for years and years. Everything was laid on the backs
of the "workhorses" they had in the new government, parliament, local
administration, and the mass media (journals, radio, and television).

Overnight, the new representatives of the old anti-ecological interests became the main opponents of environmental protection. They
referred to previous legislation, expounded the necessity to export
goods at any price, and emphasized the need to save jobs, even though
saving them entailed retaining outmoded, polluting production processes.

This new backlash against environmental protection is typical not
only of Slovenia, but of all medium-developed countries that are trying
to extricate themselves from poverty and to hide their lack of political
culture. By destroying natural resources, they imperceptibly slide
below the limit of social prosperity. Ordinary data about gross national
income presents an illusion of prosperity. But we can only talk about
the well-being of a country when its gross income takes into account

qualitative criteria, such as air quality in towns, level of pollution of rivers, and quality of underground water and soil, and includes the cost of making the public safe from the long-term toxic effects of industrial plants and products.

The European Community's introduction of product quality standards for 1992 represents today a major threat to Slovenia. The country would like to join Europe and find a place in the world market for its goods. Under EC regulations, rival European enterprises will be able to initiate antidumping suits against Slovene exporting companies that can only be competitive in Europe if they destroy the environment at home. The implementation of the EC standards will at one swoop end the good times for industrial polluters in Slovenia and their ties to the world market. So far they have been competitive at the expense of the health of the population and environment of Slovenia and her neighbors. Now they will have to build purification plants or change technological processes if they want to sell in foreign markets.

Industrial polluters will experience a severe shock. In the years to come, European environmental legislation will force them to take precautions against their own unfair competition and pollution of communities and infrastructures at home in Slovenia. The Greens pointed out long before 1992 that radical changes in legislation and investment in environmental protection were not just wasting precious money on the Greens' political aims but were an economic necessity to bolster the international competitive position of the entire Slovenian economy. The budget for the year 1991 shows that government support of economic restructuring has remained largely symbolic and there is not yet a real commitment in this direction. The amount in 1991 allotted to the environmental clean-up fund, which is normally increased by one quarter every year, was virtually the same as the year before. However, there was an increase in funding for clean-up activities of big industrial plants. These chronic economic patients have been getting help from three sources: direct financial subsidies, subsidies to cover the costs of electrical energy (although they are big users of electrical energy), and the privilege of noncompliance with important air, water, and other antipollution measures.

One reason for the monopolies' success was their quick infiltration of the new political parties, each of which responded differently to them. But most important, they began to realize generational changes within their own power structures. As a result, those individuals who had some time ago personally stopped believing in socialism or simply changed their party after the first democratic elections, acquired the most political clout.

Before the elections, environmental projects were very popular aspects of the government's program, especially the shutdown of the nuclear power plant in Krško. After the elections, the political climate gradually changed to being less favorable toward ecology. But this change, in my opinion, does not express a general trend in Slovenia. There was an effort to assert environmental issues in the new government and parliament, only to have them once again defeated by the industrial monopolies, who simply stonewalled any exercise of governmental authority.

But the environment will make it to the fore in a big way after 1992. Quick changes are just around the corner. They will come after exports from Slovenia into the EC are limited after 1992 for failure to meet EC environmental standards. Even the present government has introduced the "polluter pays" principle. The government also discussed the proposal that major consumers of electric power (iron works, aluminum plants, and big metallurgical firms) stop paying the 20 percent tax on electricity. By demand of the Green ministers, this proposal did not pass, but the big electricity consumers received subsidies approximating the value of the taxes they would pay on electricity. The compromise at first sight was a defeat for the Greens and a victory for the biggest direct and indirect polluters of the environment. The term "direct polluter" refers to those enterprises who have chronic low productivity and lack the profit to finance the building of purifying plants. "Indirect polluter" relates to enterprises that use energy, especially electric power, inefficiently, since the generation of electric power demands the construction of steam power plants fueled with polluting brown coal, which also do not have purifying plants. "Indirect" also refers to the long-term problems posed by the only Slovenian nuclear power plant, at Krško.

The Greens and the Issue of Nuclear Power

Slovenia does not have a waste disposal site for low and medium level radioactive waste, despite the fact that the government established a public enterprise responsible for constructing one. Everywhere the site could be located, the people in the local communities and communes voiced strong objections. The intense public reaction indicates that this problem will not be solved for years to come and that the radioactive waste must continue to be stored in a temporary storehouse on the plant grounds.

The Greens demanded that the nuclear power plant in Krško be shut down by 1995 as a precondition to their entering the government, and it is an indication of their success that the new government accepted the condition and put it in its program.

Then a paradoxical situation developed. Public opinion research showed that 60 percent of all Slovene citizens were for the shutdown of the nuclear power plant in Krško by 1995. Sixteen percent were even for immediate shutdown in view of the fact that it is located on an active tectonic fault. But at the same time newspapers launched an extremely intensive campaign to convince the public that the early shutdown of the plant would be meaningless, premature, ecologically unproductive, and economically harmful. Most journalists apparently understood the new freedom of the media as a chance to contradict the government and so expressed their political independence by a pathetic justification of the plant. In so doing, they were supporting the obstruction of Slovene economic reconstruction. In three years, Slovenia spent only half of the $90 million credit from the World Bank to rationalize the use of energy in the economy. Then in November 1990, there were catastrophic floods, and the government transferred the remaining $45 million to help the affected areas.

The Secretariat of Power Engineering developed two scenarios for energy development in Slovenia for the five years beginning in 1990. One anticipated the closing of the nuclear power plant in Krško in 1995; the other did not. The scenarios showed that long-term economic results would be better if the plant were shut down, but that short-term energy needs required 900 million ECU over the next five years, or some 500 million dinars in 1990. The Secretariat of Finance did not budget that amount of money and recommended instead that the government increase subsidies for mining expenses and the unpaid bills of the large energy consumers by approximately one third. The Greens in Parliament demanded a change in the budget on that one point. In our view, it was impossible for the government to pass a budget that was inconsistent with its own program calling for the shutdown of the Krško power plant in 1995.

The Secretariat of Power Engineering began to reorganize the bureaucratized, unified, state-owned electric power industry and set up a public enterprise known as ELES. The new company would only be responsible for buying and selling electric energy and would be dissociated from power production. The plan was to introduce market rationalization in the distribution and production of electricity. Unfortunately, however, the man chosen to be the manager is fanatically in favor of nuclear energy and radically opposed to shutting down Krško in 1995. The nomination of this man made a mockery of the Greens and their participation in the government. At the same time this is a problem that involves the entire government, since a government official has publicly voiced views and arguments that are directly opposed to the government's program.

Then the manager of ELES ran into conflict with his own company. His enterprise could not even begin to organize the electric energy market unless the big users of electric energy, accustomed to all kinds of privileges under the old regime, started paying for most of the electricity they consumed. The manager took the Greens to task for demanding the shutdown of Krško, although the success of his enterprise depended entirely on forcing big users of electric energy to pay the electric bills regularly under the same conditions as everyone else, or go bankrupt.

The shutdown of the nuclear power plant in Krško has an international component as well. Half of the plant was financed by the Republic of Croatia, which uses half of the energy. In contrast to the Slovene government, Croatia has not expressed support for a shutdown by 1995, although there are no signs that it would take over the problem of disposing of the radioactive waste. In principle, the user covers all the expenses of the plant. As the plant stands on Slovenian territory, it is understandable that the country stands on its sovereign right to determine the extent of risk and decide when the plant will be closed.

Long-term questions regarding the disposal of high-level radioactive waste persist. This waste will remain radioactive for up to a million years and could potentially threaten innumerable future generations. At the same time, it is clearly technically impossible and economically unproductive for Slovenia to solve the waste problem by itself. In other words, Slovenia is burdened with this waste, and lacks the capacity to solve the problem at a time when the transportation of such waste to other countries is restricted or prohibited by international conventions. Statements by journalists that, with the hundred or more nuclear reactors currently in operation around the world, the Krško plant may be considered just a drop in the sea are misleading and nonproductive.

While the nuclear energy industry tries to find new technical solutions to the high level radioactive waste, consignments of fuel and waste are being lost all over the world, and the quantity of radioactive substances increases enormously throughout the planet. The long-term solution to this problem will definitely have planetary repercussions, but there can be no solution that does not devolve upon the individual country. The fact that the waterworks at Brezice contain tritium shows that there are local reasons as well that make the shutdown of Krško reasonable and urgently necessary.

Green Input into New Environmental Legislation

Since the communist regime fell, Slovenia has been trying to extricate itself from the old political and economic structure with the privatization of enterprises as public property and with denationalization (giving back property to former owners or their heirs). On the one hand, the Greens consider the privatization of enterprises sensible from an environmental point of view because it ends the period in which the state was both property owner and monitor of the environmental impacts of property development. It was a characteristic of the former system to declare certain industrial programs strategic and of national importance. These included steel, iron, metallurgy, and the state-run agricultural industry. They were considered so important that their development superseded the necessity to preserve the environment. The low productivity of these gigantic industries was offset by their brutal degradation of air, water, and soil quality.

With the privatization of enterprises the state will stop acting as both manager and guardian of the environment and people's health. Instead, the government will focus on the role of guardian that it completely neglected before. There is little doubt that governments are not particularly innovative, consistent, or persistent if not pressured by the public at large, environmental groups, and those industries that have already accepted certain standards of environmental protection and are fighting competition that still pollutes intensively.

On the other hand, private ownership may stimulate production and new production processes that entail environmental risks not known before. Thus, private enterprise must also be restricted and regulated.

The solution, which is not perfect, lies in the distribution of political influence in the government in such a way that private economic initiative is restricted and regulated by the public's interest in preserving the environment.

The main category of regulations that are now being developed in the wake of the passage of the new act on environmental protection is the development of environmental impact assessment (EIA) procedures to evaluate the acceptability of an individual process or product, or a communal, industrial, or municipal project. In this connection, the Greens believe the Slovene government should accept the proposal of the Greens and other ecological groups demanding the legal adoption of the principle that the polluter pays for the damage he causes.

Transportation

Slovenia is a typical transit country because road and railway networks fan out over its territory and link west, north, and central Europe to Greece, Turkey, and the Near East. Under the old regime, although the state was given the necessary credits, it completely abandoned road and railway construction and neglected to make necessary repairs. The same official attitude prevailed in the post office and especially the telephone system. The Republican Secretariat of Transport and Communications has prepared an extremely ambitious program for the construction of motorways in the coming years, to the neglect of the railway system. The Greens have supported the building of basic motorways in Slovenia, such as the motorway from Sentilj and Maribor to Koper and Trst and from Jesenice to Zagreb as well as secondary ones from Maribor to Zagreb and from Trst (Trieste) to Rijeka. If the expansion of the railway system does not take place at the same time, the motorway system will have very negative environmental and economic consequences. The Secretariat of Transport has announced plans for the gradual diversion of road traffic to rail. But the budget only includes money for building motorways, with no funds allocated for road traffic diversion. The Greens argue that the implementation of such a policy will raise air pollution levels in particular, and increase noise levels by increasing international road traffic between central and northern Europe and Greece, Turkey, and the Near East. Traffic diversion to rail would be especially rational for long-distance travel from Munich to Istanbul or Athens or even farther. Our glittering motorways will only fill Slovenia with traffic, noise, and dirt. We shall suffocate from polluted air and we shall weep for our ruined forests. Our country will not be well integrated into Europe's successful railway system.

The building of motorways is highly controversial because of the great financial and political power of the road lobby. International financial corporations from Austria, Germany, and Italy are prepared to underwrite the construction of motorways in Slovenia and its neighbors. But their demands are very unfavorable to Slovenia's economy and environment. They want to build at the lowest possible cost over the richest and most important underground water reserves. The procedure is wrong. Motorway developers prepare their documentation before the authority that issues building and construction permits, the Secretariat of Environmental Conservation, has checked on the environmental impact of the project. Thus, the Secretariat can make only minimal corrections, and cannot protect the population, residential areas, agricultural land, or underground water.

The motorway project from Nova Gorica to Razdrto, a motorway of local, not international, importance, is a typical example. A project of international importance is the motorway from Trst to Ljubljana. At the turning at Vipagva, the road passes over the spring that supplies water for the entire region. Another example is the motorway from Maribor to Zagreb, which is planned to be built on prime agricultural land and over the largest underground water reserves and springs providing water for the region.

In Slovenia the legal requirement of an environmental impact statement (EIS) for the construction of a motorway is not yet in force. The developers have offered two different planned roadways for the Institute of Cultural and Natural Inheritance to study thoroughly. The first variant is planned directly along the old riverbed of the Drava river. All the underground waterfrom Dravsko Polje runs into it, and the site contains the largest potential reservation in Slovenia for animal and plant species in danger of becoming extinct. The second variant is parallel to the canal of Srednja Drava 1, which crosses the bird sanctuary of Miklavz ponds and runs down the whole length of Drava Polje and over the most important springs.

The Institute of Natural and Cultural Inheritance in Maribor had the choice of deciding between two plans that were both ecologically and economically unacceptable. But it did not have the choice of rejecting both of them and suggesting the shortest crossing of underground water in Dravsko Polje south of Maribor through the forest at Dobova to an already built motorway at Hoče. The connection to Zagreb could be built over an area rich with underground water from Slovenska Bistrica to Krapina. The problem is that motorway developers lay out roads independently of environmental considerations. Once the plan is completed, they make only minimal corrections to accommodate demands for environmental protection.

Tolls on the motorways are not collected in the countries north of the Alps, while in the countries south of the Alps they are. The Greens believe that toll collection is unacceptable both from the environmental and economic points of view. For one thing, toll collection makes the cars stop and idle for a time, producing additional burdens on the environment. Tolls also divert some traffic from motorways to parallel roads, widening the negative impact on the environment. The construction of toll collection points means the widening of both access roads and the toll booth plaza area. This means pouring 5 percent more concrete over the best soil, which is lost forever.

In many regions in Slovenia the population is dissatisfied because the building of motorways stopped. Because of the old regime's bad management, Slovenia itself cannot afford to build the basic network of motorways for probably ten years. Some building firms and banks from Austria, Germany, and Italy have offered to build these roads much sooner, but they demand the introduction of toll collection. They want to achieve higher profits at the expense of the environment. Calculations show that a thirty-year concession would bring them a 30 percent annual rate of interest. If the Republic of Slovenia itself assumes the commercial credits and if the interest rate is 12 percent, it can build the motorways and at the same time earn almost 20 percent in annual interest. It could pay back the capital with money collected from gasoline taxes. In other words, there would be virtually no expenses if tolls are collected. But collecting tolls and building over the most delicate areas containing underground water and prime agricultural land could be avoided.

In the budget for 1990 the government anticipated investing the money gathered from taxes on telephone services in other areas. One-third of the money belonging to the post office has been spent elsewhere, but this fact has provoked no objections on the part of the public. There has been quite a different reaction to spending money from gasoline taxes for other purposes. Failure to develop our telephone and high-tech communications systems will impact negatively on both the environment and the economy. Telecommunications are faster, cheaper, and less dangerous for the environment than communication by motor vehicle.

Agriculture

Slovenian agriculture has become the source of the biggest and most problematic environmental pollution. Huge pig farms, which produce 40,000 to 100,000 pigs yearly, are the major polluters. These farms are the direct inheritance of the former socialist system, in which the regime created impossible conditions for individual farmers both politically and economically, restricting private farms to 10 hectares of farmland and 15 hectares of woods. At the same time the regime lent large sums of money to the enormous pig farms, where dubious economic success was combined with more and more insensitive methods of production.

Not long ago, I visited one such farm in Nemsčak (Prekmurje). Here, they tried to economize production by keeping a large number of pigs on two levels. When entering the farm I experienced a strong odor of ammonia, as if I been slapped. Living in such crowded conditions, the animals are exposed to all the various animal diseases and sudden death. Their suffering is indicative of human insensibility and cruelty to animals. The Greens of Slovenia propose to abolish these farms and to distribute this production to individual farmers. The chief criterion should be the environmental impact of the farm. The insoluble problem of liquid manure which pollutes surface water and filters down into the ground water should not be allowed to spread from a few catastrophic points all over Slovenia. The solution proposed by the Greens is to accept the European standards of pig production and start rearing pigs on straw, not on a plastic floor. The breeding of pigs and other domestic animals should be organized in such a way that they can be considered contented pigs.

A second major environmental problem caused by agriculture stems from water improvement projects that have been carried out on 500,000 hectares. First, all the bends in a river are made straight; then the riverbeds are changed into mountain torrents. This was a national program to open new agricultural areas. For twenty years, this program was a top government priority. It involved the draining and leveling of fields as well as the destruction of forests along the river banks, meadows, and swamps on state farms and private farmland. Areas drained in this manner became new fields of dubious value, as these are not fields that have been cultivated for centuries but consist of very dry and poor soil that needs enormous quantities of fertilizer. Plants cannot use this fertilizer since it is quickly washed away, and it often seeps into underground water, streams, and rivers. Production becomes expensive and uneconomical. The growing of grass and cattle breeding is changed to the raising of rape, maize, or wheat, entailing extremely high direct costs and severe degradation of soils, streams, rivers, swamps, swampy forests, and meadows. In Slovenia these areas used to be the richest in plant and animal species. Here, with their former habitat gone, the gray heron and stork are in danger of becoming extinct.

Agricultural pressure on these lands has been very aggressive. One of the unique protected areas, where the rare swamp tulip *(Fritillaria meleagris)* used to flourish near Ptuj and Lenart along the Pesnica river, has been destroyed. The area where this plant was located was declared protected by the Institute of Natural and Cultural Inheritance in Maribor, and confirmed by the legislative assembly at Ptuj. A few years later, after regulation had transformed the Pesnice River into a mountain torrent and the state agricultural industry had systematically checked out rivers and streams all over Slovenia, the industry decided to settle in this area. The Slovenian central authorities then demanded that the commune invalidate its declaration, setting aside the protected land. Despite the protests of ecologists, the area was destroyed.

The regulation of streams and rivers and their transformation into mountain torrents has had another disastrous effect. Slovenia experienced it at the beginning of November 1990. Rains filled the streams and rivers in only a few hours. Huge quantities of water were released from large catchment areas and poured down instantaneously because the ten-year plan of the people in charge of water management was that water should pour down immediately. The result was an extremely destructive flood that caused enormous damage equivalent to one-third of Slovene national income.

The Greens are going to demand a change in the entire concept of river regulation. Mountain torrents should be changed back into streams and rivers, and meanders should revert to swampy areas so as to prevent streams and rivers from causing floods. At the same time, water flow would be distributed over a wider area, replenishing underground water reserves as well. The end of the practice of regulating rivers would return their habitat to many species of animals and plants, including the swamp tulip *(Fritillaria meleagris)*, the black alder *(Alnus glutinosa)*, the gray heron *(Ardea cinerea)*, and the white stork *(Ciconia ciconia)*.

Forests

With the fall of socialism the status of forests in Slovenia changed dramatically. Slovenia is very rich in woodlands, as half its territory is forested. After 1945 most of the forests came under state ownership and state management. There was rigorous control of woodcutting even in woods belonging to individual owners. These could cut down only those trees marked by a forester according to a plan that promoted forest growth over wood harvesting. Very early on in the new regime, clear-cutting, which constitutes such an environmental shock for a forest, was outlawed.

But the socialist management of woodland had its faults. It was dedicated to one purpose only, bigger growth of trees. Every rotting, damaged, or old tree was carefully removed, and timbered areas were replanted with pine because these trees show a large growth of wood in a short time. As the years passed, the composition of the Slovenian forests changed from mixed growth to a pine monoculture. The forests became ecologically sterile: there were no more hollows in which birds, squirrels, and dormice could make their nests. There were no rotting trees, the main source of food for most animals and plants in the woods. Intensive building of logging roads leading to all parts of the forest gradually destroyed the big oases of wilderness that were home to species in danger of becoming extinct. A special problem is people who gather mushrooms, berries, and chestnuts not for their personal use but to sell. In Italy the gathering of edible forest plants and produce is restricted or prohibited, so Italian berry pickers come to Slovenia. And commercial companies that trade in edible woodland products organize trade fairs all over Slovenia. The Greens have proposed legislation that would divide the forests into those where gathering is allowed and those where it is prohibited. The latter would provide conditions for plant and animal species to live peacefully.

The fall of communism brought new dangers for forest management and protection. The Farm Party, for example, demands the restitution of all woods taken from the original owners after the war and the abolition of all restrictions on lumbering. Under the old system the state forestry industry employed too many workers. There was a regulation that ordered a specific amount of timber cut down yearly. In addition, the regulation stipulated that a certain minimal number of board feet had to be cut in every forest each year, as the sale of this wood paid the many workers. The reduction and rationalization of the forest service is inevitable, but there should be legislation guaranteeing that in every forest there will be a chance for animals and vegetation to survive. Such legislation would change the focus of forest management away from being solely concerned with the optimal production of wood and shift it towards the problem of how to improve the forest environment as a habitat for animals and plants.

It is gratifying to realize that in many large forests in the southern part of Slovenia, especially the area around Kočevje, bordering Croatia, there are some species that cannot be found anywhere else in Europe. But recent political changes had their impact here. These so-called hunting grounds were protected by the old regime and intended solely for hunting parties of high state functionaries and rich foreigners. Kočevje should become a national park. The difficulty is that only the government has the authority to proclaim national and regional parks. The responsible government officials are already overloaded with traditional cultural issues. In 1981 the first and only national park in Slovenia, Triglav National Park, came into being. Since then no other important natural areas have been protected, although the documentation for several regional and national parks has been in the drawers of the Secretariat of Culture for years.

Climate

In agriculture, the specific method used to protect fields from hail presents a special problem, well known to the East European countries during communist rule, but not known before. Whenever a hailstorm threatens, rockets are shot into the clouds, or the clouds are sprayed with silver iodide from planes. The World Meteorological Organization has determined that such methods are not environmentally safe. However, the new Slovene Parliament did not immediately abolish the practice even though silver iodide washes off the clouds into streams, rivers, and groundwater. Its continuation threatens to pollute the drinking water, and this pollution can reach the cleanest and most remote areas in Slovenia, where there are no other chemical pollutants except acid rain, carbon dioxide, and nitric oxide.

Conclusion

This presentation of ecological problems in Slovenia is not complete. Only those questions and problems that have significantly occupied public attention have been presented. Recently there have been many public opinion studies in Slovenia. They show great concern for environmental problems but an unwillingness to support legal measures for their solution. It is very important to understand how environmental problems become a part of public opinion and how they become the object of common attention. The process by which the public becomes aware of an environmental problem is closely connected to scientific research into the same problem and to its subsequent regulation or solution. These developments do not occur all at the same time and are not parallel, because many political, social, and economic interests confront each other in every environmental issue. Sometimes there seems to be no intellectual concern, no ethical consciousness, no sense of the need for law. Then there is a sudden change in public opinion stimulated by events all over the world. This change opens the way to a possible solution where only yesterday humanity, fauna and flora, and all our natural inheritance seemed to be without a future.

————————————————**11**

Soviet Greens: Who Are They?

The View from Inside

Evgenii A. Shvarts and Irina Prochozova

A Soviet ecological, environmental, "green" movement! These words meet with the same curiosity both inside the former Soviet Union and abroad. But the actual reaction is a little different. The average Soviet citizen asks, "Oh! Do we really have any Greens? That is great! And what have they managed to do, what are their achievements?" The average Westerner exclaims, "Oh! Do they really have any Greens? That is great! If they have managed to become known abroad, they must be very important and more green than all the other Soviet Greens!" A lot of good people from a variety of professions from time to time attend this or that international conference, seminar or meeting. These tend to represent themselves as the leader of the environmental (ecological, green) movement of the former USSR.

At the outset, we would like to make clear that an environmental movement covering the whole territory of the former USSR does not exist in terms of an organized public force. We do not want to unmask anybody in this article, and we do not pretend to convey a full scien-

The authors are affiliated with the Institute of Geography, Russian Academy of Sciences and the Department of Sociology, Moscow State University, respectively.

tific description of the present-day situation. This would be impossible within the framework of one short article. What we would like to do in this article is to provide a brief survey of what we consider the most important green organizations in the former USSR. Then we shall give some history and some current events in an attempt to explain the origins, specific features, problems, and potential trends in what was once called the Soviet green movement. Our view will be from the inside, because we have been involved with the movement for a considerable length of time.

Before we begin, it is important to point out that any description of or research on a public movement in the former USSR generally becomes outdated in a month or even in a week. For this reason, we will not attempt to describe the daily appearance and disappearance of new groups, unions, and even political parties. Very often, unfortunately, they have no background in environmental issues, which frequently represent the public façade of their private agendas. We will discuss the possible reasons for the emergence of the environmental "ghosts" later. This first section focuses on organizations, that, to our mind, have had a greater or lesser influence on the political climate not only within the environmental movement, but in the public life of a region or even the country as a whole.

The first organization is the Student Druzhina Movement (DOP). *Druzhina* is an old Russian word whose original meaning was "defense group, personal guard, troops." To understand the current situation in which the movement finds itself, we must first look at the history of the movement of local groups (*druzhiny*) for nature conservation. The movement originated in 1958–60 from the group for nature conservation that was organized in the Department of Biology at Moscow University, and from a circle on nature conservation in the University of Tartu, Estonia, and the Academy of Agricultural Sciences of the Estonian Republic.[1] The formation of these groups was made possible by the great changes in the domestic policy of this country brought about by N. S. Khrushchev and by the 20th and 22d Congresses of the Communist Party of the Soviet Union (CPSU). That period brought to life the rudiments of democracy in our society in the form of "informal organizations and movements," as they were called in the contemporary terminology of Soviet society. During what were called the "times of stagnation" under Brezhnev, some of those informal organizations were forced to relinquish their love of freedom for official status as the whole might of the command-administrative system was brought to bear upon them, and they reverted to typical components of the state administrative machinery. These were the Voluntary People's Patrol and the students' construction squads. The latter mutated into working squads that operated in the different trades, so that there were loaders' squads, construction workers' squads, stewards' squads, medical nurses' squads, and squads for teachers in summer pioneer camps. Other informal organizations were unable to resist the destructive force of totalitarianism and, consequently, were disbanded. Still others went underground. When they did, the members were effectively denied work and active contacts with society. Examples of these groups include the organization of communards, many student unions, including unions of creative youth. One of these, *Fakel* (torch) in Novosibirsk (Siberia), earned the reputation as a prototype of the present-day unions of young scientists and engineers (NTTM).

With the exception of the dissident movement, which was well known in the West, the movement of groups for nature conservation and, to a lesser extent, the singers' clubs (amateur songwriters and singers—KSP) remained the only informal organizations that managed to retain their original character. The club of student singers probably was able to survive because it had a truly nationwide character and involved large numbers of young people. Its massive informal membership was the main reason why so many Party and Young Communist League (Komsomol) officials focused their attention and propaganda on the organization. But the reasons for the survival of the DOP were not so simple.

One reason for the long history of the movement of groups for nature conservation has been the steadily increasing importance and acuteness of the problem of controlling environmental pollution. This issue brought into the movement the most courageous people, who were by and large politically in good standing and generally educated. Most were students from established universities. Another explanation may be found in the restricted admission of new organizations into the movement. This is the view of S. Kushnerev, a member of the editorial board of *Komsomolskaia pravda*, an organ of the former Young Communist League. However flattering these assessments might sound, neither of these conditions, although necessary, can be considered sufficient reasons. The communards' organization and the *Fakel* union from Novosibirsk both had similar features.

The authors hold the view that the decisive reason for the survival of the movement during the time of stagnation was that the movement purposefully and deliberately based its work on what might be termed "embryos of the legal state" brought about by Khruchshev's thaw. These embryos were the by-laws of different inspectorates for nature preservation. The by-laws armed the groups with the powers of governmental organizations and permitted them to monitor the observance of laws on nature preservation. The multifaceted nature of the organizations concerned with nature conservation also played an important role. Since the groups were incorporated into the by-laws of different inspectorates, they were able to retain their voluntary and independent status rather than become a subordinate component of one specific agency of the governmental mechanism with all its negative consequences, as happened to the Voluntary People's Patrol.

From the legal point of view, the movement managed to survive only because it was a legally registered, rather than permitted, organization. Under the conditions of the branch management of natural resources, every Soviet ministry had its own public inspectorate for nature preservation that enjoyed broad and, to some extent, similar rights. If the members of a group for nature preservation happened to catch red-handed an inspector from the State Inspectorate for the Preservation of Wildlife poaching, they would probably come into conflict with the corresponding state-run organization. This conflict could happily be avoided. In this case, they could go to the regional inspectorate for forestry and produce their mandates as public inspectors. Should they catch a forest ranger, they could report his activities to the local inspectorate for the preservation of water life. If an inspector was caught red-handed, the activists could report his activities to the local chapter of the Society for the Preservation of Nature that used be attached to every territorial Executive Council.

In other words, the abundance of inspectorates outnumbered the possible conflicts that a single group of nature preservationists could run into. When they reached the upper levels of power, i.e., the Regional Party Committee or the Executive Council of the Regional Soviet, they were supported by the whole movement. Letters were mailed by all constituent groups of nature preservationists to the corresponding high-ranking official organization. Campaigns of protest were launched in the local and national press. There was "harmony" between the DOP and the state.

Clearly such a situation could not long continue. The further development of the DOP required the formation of democratically organized coordinating and executive organs or some kind of regularized conduct of official conferences of the movement. The conflict between the movement and elements of the governmental machinery for nature preservation at both the national and republican level is of recent venue and came into being on the eve and during the first years of *perestroika* (restructuring), 1984–86. In Russia, Ukraine, and to a lesser extent, in Belorussia, tensions flared up between the groups and the republican Societies for Nature Preservation, the Young Communist League Central Committee, and the organs of nature protection, *Goskomprirody*, of the constituent republics. At issue were attempts to control the movement through control of one of its principal executive organs, the Methods Coordination Council.

The first coordinating council of the DOP, which existed from 1977 to 1979, was not reelected and dissolved itself as a result of the political attack by a communist activist from Tomsk University, Nikolai Laptev. Thanks to Laptev, five Obkom Komsomol members and a corresponding number from the local KGB organs conducted a personnel investigation of the leaders of the movement in Moscow, Kazan, Tomsk, Kirov, and Irkutsk.

Fresh efforts by a new generation of movement leaders to open a dialogue with the official structures, in which many new leaders continued to see allies in conservation work, led eventually to a denunciation of the movement by these structures (i.e., the Komsomol, the official republican Societies for the Protection of Nature of Russia and Ukraine, the State Committee for Nature Protection of Ukraine), which more than anything were interested in the liquidation of a youth organization that was independent of the state machine. In February 1984, an initiative of the student department of the Komsomol Central Committee and the Ministry of Higher and Secondary Specialized Education of the USSR *(Minvuzom)* resulted in the authorities forbidding the holding of the regular all-union conference of the movement scheduled in Sverdlovsk (Ekaterinburg). Convening the meeting under these conditions could be considered a relative success, in that a majority of delegates were able to get to Sverdlovsk.

In Ukraine and other areas a different situation prevailed. A democratically formed grass-roots organization, the Methods Coordination Council of DOP Ukraine, had existed within the Ukrainian Society for

Nature Protection since 1983. It was thus much easier for the Komsomol and other bureaucratic structures to operate in their traditional manner of "seizing the initiative." At the end of 1985, the Central Council of the All-Russian Society of Nature Protection (VOOP), with the participation of the Komsomol and branch institutions, created by bureaucratic methods an organ called the Methods Coordination Council for the Work of Student Druzhinas of Nature Protection attached to the Presidium of the Central Council of the All-Russian Society for Nature Protection. Out of 40 members of this council, there were 30 representatives of the bureaucracy, essentially from those institutions whose activities had been in constant opposition to the *druzhinas*. The council contained not one leader proposed by the *druzhinas*. Included in it was N. Laptev, who had by this time become the deputy chairman of the Tomsk oblast VOOP Council, functionaries from the Ministry of Water Management, the Ministry of the Riverine Fleet, and other interested institutions.

These actions called forth a strong protest and open confrontation. On one side were the state bureaucracies in the form of representatives from the *apparaty* of the Presidium of the VOOP Central Council, the student section of the Central Committee of the Komsomol, and the Ministry of Higher and Secondary Specialized Education of the RSFSR. On the other was the student movement. The leaders of the DOP had acquired a deep understanding of this oppositional relationship through their experience of working with the bureaucratic structures. They arranged for the movement at the beginning of February 1986 (a month before the 27th Congress of the CPSU) to hold an all-union conference officially endorsed by the Ministry of Higher and Secondary Specialized Education of the USSR, regardless of the active opposition of VOOP and the student section of the Komsomol Central Committee. With this action, the conflict between the Movement and VOOP came out into the open.[2]

Similar developments were taking place at the same time in Ukraine, where functionaries of the Society for Nature Protection and the State Committee for the Protection of Nature were trying to change the composition of the Coordinating Methods Council as well as the democratic way in which it was formed. However, there was one difference: the principal opponent of the *druzhina* movement in Ukraine was the State Committee for Nature Protection *(Goskompriroda)* of the UkSSR. The *druzhiniki* had publicly criticized the committee's performance in journals published by the central, all-union press, because the publication of ecological problems in the republican press was for all intents and purposes completely controlled by the functionaries at *Goskompriroda* of the UkSSR. At the same time, the secretary of the Central Committee of the Ukrainian Komsomol, B. Matvienko, supported the activities of the DOP and the Methods Coordination Council of DOP UkSSR.

A solution was found only at the republican conference of the Student Groups for Nature Conservation (Ukraine) held in November 1987. The conference declared the organizational independence of the Methods Coordination Council of the Movement of Student Groups for Nature Conservation in Ukraine and all other movements from the official Ukrainian Society for Nature Protection. The all-union conference of the movement was held in December in Dolgoprudny, in the Moscow region. This conference adopted important guidelines for the movement. At Dolgoprudny, it established nine basic criteria for membership in the movement, and elaborated draft statutes for the Student Groups for Nature Conservation. The statutes took their legal basis from Directive No. 143 of July 17, 1988, signed by V. D. Shadrikov, Minister of the USSR, which defined the DOP as a voluntary public independent organization. The draft statutes stipulated that the movement, as a legal organization, enjoyed the right to have elected organs for coordination of methods and to work with other groups, organizations, and unions with similar interests. The conference also adopted a draft statute for the Methods Coordination Council for the movement, and elected members of the council.

The right to have elected organs allowed the movement officially to promote the organizational independence and the voluntary character of the movement on an all-union basis. The same conference adopted a decision by which the Methods Coordination Council for the DOP attached to the Presidium of the Central Council of the All-Russian Society for the Preservation of Nature was no longer recognized as an authoritative organ of the movement. It was thus stripped of all its former powers. In line with the decision, the movement recalled its representatives from the council and stopped its work in the council. On December 24, 1989, the decision was brought to the notice of the Presidium of the Central Council of the All-Russian Society for the Preservation of Nature, some of whose members had been elected by the Methods Coordination Council that had worked at the Presidium.

However, the Methods Coordination Council that worked at the Presidium from the beginning of 1988 had been appointed under the conditions set forth in the old statutes, and had not been elected in accordance with the stipulations of the new draft statutes. Most of the members of this council were representatives of different ministries and enterprises. However, even though one-fourth of the membership on this council were activists themselves, the former Methods Coordination Council was legally obliged to stop work.

It is worth mentioning the broad democratic basis of the movement. The new Methods Coordination Council of the movement, according to its legal status and name, is only a consultative organ. Members of the council are now elected, rather than appointed by the higher authoritative bodies. Whenever there is a difference of opinion on fundamental questions, the minority enjoys the right to organize its own methods coordination council according to the aforementioned draft statute of the Student Groups for Nature Conservation. Moreover, the same article of the statute allows the constituent groups to organize the necessary work coordination organs at all levels: national, territorial, regional, city, or district.

Another important feature is the draft statute of the Student Groups for Nature Conservation. The draft statute can be used by any voluntary student organization interested in monitoring pollution. A student group may use its articles as the basis for its work, regardless of whether this particular student organization is incorporated within the movement. What adoption of the statutes signaled was that public life had begun to lose its subservience to the state bodies. Both the statutes and the national movement now exist independently of each other. In a legal sense, the statute is much broader than the movement, since the statute can serve as the legal basis for any voluntary student organization charged with monitoring environmental pollution. The movement itself has stopped being an organization of students only. None of the nine criteria for membership in the movement restricts either age or social background of the membership.

As of this writing, the situation is to a great extent a compromise between meeting the legal requirements stipulated in the Law on Public Organizations (1932), and the movement of the Student Groups for Nature Conservation. But the text of the statute was conceived with the bureaucratic practice of the time in mind so that, thanks to it, a whole series of social ecological organizations not connected to the student movement for nature conservation were able to register, on the eve of the first democratic elections in 1989 and 1990, as legal social organizations, with the right to nominate candidates and to take part in the elections.

As time passed after a solution was found to the most urgent "external" problems and conflicts that hampered the successful work of the movement, it became increasingly evident that events were snowballing into a crisis. But this time, the problem derived from conditions within the movement rather than from its relations with the state agencies. The pressure exerted by the command-administrative system had served to consolidate the movement. In the absence of such pressure, all the politics that had long been simmering in the movement became open to view.

The movement of Groups for Nature Conservation started at a time when the idea of nature conservation—the protection of the environment from damage caused by "our Soviet man" and "our Soviet enterprises" operating in a socialist planned economy—sounded blasphemous and offensive. Under such conditions, the exercise by DOP groups of an independent monitoring function over environmental pollution or nature preservation was a political activity, in the literal sense of the word. It was not merely romance, like listening to the rattle of the forest ranger's motorboat on the river in a cold piercing wind. At a time when every tenth poacher was a party, Soviet, or Komsomol official, and 10 percent of those poachers who were caught were militiamen, criminal investigators, local KGB men, and prosecutors, the work of the student groups was regarded as the embodiment of people's democracy, as the realization of societal control over the party and state aristocracy, whose members strongly believed in their immunity from the law.

However, up to the present writing, the other activities of the groups for nature preservation had quite a different character. These had no political overtones whatsoever and included, among other things, the setting up of temporary nature reservations. This work was essentially altruistic, done out of sheer commitment. It required a great deal of energy and effort on the part of the group to make its point of view prevail in negotiations with Soviet officials and land managers.

By the mid-1980s the situation had definitely changed. Nature conservation was no longer a lollipop of the intellectuals, but a national concern. It became clear that members of the groups for nature conservation were fighting the consequences rather than the reasons for the widespread social illness of environmental degradation. The campaign for nature preservation became more and more limited to the struggle for human rights. This became especially clear to the groups for nature conservation that stood sentry against poachers, in what was known as the *Vystrel* (gunshot) campaign. Most cases of poaching in the woods and in rivers had no effect on nature preservation per se. Poaching by and large was the direct consequence of an unreasonable and tight control of forest and wildlife management, both in terms of ecology and in terms of law. However, research into optimum rules for nature management were long denied proper attention in the work of the groups. Paperwork is less romantic in comparison to swoops on armed poachers. You can hardly impress a fellow student or the public, common hunters and fishermen among them, with achievements in this area. The *Vystrel* campaign was brought to a successful conclusion, but the biggest number of requests forwarded by the subsection of the movement concerned with the antipoaching campaign at the national conference of the movement in 1986 were answered by *Glavokhota* of Russia, the Inspectorate for Wildlife Management, independently of the groups. The same thing happened to other aspects of the movement's work.

It was recognized that, if it wanted to continue to exist, the movement had to reform itself and shift its focus away from the old altruistic approach toward an active contribution to the direction of nature preservation, and first and foremost, to the preservation of a healthy habitat for humankind. It was probably wrong to separate preservation of wildlife from preservation of the human habitat. But in terms of the organization's philosophy of work, it was quite feasible, since no solution to urgent national social and economic problems is found without broad public support. Ordinary people had become concerned about the deteriorating environmental situation and had become involved in the environmental movement not through appeals by scientists but after having begun to understand the real threats posed to their health and life, and what is even more important, the threats to the health and life of their children.

What is absolutely clear is that the social background of those involved in proenvironmental activity seriously changed, particularly after *glasnost'* (more or less, "openness") enabled a great deal of shocking data on the environmental situation to become public knowledge. On the other hand, individuals who had been the core of the *druzhinas* movement had grown up and were no longer eligible to work in it. The majority of them could not imagine themselves without environmental activity and tried to find a place in the public movement, where there would be an opportunity to use their experience, their knowledge, and their good-will.

In the middle of the 1980s, a group was formed known as the Alumni of the DOP Movement (*Gruppa sviazi vypustnikov dvizheniia DOP*). This organization allowed DOP alumni who had gone to another city or nature reserve or had simply gone to other organizations of the same city where there were no *druzhinas* to retain contact with the movement and work with it. At that time, there was an especially large number of DOP alumni working in the nature reserves in Turkmenistan, who called themselves the Turkmen Dekant. However, a great many organizational problems piled up as the alumni tried to formalize their relations with the parent organization. One of the most difficult of these was how to admit into the alumni activists who had not worked in any *druzhinas* movement during their student years. Another was the widening break in the form and way in which conservation work was carried out in the two organizations. It was not long before it became obvious that a new independent organization had to be created.

From these origins and organizational framework came the Socioecological Union, an umbrella organization that has today about two hundred member groups all over the former Soviet Union and approximately ten to fifteen thousand individual members. The Socioecological Union is very closely connected with the student *druzhinas* movement. But the average age is no longer in the twenties, but between 35 and 45.

There are certain differences in aims and activities between the movement and the union. In the union, in addition to the practical environmental work of local groups, a great deal of attention is paid to political work: protest campaigns, meetings, active participation in elections at every level, work with the new People's Deputies, efforts with the help of specialists (scientists mostly) to influence not only a concrete decision on a concrete problem, but even to take part in the creation of legislation, especially at the republican level.

The conference that announced the birth of the Socioecological Union took place in 1987. It marked the start of a prolonged period of creating an environmental movement, very often from nothing. We emphasize creating, because the union did not just provide some central organizational structure to already existing groups or unions.

There are three very specific factors that made such a phenomenon possible. It is very hard to identify which was the most important, but let us at least try to name them.

First, the period of perestroika made possible different forms of public activity. But up to the abolition of Article 6 of the USSR Constitution and the leading role of the Communist Party, serious political, especially opposition party, work was dangerous, at least in terms of a personal career. At the same time environmental slogans encountered a mostly loyal reaction from the official spheres of the party and government leadership and administration, especially if they were speaking only about global, general, or, even better, theoretical problems that did not name specific state organs, ministries, plants, or factories. So on the one hand ecologists gained a reputation as political activists, and on the other they seemed to be at no risk.

Accordingly, there rather suddenly appeared a great number of different organizations at different levels, most of them carrying on discussions about the environment without any results to show. Usually they had a lot of facilities and were very well equipped, because they were ready to play the official leadership's tune or, at the very least, guarantee that they would never cause a scandal. They were always polite and obedient, and constituted what might be called a kind of "pocket" green for the government to show off to everybody, mostly to organizations and people abroad. You can find them at every official meeting and find their fax or telex number in every official directory.

Closely connected with the political factor and corresponding type of "green" organization, there is, let us say, a commercial factor. Very soon it became evident that environmental activity could be very profitable. And one could acquire money by merely professing environmental expertise or advocating environmental protection. It is very sad, but there were announcements of the formation of a great many foundations. The environmental goals and concepts in the statutes of these organizations appeared to be just enough for several people or several groups. Certainly, we do not want to condemn all foundations dealing with environmental problems. Many problems were impossible to solve without foundation support. But citizens should do their homework and make sure they can identify the primary concern of an organization to which they donate funds: Is it money or the environment?

A final reason is typically soviet. The trend to unite, to organize, and, most important, to lead still exists as part of the fabric of our country. The totalitarian system, with its regime of subordination and dependence and its territorial structure, had too long a period of domination. Whether they understood this or not, many new leaders brought the old authoritarian habits to the creation of a new association, union, or organization. The idea was to "bring order" among different local groups. All over the former Soviet Union, people wanted to stand at the head of a new structure, what might be called a post-totalitarian variation on the "strong leader" syndrome. It was not uncommon that a new organization appeared only because of the energy of one person, who decided to have his own organization and to be its sole leader. The exact kind of association that he should head was not so important to him: It could be a green movement, an agricultural union, or an independent television station. But even the short time that has elapsed since restructuring began shows that this kind of artificial green structure is not sustainable. It either breaks down, or it tries to join some bona fide organization.

A very important factor that unexpectedly aroused great interest in the Soviet environmental movement came from abroad. Participation and leadership in any organization, plus knowledge of a foreign language, allowed and allows many Soviet citizens to go abroad and thereby earn not a bad profit, from the Soviet point of view. The "foreign card" was responsible for the appearance of a great number of green organizations that preferred to protect nature somewhere in the West rather than inside the Soviet Union.

It is not by chance that we stress the negative motivations for founding a green organization. These reasons may be said to be precise reflections of the real situation in our country in this particular period of time. By contrast, the "positive" reasons leading to the establishment of a Green movement or party are fairly typical and approximately the same in every country.

The end of 1989 to the beginning of 1990 was the high point in the creation of an environmental movement. Within less than five months there appeared five organizations at the USSR level.

1. The Green Movement of the USSR was organized by a former Komsomol leader, now a minister in the democratic government of Russia. Today, the Green Movement is moving closer and closer to the Socioecological Union, but it is much weaker. Nearly 60 percent of the local groups in the Green Movement are member organizations in the Socioecological Union. The movement's principal aims and activities are nearly the same, and as of this writing the complete unification of

the Socioecological Union with the Green Movement is only a matter of time. The coordination and information centers of the two organizations have already been consolidated.

2. The Ecological Society of the USSR. In the spectrum of the green movement, the society seems to be closest to the "right" in the Soviet meaning of the word, with a strong nationalistic ideology. Its activities are typical for grass-roots movements. Since 1991 we have no information on the activities of and persons active in this society.

3. The Ecological Foundation of the USSR has very close historical and organizational ties with the Ecological Union of the USSR. They are very closely connected. According to a statement by the head of the Ecological Union, "the most important feature distinguishing (the Union) from other green organizations is its creative objectives on the biosphere level."[3]

4. The Green International. This is an organization that may have absolutely clean aims. However, it gives the impression of people who think that they are professionals in business and in science and that they are the first in the world to deal with specific environmental problems, for example, the ozone layer, and, certainly, the only ones who can solve the problems. The Green International appeared approximately a half year after all the other nature protection organizations had been created. The complete independence of its founders separates them from the social activists of the ecological movements of the 1970s and 1980s.

5. The Association "Save Peace and Nature." This is a typical semi-official green organization, yearning to get into international affairs. From time to time, it has done rather useful things, especially in trying to attract public attention to this or that specific environmental problem. Public awareness is one of the stated aims in its statutes. The type of ecological initiative the association chooses to support, our research suggests, coincides in large part with the material interests of its founders, Igor Altshuler and Ruben Mnatskanyan.[4]

Material from the regional and "green" press in Russia and the Russian-speaking oblasts of Ukraine is well worth a brief analysis. A review of a large number of regional and "ecological" publications presents a picture of the Socioecological Union as an organization with broad public support totally dominated by one or at best a few leaders. Regardless of the huge authority of the leader of the DOP for many years and now leader of the Socioecological Union, Sviatoslav Zabelin, the majority of the published materials are articles by individual members of the Union or by leaders of the regional sections (Moscow, Samara, Nizhni Novgorod, Altai province, Odessa, Kharkov, etc.). There are significantly fewer references to "the Green Movement" (Leningrad/St. Petersburg). The activity of the "Ecological Fund" may primarily be seen in its sponsoring of initiatives, competitions, and other events, including the publication of the journal *Green World* (*Zelenyi mir*). *Green World* is the official organ of *Goskompriroda* (the Ministry of the Environment RCFSWR, the Central Committee of VOOP, etc.). But the fund's interests are also reflected in publications by individual activists in the union's regional sections, such as the journal *Survival*, published in Tula. Despite the considerable quantity of publications tied to the activities of the Ecological Fund, all of them contain articles by or interviews with its chairman, Professor and Doctor of Biological Science, N. F. Reimers. During 1990–91, we were unable to find publications linked to the activities of the Ecological Society.

The list of so-called Soviet nongovernmental organizations of green orientation could go on and on. But a few words about the Green Party seem in order. The most surprising thing we can say is that a green party exists. It is very young, weak, and small, but it has already split into three branches, and they cannot find common ground between them. It is characteristic that people tend to come into the Green Party, especially into its leadership, who are not from practical environmental work but from humanitarian spheres. Party members include historians learned in theories of Western experience, or people who have already tried to find themselves in some other kind of political activity, such as a professional party organization. So far the Green Party has had no visible successes or achievements. The Socioecological Union performs party functions much more successfully. The topsy-turvy nature of green movement behavior becomes understandable when one realizes that the process of power structure formation in the USSR began much earlier than the process of formation of public movements. After the elections in Estonia, one of the leaders of the Estonian Green Movement turned to the new deputies at each administrative level who were working on environmental issues, with the aim of creating a parliamentary Green Party. The situation is absolutely opposite to the usual one, in which there is first a process of organization and growth of a party, and only after that does the party introduce its members to election campaigns. To continue the example of Estonia, and to be perfectly objective, we have to say that there is already a green party in Estonia, the Estonian Green Movement.

As far as the ideology of environmentalists is concerned, once again the situation is very unusual from a Western point of view. On the one hand it is important to understand that those whom we call leftist democrats and with whom the Greens mostly cooperate are without any doubt supporters of a free market and the more or less traditional, conservative Western way of development. At the same time, among those whom we call rightists are many supporters of communal ideas. They would like to return to the so-called natural, traditionally Russian way of life. Unfortunately, these ideas have become the slogans of openly nationalistic organizations like Pamyat (Memory). There is apprehension that as the green movement develops and works out its philosophy and strategies for future development, the movement could side with the nationalist right, in terms of the contemporary political situation in the former USSR. In order to avoid this alliance on the one hand, and not allow the country to repeat all the mistakes of Western development on the other, the new democrats who have come to power must pay the most careful attention to the environmental aspects of their economic programs, something we have not yet seen. Last but not least, the green movement should be mature enough to generalize its experience (in scientific terms too) and to combine it with theory in order to bring the best, the most sensible and useful aspects of the movement to new environmental programs and legislation. This development is probably only possible on the republican level.

Whether this maturation process will take place or not, only the future will show. But let us trust that we in the lands of the former Soviet Union still have time and, therefore, some hope of success.

Notes

1. D. R. Weiner, "The Changing Face of Soviet Conservation," in D. Worster, ed., *The Ends of the Earth* (Cambridge and New York: Cambridge University Press, 1988), pp. 252–73.

2. V. Mokievskii, I. Chestin, and E. Shvarts, "Prirodu ne obmanesh" [You Can't Fool Nature], *Komsomolskaia pravda*, September 5, 1986.

3. "The Changing Face of Environmentalism in the Soviet Union," *Environment* 32, no. 2 (February 1990): 4–9, 26–30.

4. N. Ph. Reimers, *Prirodopol'zovanie* [Exploitation of Nature] (Moscow: Mysl', 1990).

12

The East European Environmental Movement and the Transformation of East European Society

Barbara Jancar-Webster

The 1980s saw the proliferation of spontaneous popular movements in Eastern Europe. During the decade, public participation in these movements progressively expanded from the activities of a small core of dissidents to demonstrations by thousands. By 1989 the protest movements had succeeded in eroding the power of the established communist regimes. When Gorbachev refused to back the perpetuation of the communist command-administrative model, one by one, in rapid succession, the regimes crumbled and fell. Only in Romania and Bulgaria was the transition accompanied by violence.

More than any other issue, the environment became the focal point of public demand for the end of the old regime. Starting with Poland in 1980, when environmentalists succeeded in getting the big aluminum mill outside Cracow closed down, revelation of ecological crisis or of some gigantic government project harmful to the environment precipitated public response and a call for the end of the Stalinist order.[1] In Czechoslovakia, air and water pollution were the catalysts. In February 1987, some three hundred people from the Chomutov District of North Bohemian kraj signed a letter sent first to the chairman of the district National Council and then to the Czech prime minister and the presidium of the Communist Party, complaining about an inadequate warning system to alert people to an increase in air pollution in the district. On November 11, 1989, just a week before the student demonstration in Prague that ended the old regime, there was a protest demonstration against living conditions in the North Bohemian town of Teplice, where coal mining had turned the land into craters and made the air unbreathable.[2] In the preceding weeks, a determined group of women known as the Group of Czech Mothers staged demonstrations in the streets of the capital against the quality of water. Everywhere, water treatment had not kept pace with water contamination, so that there was virtually no drinkable water in the whole country and mothers were advised not to make infant formulas with tap water.

In East Germany, environmental groups such as the Environmental Library and the Green Network "Ark" were long active under the aegis of the Evangelical Church. Then came the emigration crisis and the formation of four large independent organizations with specific democratic agendas, which overshadowed the earlier grass-roots movements. The later organizations were in turn completely outclassed by the invasion of the highly organized West German parties and gradually faded out of the picture. But environmental pollution was a major political issue at the Leipzig rallies in 1989, and the greens were able to profit from it despite the rapidly changing political climate. Three East German green parties registered for the March 18, 1990, elections and won between them 8 seats out of the 400-seat parliament.

In Hungary, the catalyst for change was the controversy generated by the government's insistence on continuing the building of the Nagymaros Dam across a historic and enchanting bend in the Danube River. In October 1988, forty thousand people filled the area in front of the Hungarian parliament to demonstrate against the dam. The air was full of tension, since it was the first time there was a demonstration on that site since the Soviet invasion of 1956. The construction of the dam, according to Judit Vesarhelyi of the Independent Ecological Center, symbolized to many the regime's gigantomania and arbitrary methods of rule. Its broad popular appeal made it possible for the antidam movement to become the Hungarian pioneer of peaceful methods of protest within the framework of existing Hungarian law. (Samizdat was excluded.) For years, the "Blues" walked a tightrope between legality and illegality. When they placed advertisements in foreign newspapers, they were quickly accused of going back to "the ugly thirties" and of using foreign support to influence national politics. But the movement persevered. The Danube Circle was the first to hand out handbills in the street. In the spring of 1988, the group organized one demonstration at Nagymaros itself. It was supposed to be a march of women and children, but so concerned were the fathers about the safety of their families that they marched along. The women handed petitions through the construction gates and chatted with the engineers and workmen. In this and many other ways, the ecological movement developed and taught large numbers of people democratic methods of protest.

In 1988, Bulgarian public protest spilled over the boundaries of scholarly and intellectual discussion. Air pollution in the Danube town of Ruse had reached such proportions that it severely threatened the health and life of the resident population. The pollutants were being carried across the Danube River from chemical plants on the Romanian side. Public health statistics increased the mass discontent, forcing the Bulgarian government to take issue on the matter with the Romanian government. The protests evolved into the first full-fledged independent environmental movement, the Independent Committee for the Protection of the Environment. By 1989, independent groups had formed in virtually every large Bulgarian city. Leading the movement was Ecoglasnost. In October/November 1989, that organization sponsored a series of protests in Sofia during the Helsinki conference on environmental cooperation. The subsequent imprisonment of the demonstrators contributed in no small part to the fall of the Zhivkov regime.[3]

Environmentalism in Romania is still in its infancy. Under Ceaucescu, environmental activism was ruthlessly suppressed, and all information on the environment was kept secret. Nevertheless, Ceaucescu's campaign to destroy the Romanian countryside and turn the Danube delta into agricultural land did not pass unnoticed. In the spring of 1988, an underground opposition group calling itself Romanian Democratic Action issued a document entitled "The Green Report of the Romanian Democratic Action on the Environmental Situation in Romania." The first material of its kind to reach the West from Romania, the report stated that the sociopolitical and economic crisis in that country was turning into "an ecological disaster." Significantly, the second half of the report contained a 12-point program that the signers believed would halt further environmental deterioration.[4]

The first organization to register officially after the December 1989 revolution was the Ecological Movement of Romania, which quickly allied itself with the ruling National Salvation Front (NSF). Six days later the Romanian Ecological Party was officially registered. The group has been generally critical of the NSF's activities. Numerous smaller local groups and parties have subsequently registered, each fighting a serious local pollution problem. One such is the Democratic Ecologist Party in the town of Turda in Transylvania, where the *Wall Street Journal* described air pollution as "a beige mist from a forest of (cement works) smokestacks."[5]

In Yugoslavia the environmental movement has played a very uneven role over the past twenty years. In the mid-1980s a nationwide effort led by scientists and professional organizations was successful in getting the federal government to rescind its decision to build a hydroelectric station at the Tara River Canyon, one of the most scenic gorges in Europe reserved under the United Nations Man and the Biosphere (MAB) Program.[6] A second success was the stop-nuclear-power movement initiated by a Belgrade student, which spread across the republics and resulted in the federal legislature's vote for a moratorium on nuclear power until the year 2000.[7] Each of these movements developed means of action within the framework of the Yugoslav constitution and were training grounds for democratic action.

The republic where the environmental movement has so far put down the deepest roots is Slovenia. Started in the late 1960s by a group of courageous students, the movement moved to the forefront of democratic activism in the mid-1980s and in 1989, without official approval, declared itself a party. In the 1990 elections, the party allied with DEMOS, the coalition of national democratic forces, and won.

All over Eastern Europe, then, the environmentalists were leaders in demanding political change and in developing constructive methods to induce that change. In 1989, the greens of Eastern Europe led the world in publicizing environmental degradation and demanding environmental remediation. In 1990, the region held its first democratic elections. But the saliency of the environmental issue did not transform itself into a massive green victory at the polls. With environmental slogans on the lips of every candidate, unless the greens could expand their platform beyond the single issue, it was impossible for them to win on an independent ticket. In fact, they generally fared best when they joined the leading coalition.[8] Every legislature, with the possible exception of the Croatian, included a small group of deputies elected for their proenvironmental stance. Thus, while not indicative of heavy popular support for the environmental movement, the election results in all the countries would seem to have placed environmentalists in a relatively strong position to exert pressure from within the newly elected representative institutions. Yet, when the author conducted interviews in Hungary, Czechoslovakia, Croatia, and Slovenia in the summer of 1990, she found environmental activists and officials very pessimistic about the ability or interest of the new governments to implement the necessary environmental programs. Environmentalists were even more pessimistic about the public's commitment to environmental protection. In the aftermath of the elections, the environmental movements in Eastern Europe seemed to be in profound disarray.

The authors in this book lean toward the view that an environmental movement committed to environmental protection per se may be a misnomer in predemocratic Eastern Europe. The public took up environmental issues because for many years the environment was the only "public talking space" and could be used to pursue other agendas. Indeed, the giant projects so harmful to the environment undertaken by the communist regimes were opposed not so much for their ecological risk as for their symbolic value as examples of what the Czechs call the *totalita* of the old regimes' rule. As Judit Vesarhelyi of the Independent Ecological Center in Budapest put it, the Nagymaros Dam more than anything the academics could say or do was a symbol of the inefficient and disastrous mode of governance of the Stalinist system.

If one follows this argument to its conclusion, there is little that predemocratic environmental movements can bring into the new situation. As the old consensus fractures, a new environmental movement will have to be constructed from the ground up through such means as consciousness raising, education through the mass media, new forms of organization, and strong Western support.

As an alternative to this view, this chapter proposes that the old environmental movements have not become irrelevant with the advent of democracy. On the contrary, their predemocratic experience makes them more capable of capturing a mass following and more knowledgeable about local conditions than any of the myriad new parties formed on the eve of elections. Even more significantly, the environmental movements do not hark back to a precommunist era. They are not interested in refighting the political and national battles of 40 years ago. As such they are in a position to become spokesmen for contemporary solutions and advocates of new approaches to old problems. The predemocratic experience of the environmental movements injects three important new dimensions into political arenas becoming increasingly bogged down by the unfinished business of the past. These dimensions are: (1) a global democratic ideology that offers an alternative both to the Western free-market technocratic ideology prevailing in government circles and to the narrow interest-based ideologies relying on specific national or economic segments of society; (2) an alternative and as yet untested form of political organization that attempts to blend mass movement and political party; and (3) a new, relatively unstructured, nonbureaucratic global network of international contacts. None of the political parties has this unique mix of local activism, global scope, and global ideology. However, the ecological movement does not possess the same capability in each country of utilizing these dimensions to influence the national political agenda. Each movement, for a variety of economic, cultural, and political reasons, finds itself in differing stages of development from popular movement to stable political entity, be that entity a political party or a permanent nongovernment organization (NGO). The core of the paper will attempt to support this thesis.

Before we proceed further with the discussion, some clarification of terms is useful. According to Alberto Mellucci, a social movement is basically a system of actions that concentrates most on "a general orientation and concrete actions in support of that orientation." A party, by contrast, focuses on organizing to gain political power through leadership and a unified platform.[9] It is perfectly consistent that an environmental movement "act locally and think globally." A political party, however, must develop a platform and leaders capable of winning votes. If successful in the election, the party must do something to implement its program but must always think ahead to the next election and to keeping its hold on political power. A movement, then, may be more radical, less organized, and less answerable for its orientation than a political party.

In his study *Social Movements,*[10] Othein Rammstadt identifies seven steps in what he considers to be organic growth from social movement to political party: propaganda on the source of the chosen crisis, articulation of protest, intensification of protest, articulation of ideology, broadening of participation, organization, and institutionalization. If one generalizes these stages to all social movements, the record suggests that the majority of the East European environmental movements have gone through the first two stages; most are in the process of working out the next three. It is a question how many of them will settle down into permanent institutions. Possibly the Greens of Slovenia have reached the last phase, with their decision to become a party and their publication of a constitution. But it is by no means certain how long they will endure in their present organizational form.

The Development of an Alternative Ideology

All the East European environmental groups, as well as Western environmentalists, are in the grips of an ideological tug of war. There are two central issues dividing the environmental movement. The first is identifying the root cause of the ecological crisis. The second, which derives from the answer to the first, is choosing the appropriate response to solve the crisis. As regards the first issue, making public the fact that there was a crisis and organizing protests were relatively simple matters in Eastern Europe, once fear of police reprisals had eased. People living in the heavily polluted areas were becoming increasingly aware that something was wrong. However, in the beginning there was tremendous personal cost involved in protesting, and this cost continued unabated in Bulgaria, Czechoslovakia, East Germany, and Romania until the very end. In Poland, there were no environmental protests until the emergence of Solidarity. Jail sentences were the rule in Czechoslovakia, Bulgaria, and Romania. In Hungary, considered by the West as the most liberal of the East European countries, protesters risked loss of job, denial of a visa for foreign travel, denial of admission to higher education for their children, even denial of permission for children to travel abroad. In the words of Judit Vesarhelyi, "our children became orphans of the movement."

For scientists, these risks were compounded by the additional fear of losing what privileges they enjoyed, such as access to vital environmental information, research trips abroad, foreign contacts, and, most important for some, the foreign financing of research. In addition, there was a tendency among many scientists to see employment in the institutes of the national academies as a special symbol of status that they were loath to lose. Hence, while many scientists were concerned about deteriorating environmental conditions, almost none chose the path of dissidence, of open contest with the regime, until open contest became politically possible. For example, for over twenty years Polish scientists have been conducting population studies of the effects of air pollution on human health in the most heavily polluted areas of the country. The study has been funded in part under the U.S./Polish scientific and cultural exchange program.[11] Yet data from those studies only reached the international press in 1989. When Polish scientists did come out in the open in the early 1980s, many took the lead in founding environmental groups. But those that engaged in this activity were generally less nationally or internationally visible researchers.

In Hungary, the government evidently so intimidated the members of the Hungarian Academy of Sciences' commission that opposed the continuation of the Nagymaros Dam that the commission's entire report was quashed. In 1987, this author was assured by an official from the environmental authority that no report had been made. Only recently did the scientists on that commission come forward and reveal their identity. Janos Vargha was thus very much a maverick in the scientific community. Those individuals who formed the core of the Danube Circle were recruited mainly from the ranks of journalists, writers, and students.

In Czechoslovakia, no scientist went into open opposition. However, working persistently behind the scenes was a core group of highly trained and concerned environmentalists officially organized into a unit called the Ecological Section of the Biological Sector of the Czechoslovak Academy of Sciences. The group was responsible for the first nationwide assessment of ecological damage, undertaken at the beginning of the 1980s, and their proposals for solutions are now being updated and reworked to be turned into law.[12] By contrast, the founder of the first and only Czech underground environmental movement, the Ecological Society, was an engineer by profession, Ivan Deimal. Deimal also edited the only underground journal devoted to environmental issues, *Ecologicky bulletin* (Ecological Bulletin).

In Slovakia, scientists also worked actively behind the scenes in their institutes and in the officially recognized Society for the Defenders of Nature. Their core group was responsible for the unofficial publication of *Bratislava nahlas* (Bratislava Outloud), a document that described the seriousness of environmental pollution in the Slovak capital. But the unofficial environmental movement was started by university students.

The approach of the environmental scientists goes to the heart of the dispute over the movement's ideological stance. Accordingly to Deimal, there was a big discussion among Czech scientists as to whether the environment was a political or a social problem. To state that it was a political problem meant challenging the regime. If the environment was considered a social problem, then in principle the regime would be open to arguments and pressures for doing something about the deteriorating situation. In the words of Janos Vargha, "the environment recognized no political system." This argument is not unlike the division in the United States between the "politicos" and the "greens." The former consider the current system democratic enough, and hence focus on getting laws passed and regulations implemented. The latter believe the environment can be saved only through a fundamental transformation of Western society from a corporate economic and political system into a more just and ecologically safe community through the practice of what Barry Commoner calls ecological democracy.[13]

The social-problem approach had its results. During the late 1970s and early 1980s, concerned East European scientists and other individuals received permission to set up conservation organizations and were given sufficient state financing to enable them to carry out important mass education programs, youth nature study camps, and similar nature conservation activities. Over the years, some of these organizations built a sizable membership, a national reputation, and international contacts through membership in the International Union for the Conservation of Nature (IUCN). People welcomed the opportunity to participate in environmental activities because they believed they were doing something that carried no political constraints. In Czechoslovakia, the Czech and particularly the Slovak Societies of the Defenders of Nature recruited many enthusiastic supporters. A very active youth group attached to the Communist Youth Movement, named Brontosaurus, attracted large numbers of young people to its summer camps, which aimed at teaching them how to live an environmental life-style. In Hungary, the work of the Hungarian Ornithological Association became internationally recognized. The mass environmental organization in Poland lost its following when unofficial groups began to organize after 1981, while Yugoslavia never had an official mass movement. As of this writing, the successful organizations continue to benefit from state financing, and during the early stages of the transition were the only environmental groups that did. Over and over their representatives insisted to the author that they were not political but social organizations. They planned to cooperate with the new government, as they had with the old, in promoting conservation and helping solve environmental problems. The main difference they saw was in the greater freedom and scope of cooperation with environmental organizations abroad.

The actions of the unofficial environmental groups automatically put them in the camp of those who believed that environmental deterioration was a political problem. To come out in the streets against Nagymaros, nuclear power, or air pollution was to come out against decisions by the regime. The very act of protest was antiregime. Moreover, given the number of those who participated, the majority had to be ordinary people, not scientists, or even committed environmental activists with inside knowledge of the problem. The demonstrators' simple agenda was to stop the people who were responsible for agreeing to the dam or nuclear power plant in the first place. Once an individual had decided to protest, politics surpassed the environment as the primary motivation. Judit Vesarhelyi described her own feelings: "In coming out in the open, in assuming personal responsibility for my actions, I felt myself become a person."

The old system ended in most of the East European countries with astonishing ease, forcing those persons who had been active in the demonstrations for change to rechannel their interests and energies into their personal expectations of democracy. The transition also brought the experts who had been working behind the scenes out into the open, and in many of the countries, almost immediately into the government. Almost overnight, the organized, environmentally supportive public appeared to have evaporated, and the only money to finance a movement was that which had been allocated to the conservation organizations under the old regime. In the Czech lands, representatives of Brontosaurus were coopted into the Ministry of the Environment, along with the social and natural scientists of the Environmental Section of the Biological Sector of the Academy of Sciences, who had done so much to assemble the data and to prepare the assessment of Czechoslovakia's environmental damage. The recruitment of the core of the Environmental Section into the government deprived the Ecological Society of scientific leadership. Not unnaturally, the organizers of the former unofficial environmental movement felt unjustly excluded. In addition, they were concerned that the democratic changes would lead nowhere, since the old specialists and bureaucrats were still in power.

In Slovakia, the transition ideology was definitely political. In contrast to the Czech scientists, in 1988 the core group of Slovak scientists went openly over to dissent with their unofficial publication of *Bratislava nahlas*. The study sharply accused the ministries in the federal government of being the chief culprits responsible for Bratislava's severe pollution. While the federal government condemned the study as subversive, its nationalist overtones appealed to Slovak intellectuals dissatisfied with the existing federalist system. Nationalism also influenced the activities of the officially organized Slovak Society of the Defenders of Nature. Here, too, the scientific leadership, with some justification, saw Slovakia as unable to defend itself from the environmentally unsound decisions of the central ministries. When the time for elections came, the environmentalists were able to mobilize support for the Green Party through this combination of environmentalism and nationalism, depicting Slovakia as defenseless victim of central government *totalita*. As a result, when the editor of *Bratislava nahlas* and the core of environmental scientists were recruited into the government, popular support did not seem to vanish as it had in Prague. Much of it remained in the Slovak Society of the Defenders of Nature, which enthusiastically endorsed the Green position: Slovakia should be as independent as possible from Prague. Since Prague had sponsored all the damage, Slovakia needed a Slovak solution to Slovak environmental problems.

In Hungary and Croatia, the controversy regarding the causes of environmental pollution is still going on. To be against a dam is not a philosophy. When the dam issue was resolved, the movement fragmented into its local constituent parts. There was no ideological glue to hold it together. The elections were fought on other issues. In Croatia, the formation of a nationwide environmental network, the Croatian Environmental Alliance, came too late to resolve the ideological issue before the May 1990 elections. As a result, the alliance went into the elections with no comprehensive platform and severe divisions along local group lines.

Slovenia provides the best example of the successful development of a comprehensive ideology. With long years of experience in operating unofficially, the Slovene Greens had time to develop solid ties with the German and Austrian Green parties and to work out their own political philosophy. The party's political objectives are set forth in its Constitution: democracy, private property, economic competition, and a moderate nationalism.[14] Behind these values lie the postmaterialist values of the European Greens. As Peter Jamničar, then secretary general of the Greens of Slovenia, explained to the author in 1990, the values are global, not related to interests of a specific group as are the values of the old and reformed political parties. In addition, the focus has changed from quantity to quality of life. For Jamničar, quality of life is best improved by resolutely opposing all forms of bureaucratization, including technology. He sees modern society run by a vast consuming machine. There is little room for spontaneity or creativity. Everything is subsumed under this machine, including the scientific establishment in Slovenia and elsewhere. But society is in the process of trying to escape this inhuman control. The Greens' alternative ideology calls for a shift to alternative energy sources, to a less hierarchically structured mass society, and to a return to recognizing the value of the individual and his responsibility for himself and his surroundings. Finally, the ideology calls for a shift from seeing progress in technological and material terms to seeing progress in psychological, spiritual, and cultural relationships. What one needs in modern society is space to assert one's individuality and one's identity in harmony with the environment. For Jamničar, the essential break with bureaucratization occurred in Slovenia with the end of the communist monopoly ideology. This ideology celebrated the destructive aspects of modern society: bureaucracy, technocracy, political hierarchical power. In his view, the West will never adequately resolve its environmental problems until the economic monopolies are brought down. But he declined to offer a methodology. In keeping with his party's democratic views, he believes that environmentalists in each country must work out their own ideologies.

The philosophy of the Slovene Greens would seem to be a derivative of the experience of living in what Václav Havel called the "parallel society."[15] As Jamničar explained, when he and other students made the decision to bring environmental dissent into the open, they rejected all aspects of the totalitarian bureaucratic structure, with a view to building new structures and new relationships. When asked what new relationships his party would attempt to build in Slovenia, he pointed to the nonhierarchical organization of the Greens and to the penetration of Green sympathizers into all echelons of government. He also stressed the positive approach of the party. "We do not just criticize," he said. "But we try always to offer constructive solutions." He admitted that the public might not yet be ready for a postmaterialist ideology, but insisted that the continued implementation of the old materialist economic values would ultimately lead to the economic destruction of Slovenia. The Greens believe their postmaterialist values will survive closing down coal mines and nuclear power plants, and even the unemployment resulting from the closings. Jamničar insisted, "We will have difficulties, but as long as there are men of good will, we will survive."

The ideological contribution of the environmental movement to the fledgling East European democracies is in delineating the boundaries of the conflict over the cause of pollution. The popular demonstrations represent a form of Commoner's ecodemocracy, a Green objective. The scientists working in the wings on concrete solutions may be viewed as proponents of environmental problem-solving as essentially a process of meshing technology with the passage and enfocement of legal regulations. The second position sees the new government as a vehicle to achieve the requisite regulations. The first remains suspicious of the composition and objectives of any government that practices what Eric Lykke has termed closed or "exclusive" (confined to immediately interested parties) rather than open or "transparent" (democratic) decision-making.[16]

The new governments would be ill-advised not to take note of the incipient demands for ecodemocracy that accompanied the pretransition environmental movements. Where the movements can present a unified ideological face, the presence of greens in the East European legislatures is a force for more radical changes in economic and political structure, including the closing of nuclear and polluting industrial plants (Slovenia) and deep democratic reform (Bulgaria and Romania). Where the movement is fragmented, as in Hungary or Croatia, popular ideological influence on the government may be marginal but nevertheless will strengthen the hand of the problem-solvers in their efforts to devise concrete solutions.

Alternative Political Structures

During the predemocratic system, environmental movements, like other dissent activities, operated underground. The key people knew each other, but the individuals they recruited tended to know no one but the recruiter and members of their own circle. Local initiative was at a premium, as any kind of central coordination was difficult. In consonance with the antihierarchical spirit of grass-roots environmental activities worldwide, those who did operate at the center were not considered leaders in the strict meaning of the word and conducted their affairs through suggestion and discussion rather than command. As with all movements, the focus was on local action under an umbrella general orientation. This experience taught participants democratic behavior and developed personal responsibility and initiative. However, it was not easily transferable into the new democratic order for two reasons—a question of trust and disagreement on structure.

Those individuals who made the hard decision to go into dissent necessarily built a network of trust between themselves and tended to distrust those who remained within the official system. Many dissenting environmentalists were Communists who left the party or who were forced to resign. After the democratic change, the problem of trust increased. There has been much accusation and pointing of fingers: "So and so is a Communist," "They are all Communist in the ministry," "You cannot trust the Greens, they are carryovers from the Communist Youth Movement."

Accusations of this kind have a basis in fact. In every country, personnel was needed to staff the new ministries. Most of these were recruited from the academic institutes or the other pretransition bureaucracies. Assuredly, they were former Communists, as virtually no one could receive a higher education who was not a member of the party, but they had little or no commitment to the party. Most scientists and specialists joined in order to become eligible for university and to pursue their careers. Jiřina Šiklová of the Department of Sociology, Charles University, argues that under the former regime, people's hands were neither completely clean nor completely dirty. Rather, there was a gray area where individuals complied with regime regulations and demands in order to have a little personal peace.[17] Communism as a belief in an ideology had long since disappeared among most party members, from whose numbers were recruited the functionaries and bureaucrats. Still, although they could not be termed true believers, they nevertheless had been educated in certain habits of bureaucratic management and behavior. The new governments had to turn to them because of the virtual absence of skilled administrators and policy makers trained in Western methods. While Czech President Václav Havel's own noncommunist credentials were impeccable, he was accused of having an inner clique composed primarily of former communists.

Furthermore, not all the new staff members were hired on the basis of merit. In many cases, additional personnel were brought over from other ministries where budget cuts had severely reduced ministerial staff and left state functionaries out of work. In the Czech Ministry of the Environment, many of the new positions were filled with former employees of the Ministry of Energy. It was rumored that these had obtained their new jobs through party connections even though their work at the Ministry of Energy had been inefficient. Such individuals brought with them a very negative reputation for being "communist." The leaders of the conservation organizations were also former members of the party, and grass-roots environmentalists insisted that the individuals behaved and acted like communists still. "Communist" infiltration of the Green parties was perceived as especially threatening. In Hungary and Czechoslovakia, former officials of the Communist Youth League joined the Greens. Accusations that the Czech Green Party was only a haven for communists probably prevented it from placing in the elections, while in Hungary, the struggle between former Communist Youth League functionaries and Danube Blues in the Hungarian Green Party split the party apart, reducing any chances it might have had in the Hungarian election. In Croatia, there was an uproar when the sole Green elected to Parliament from Split was known to have been supported by the Croatian Communist Party. Tempers did not cool when he attacked the religious beliefs of another deputy in his maiden speech to the legislature. In Slovenia, the Greens are reluctant to cooperate with the Serbian Greens, whom they accuse of being "secret communists," although the Slovenian Greens do cooperate with the Green Faction of the Slovenian Communist Party. Everywhere a fundamental problem is to broaden trust between the movement participants. While time is a great healer, the environmental parties will continue to perform poorly at elections and the environmental organizations will be hampered in their activities as long as they cannot develop trust within their membership.

The second basic problem is disagreement over structure. Grass-roots environmental groups everywhere generally operate with a structure that is nonhierarchical and inclusive rather than exclusive. The East European environmentalists differ sharply on the meaning of these words. The format typical of most countries has been to create an umbrella organization whose main function is coordination and information sharing. East European environmentalists like the Western concept of networking. Yet, in most cases, local environmental groups have developed a wider network with foreign environmental groups than with groups in their own country. Money is the main difficulty. As noted earlier, in Hungary and Czechoslovakia only the organizations postdating the democratic change received government funding in 1990. The former dissident groups had no money. The new governments have tried to promote cooperation between the funded and non-funded organizations, but bureaucratic infighting is all too common. The former dissident groups have been refused use of telephones, computers, and office help and have been assigned to the least attractive office space. Officials of the funded groups are proud of their international ties and quite naturally want to continue participation at international meetings, without having to share these opportunities with newcomers.

Western funds are not a panacea. For one thing, individuals with dubious credentials who are looking for a quick Western dollar or mark target bona fide environmentist groups searching for much-needed financing. It thus becomes increasingly difficult to distinguish the real environmentalist from the phony, a situation which does little to increase trust among the various organizations. For another, Western environmental organizations and foundations can be themselves arbitrary in selecting what they consider to be "appropriate" East European groups and in laying down conditions for funding. Representatives of Greenpeace reportedly told members of the Danube Blues that they would not be eligible to receive any financial support unless they joined the international movement. Nevertheless, Western money at present seems to be the most promising means of rehabilitating the East European environmental movements. Perhaps the most ambitious funding is the $4 million allocated by the Bush administration for the Central and East European Environmental Center that opened in Budapest in the fall of 1990. One of the tasks of the center is to facilitate networking among environmental groups within Hungary and throughout Eastern Europe.

Even if the financial problem were resolved, the most controversial issues would still remain. These are the relation of the center to the local organizations, and whether the groups should pursue the U.S. model of lobbying by nongovernmental institutions or the German model of political party. How to retain the spontaneity of the original movement in this process? How large or general should the membership be? How specific should the goals of the umbrella organization be?

There are hundreds of environmental groups in every country. The large majority of these are local and/or issue-specific, with the greatest number located in the national capitals. Frequently, the leader is a forceful, assertive individual who may carry the group as long as he is interested, but when his interest flags, the group dissolves. There are groups with such diverse associations with international movements as the Biokultura Association in Budapest, which in the summer of 1990 hosted an international conference on organic agriculture. Janos Sebeok is the founder and head of the Hungarian Biosphere Party, dedicated to preserving forests, particularly the rain forests, and proponent of the view that man should work in harmony with nature, not dominate nature. In every country, the fate of an environmental group often depends on the initiative and energy of a few individuals.

Attempts to found Western-style NGOs with Western financing may be more successful, as their bureaucratic structure and paid staff assure continuity, enabling them to lobby government for particular legislation while serving as a focus for grass-roots organizations. The Independent Ecological Center in Budapest grew out of the victory of the Danube Circle in suppressing construction of the dam at Nagymaros. It will now become part of the Bush Regional Environmental Center. Another emerging NGO with Hungarian and Western funding, the Nature Conservation Club, focuses on the Hungarian Parliament and its environmental committee. Toward this end it has prepared a list of environmental priorities in Hungary and mailed it to all members of the environmental committee and the environmental ministry. The club sees itself as a leader in the organization of a grass-roots network. Although it appreciates the effectiveness of single-issue movements in local politics, it believes that a more institutional approach is needed at the national level.

Finally, not all the countries are equally open. It is much more difficult to maintain communication among and between Bulgarian and Romanian groups than among those in Poland. The fluidity of group formation and intergroup communication frustrates the best efforts to develop a network within and between countries. A list of East European environmental groups given the author in Budapest in the summer of 1990 was already out of date.

These problems are common to the worldwide environmental movement as well as to groups in Eastern Europe, and they are not easily resolved. In most countries, environmental activists are experimenting both with nongovernmental networking and with the formation of political parties. In the networking model, the green parties may join the network, as can any group if it so desires. Most East European environmentalists, like many of their counterparts in the West, are uncomfortable with the idea of political power, and rather naively believe that their goals are so global that they may be accomplished no matter what political party governs. The ideological conflict surfaces in every discussion of structure. But all are quick to recognize that there is little impetus for radical environmental measures in the newly elected democratic governments.

The true believers among the environmentalists also find it difficult to understand the quarrels within the environmental movement. Pal Zoltan Kolchis of the Hungarian Greens told the author that when they decided to form a political party, they offered membership to anyone interested. They accepted former Youth League officials because they thought that everyone had the same attitudes toward the environment. The attempt by the Youth League members to use the party to push their own agenda and enter the power elite through the back door came as a shock to the other Greens. For them, the global goal of saving the environment remained paramount. For the former communists, regaining lost status was important.

In Croatia, the conflict over party and/or NGO status provides another insight into the movements' problems. After much discussion, it was decided to form a network, the Green Alliance for Croatia, and to make running for office voluntary for the member groups. Groups in Zagreb and the group from Split did run candidates, with the controversial election of the candidate from Split, whose remarks in the legislature the center later disclaimed as being nonrepresentative of the movement. The incident reflects the difficulties of a network approach to power seeking. If running candidates is left to the local groups on a voluntary basis, then whom does the successful candidate represent except his electoral district? What claim does he have to speak for the environmental movement as a whole? The central leadership of the Croatian Alliance is trying to grapple with this problem by writing a charter containing global principles, including organizing for political action, but delegating activism to the local groups. The leader says that this solution has already brought 48 local organizations into the alliance, and she hopes that all the Croatian groups will join.[18]

The alliance's network model, however, has come under strong attack from the Croatian media. Television especially has accused it of weak leadership and failure to mobilize the localities for appropriate action. A reporter for a leading Zagreb television station cited the alliance's mediocre showing at a mass demonstration against nuclear power in Krško and in particular the failure of the alliance at election time. The reporter inferred that the only reason a Green was elected from Split was because he had communist support, which was very strong in the area. While the media attack is fueled by friction between media staff and the staff of the Green Alliance, if the alliance is to become politically credible, it has to overcome negative perceptions, and that means a review of the network model.

The Slovenian Greens once again believe they have found the right balance between the center and the local organs. There is a general program to which all participating groups must adhere. This program unconditionally states that the party will fight for power. The party platform is broad and realistic, designed to appeal to a wide constituency. The party structure is a product of the evolution of the green movement from its underground organization. The movement was formed by a small group of twelve students who were determined to stand up publicly for the environment regardless of the consequences. Since Yugoslavia in the early 1980s prided itself on being a different form of communism than the Soviet model, the students did not fear being ejected from the university. But they didexpect harassment and difficulty in finding positions later on. According to Jamničar, the first demonstrations took Slovenian party and government leaders by surprise. They had not expected that anyone would have the courage to come out and oppose them. As the government vacillated on tactics, the group expanded its activities. The original twelve each recruited people, who recruited people in their turn. The recruitment was on a personal basis, because trust was essential. News of planned demonstrations was spread primarily by word of mouth, and the mode of demonstration was left up to the individuals in the different groups. In the mid-1980s, the environmental movement followed the peace and feminist movements in accepting the umbrella of the Communist Youth Movement (CYM).

When it broke with the CYM in 1989, the new independent organization continued its method of personal recruitment, information dissemination, and suggestions for action. Matter came to a head politically in Slovenia during the prosecution of a student who refused to do his compulsory military service. Many in the environmental movement left the Communist Party at that time in protest against what they perceived to be close cooperation between army, police, and party leadership. The leaders of the various movements within the CYM behaved totally within the law. Their main request was that the trial take place in Slovenia, where the alleged offense occurred, and not be moved to Belgrade. According to Jamničar, the party knew it was beaten when a crowd of thousands filled the main square in Ljubljana demanding that the trial be held in the Slovene capital. Following the Communist Party's call for elections, members of the environmental movement decided to become a party and run for office. To organize for elections, the Greens set up a parliament composed of all the members of the movement, a presidency of the heads of the local groups, and an executive council. The success of the elections brought some of the most active Greens and Green followers into the government.

Fearing that government office might siphon off too many Greens, the party reorganized again in June 1990. At a special conference, to which all Greens were invited, the membership was asked to elect a parliament, and a presidency from which would be recruited a permanent executive council. The parliament would be responsible for providing central direction, the presidency would work out political policy but leave autonomy of implementation to the local organizations, and the executive council would be responsible for seeing that policies were carried out. When I asked Jamničar whether this type of organization was not a replica of the typical party structure, he pointed to its nonhierarchical character and the autonomy left to the local groups. The presidency does not give binding orders that the executive council must transmit to the local groups. Each group decides for itself how to interpret the directives, and the role of the executive council is to encourage, support, and suggest. In short, Jamničar thought his organization had retained the best aspects of the informality and spontaneity of the movement and the structure necessary for a successful political party.

The Greens of Slovenia have received a very controversial welcome in some parts of the West. There is a tendency to perceive them as modern-day flagbearers of the old communist ideals, or at least the current variant of radicalism.[19] Two-party systems, like those of the United States and Great Britain, may not be favorable climates for the emergence of a Green party, although the organization of a Green party is under way in California and other U.S. states. The Greens' decision to forgo the status of NGO for political power has tended to alienate the larger, more bureaucratic U.S. environmental NGOs, who believe that public pressure exercised from outside the power nucleus is a more efficient modus operandi. Moreover, like all the East European Green parties, the Slovenian Greens have built very close ties with the Austrian and German parties. Much of the Slovene party platform is directly inspired by these parties' philosophies. The large U.S. and British environmental establishments tend to be more pragmatic and less philosophic in their approach, and they see the calls of the German Greens for a transformation of society as unnecessarily hostile to the established order.

For whatever reason, the West may have overlooked the significance of the Green experiment in Slovenia. If the Greens manage to forge this experimental party structure into some permanent arrangement that translates itself into votes at the next election, then the Greens will indeed have constructed a model that merits investigation by both Eastern and Western environmental movements. Fisher suggests that the comprehensive program and central direction of the new organization have cost it membership. However, evaluation of the experimental party structure must be postponed until another round of local and national elections can test the new party's overall popular appeal.

Networks of International Contacts

There are two kinds of relationships being established by East European environmentalists with the international world. The first is the integration of the East European movement with the global environmental movement through networking. The second is the development of formal cooperative ties with foreign government agencies and established international and national environmental NGOs, such as the International Union for the Conservation of Nature (IUCN), the World Wildlife Foundation, and the World Resources Institute.

The first type of cooperation conforms to the democratic, nonhierarchical ideology of grass-roots environmentalists, because it is basically informal. Every East European group is aware of the importance of international contact, although the capability of each to work with the global environmental movement varies. Networking has taken two directions. One well-known network, Greenway, sought to put all the East European dissident environmental groups in contact with one another, uniting groups from Bulgaria to Estonia. Communication was maintained through couriers, letters, unofficial meetings two or three times a year, and, in some cases, a newspaper. The environmental center in Budapest is now expanding this network.

The second direction has been toward the Western groups. The Polish Ecology Club was the first to affiliate with Friends of the Earth. A Greenpeace organization was set up in Moscow, while other U.S. and foreign groups have been very active helping local organizations or providing assistance for victims of Chernobyl or the Armenian earthquake. Because of their more liberal political system, the Poles, Hungarians, and Slovenians were able to develop very solid relationships with European environmental groups. The Hungarian Nature Conservation, working with Greenpeace and Friends of the Earth, was able to get 16 Hungarian NGOs to join with 46 European NGOs in signing a petition to the World Bank calling for the inclusion of a section on the environment in all loan contracts. The greatest degree of communication has been between the Western and Eastern Green parties, especially between the German and Austrian Greens and those in Slovakia, Croatia, and Slovenia and the Danube Circle in Hungary. The political climate in the Czech lands made it difficult for dissident environmental groups to make contact with the outside, and financing still poses barriers. Contacts between the Romanian and Bulgarian environmental groups and the international movement, as Fisher describes, are in their initial stages. As international environmental conferences in Europe and the former Soviet Union have proliferated, more and more East European environmental groups have been seen among the conference participants.

The end of legal and political barriers to communication between the East European environmental groups and the international environmental movement has made access to communication technology imperative. The telephone systems of Eastern Europe were by and large built in the 1930s and have not been upgraded in fifty years. Many groups have fax machines, but sending a fax over antiquated telephone lines can be a problem. It is paradoxical that even though communication with the West can be a challenge, it is far more difficult to communicate within Eastern Europe because of the dilapidated condition of basic communications hardware. Phone books are not up to date. Telephone information services are inadequate. Computers are generally only in government, in academic offices, or where a Western interest has provided one. Modems are few and far between. In addition, information on who is whom in the environmental movements is only just beginning to be collected. The Panos Foundation in Hungary is trying to keep the Greenway list of East European environmental group leaders current, but the organization of the groups is so fluid, and the commitment of individuals so tenuous, that the list has to be constantly revised. Even with the list, environmental groups outside the main urban centers do not know where to go to seek such information. Indeed, the author found herself a distributor of information between activists in the different countries.

Finally, local environmentalists outside the big cities not only do not have access to communications services, they are not accustomed to "thinking globally" and to communicating over long distances. Their entire focus is on the local problem. In countries where all outside communication until recently was severely limited and local businesses did not have their own phones, establishing contacts with groups in one's own country, let alone abroad, was far beyond a local organization's realm of possibilities. Now that international contacts are possible, people have to learn how to make the best use of what limited communications facilities they have.

The second kind of relationship being established by East European environmentalists is implicit in the need for political, managerial, and technological expertise to move the environmental cause forward. The search for outside expertise was started before the democratic changes by some of the established East European environmental organizations, which were authorized by their governments to make contacts with selected international environmental bureaucracies, particularly with the IUCN, and U.N. organizations such as UNEP. The Czech Brontosaurus Movement developed a sizable program of youth exchanges, mainly between European conservation-minded youth groups. The Slovak Defenders of Nature developed international conservation study camps for adults. And the Hungarian Ornithological Association established relations with most of the European ornithological organizations, although it was less successful in making ties with the U.S. Audubon Society. All these groups were members of the IUCN. Hungary, in particular, has stressed the importance of working through the U.N. organizations. When the democratic change came, the heads of the existing organizations and academic institutes with international contacts were well placed to broaden their international ties.

More important than these old ties has been the formation of completely new relationships with Western foundations, governmental institutions, and banks. The Central and East European Environmental Center in Budapest is one of many instances described by Persanyi for Hungary. The problem lies in the fact that no money comes as a free gift. Hungarian environmentalists with whom the author talked were sensitive that the center was as much a part of the U.S. environmental agenda as it was the Hungarian. They were proud that through their vigilance the center had been established on the Hungarian side as a bona fide NGO, rather than as an arm of the government. But they realized that there was a very real risk that the center might become a political chess game between the U.S. sponsoring agencies, the State Department, and the Environmental Protection Agency, with East European environmental needs pawns in the game. Hungarian environmentalists believe they are sufficiently politically alert and well enough organized to keep the center on its nongovernmental, issue-oriented course.

Despite the risks inherent in accepting foreign funds, the extent and scope of pollution in Eastern Europe is so great that environmentalists know their country cannot pay for the clean-up, let alone fund environmental NGOs and political parties. Equally important, they see the democratically elected governments hard pressed to handle the damage fallout resulting from the transition to a market economy. If corrective action is to be taken, it can only be with Western capital and Western assistance. While all the groups saw Western assistance as essential and were eager to expand their communications capabilities, it was possible to divide the groups into those that were fearful of too much dependence on Western largesse and those that sought to align themselves with the appropriate governmental and nongovernmental institutions in the West in positive anticipation of both communications equipment and Western know-how. The United States and the Netherlands for the European Community are regarded by many as the two leading models of environmental management. Not surprisingly, the roads to Washington and Brussels, the capitol of the EC, have become well-beaten paths not only for environmental officials but also for leaders of environmental groups. As might be expected, the Greens appeared most hesitant about the arrival of Western financing and technology. Their concern is that the Western steamroller, with foreign control of capital and technology, might crush the nascent democratic movement. The result would be the replacement of communist low-tech industrial pollution with high-tech pollution controlled by a resurgent Germany, the World Bank, or the International Monetary Fund.

One chance the national environmental movements have against such giants would be to hook solidly into the international environmental network and to cooperate with those groups whose funds do not derive from the large corporate interests and which thus can oppose them. In essence, such a tactic would probably mean closer alliance with the European Greens and the more radical U.S. organizations like Greenpeace. The Czech and Hungarian Green parties are struggling to regroup for just this purpose. Such an eventuality increases the probability of the deepening of the split in the development of international ties between those with the more egalitarian, democratically oriented environmental network and those with the bureaucratic, legal-regulatory environmental interests of Western industry. While both democracy and environmentalism are well-enough rooted in Western society to sustain such a split, division in the national environmental movements in Eastern Europe threatens both the growth of democracy and environmental protection. The environmental agencies and groups funded by the national governments simply do not have the political, not to mention economic, clout to offset the technocratic industrial interests seeking to make Eastern Europe competitive in the world market. The critical contribution that the environmental movements can make to postcommunist East European politics is the mobilization of the public for environmental measures. While the funding of pollution control and prevention hinges on contacts with official Western environmental NGOs, IGOs, and national bureaucracies, public opinion is most sensitive to global popular pressure deriving from the informal international environmental network.

Conclusion

The East European environmental groups are well positioned to influence the new democracies, if they can learn to act together and constructively. If their role in the old regime was negative, it must be positive now. Postindustrial ideals may seem threatening in the short term to people fearful of losing their hard-acquired level of economic well-being. However, in the long term, civilization depends on giving nature its place, and the environmental ideology offers constructive alternatives to the old industrial paradigm. In the West, the Greens and the environmental lobby have mobilized populations where traditional parties have failed. Part of the success of organizations as diverse as the Greens and the Sierra Club is due to their ability to keep a global orientation before large numbers of people, while leaving local action to local groups. The East European movements must decide whether to go the way of political party or NGO, but whichever way they decide, they hold out a new democratic mode of operation based on individual responsibility and freedom. Lastly, the availability of the international environmental network multiplies at long last in Eastern Europe, as it has in other parts of the world, the strength of the local environmental movements. In so doing, it provides a democratic alternative to global intellectual, technocratic, and business interests with their high-tech development programs.

Before the changes, it was easy to unite against a common enemy. Now, the need is to build a constructive platform and permanent but flexible organization. The degree of influence each movement enjoys would seem to depend on how successfully it solves the problem of spontaneity versus institutionalization and develops a generally positive platform regarding nature, the use of power, and the importance of "thinking green" to secure a better quality of life. In short, the movements now must make the transition from underground dissident to responsible political actor.

Notes

1. The oldest continuous environmental group is probably the Polish Ecology Club (PEC), although the Greens of Slovenia trace their origins back to the end of the sixties and the German environmentalists say their first organization was founded in the early seventies. Until the emergence of Solidarity in 1980, discussion of environmental problems was taboo in Poland. The PEC was the first ecological group to organize following the Gdansk strikes, forming in Cracow in September 1980. The PEC began publishing a popular monthly and soon claimed a membership of over 1000 people. Under its sponsorship, the Polish people learned for the first time of the seriousness of pollution in their country. The PEC was the motor force behind the drive to close the polluting aluminum plant in 1980–81, and its experts prepared the memorandum demanding the closure of all processes emitting fluorine and hydrogen fluoride. The PEC lost visibility with the imposition of martial law in December 1981 but it resurfaced after Chernobyl. Since 1986, it has become the leading environmental organization in Poland.

2. Much of this information was obtained through a series of interviews with ecological groups undertaken by the author in the summer of 1990. Except where

an interviewee is quoted or his/her remarks paraphrased, there will be no referencing of the interviews.

3. See the author's testimony before the CSCE Committee, Washington, DC, Spring 1988.

4. Dan Ionescu, "The 'Romanian Democratic Action' Group on the Environment," RFE *Romania SR* 8 (June 23, 1988): 45.

5. *Wall Street Journal*, January 2, 1990.

6. It is interesting to compare the emergence of the U.S. environmental movement out of the long struggle of John Muir, first president of the Sierra Club, to stop the construction of the Hetch Hetchy Dam in California, and the battles of the Danube Circle and the environmentalists in Yugoslavia who stopped dam construction in the Tara River Canyon. As John Muir thundered against the "triumphant growth of the wealthy wicked," so East European environmentalists have attacked the "gigantomania" and reckless spending of their Communist rulers. For a popular presentation of the battle against the Hetch Hetchy Dam, see Ken Chowder, "Can We Afford the Wilderness?" *Modern Maturity*, June-July 1990, pp. 61–64.

7. See Barbara Jancar, "Ecology and Self-Management: A Balance Sheet for the 1980s," John B. Allcock, John H. Horton, and Marko Milivojevic, *Yugoslavia in Transition: Choices and Constraints* (Oxford: Berg Publishers, 1992), pp. 337–64.

8. For a breakdown of the elections, see Duncan Fisher's chapter in this volume and Vladimir V. Kusin, "The Elections Compared and Assessed," *Report on Eastern Europe* 1, no. 28 (July 13, 1990): 38–47.

9. Alberto Melluci, "Kraj drustvenih pokreta?" [The End of Social Movements?], *Nase teme* (Zagreb) 83, no. 10 (1984): 1346–47. See Andelko Milardovic's discussion of this problem in *Spontanost i institucionalnost* [Spontaneity and Institutionalism] (Belgrade: Kairos, 1989), pp. 61–64.

10. Othein Rammstadt, *Soziale Bewegung* [Social Movements] (Frankfurt am Main: Suhrkam, 1976), pp. 137–44.

11. See my discussion in Jancar, "United States East European Environmental Exchange," *International Environmental Affairs* 2, no. 1 (Winter 1990): 40–66.

12. For example, "Koncepce ekologicke politiky Ceske republiky, 'Duhova Kniha' MZ CR; pracovni verze pro verejnou diskusi" [Overview of the Environmental Policy of the Czech Republic, 'The Rainbow Book', Ministry of the Environment, Czech Republic; Draft Version for Public Discussion], in *Uzemni planovani a urbanismus* [Territorial Planning and Urbanism], 3/90, whole volume.

13. For the presentation of both views, see, "Shades of Green, Beyond Earth Day: Ten Views on Where to Go from Here," *Utne Reader*, no. 40 (July/August 1990), pp. 50–65; in particular, Walter Truett Anderson, "Green Politics Now Comes in Four Distinct Shades," pp. 52–53, and Barry Commoner, "Environmental Democracy Is the Planet's Best Hope," pp. 61–63.

14. "Voleni program Zelinih Slovenije" [Electoral Program of the Greens of Slovenia], 1990 (mimeographed).

15. Václav Havel, "The Power of the Powerless," in Václav Havel et al., *The Power of the Powerless* (Armonk, NY: M.E. Sharpe, Inc., 1985), pp. 23–96.

16. Erik Lykke, "The Dynamics of Transparency: Discretion and Disclosure in Environmental Decision Making," paper prepared for the annual meeting of the

International Studies Association, Washington, DC, April 10–14, 1990.

17. Jiřina Šiklová, "The 'Grey Zone' and the Future of Dissent in Czechoslovakia," *Social Research* 57, no. 2 (Summer 1990): 347–63.

18. The original program of the Croatian Alliance elaborated in March 1990 has already been revised to clarify the voluntary nature of running for public office. See "Programska izjava" [Program Announcement], *Zelen List, Bilten osnivačkog sabora Saveza zelinih Hrvatske* [Green Paper, Bulletin of the Founding Conference of the Alliance of Greens of Croatia] (Zagreb, February 2, 1990).

19. Green parties everywhere risk being labeled "communist." See David Horowitz, "The Environmentalists Are Simply Reds in Green Cloaks," as reprinted from the *National Review* (March 19, 1990), *Utne Reader*, no. 40 (July/August 1990), p. 57. Like all name-calling, there is some validity in the title: witness the "green" direction taken by the communist parties in Spain and Italy.

━━━━━━━━━━━━━━━━━━━━━━━━━ 13

Conclusion

Barbara Jancar-Webster

What conclusions can be drawn from this disparate collection of essays? Are there indeed new trends in environmental management in Central and Eastern Europe? The essays leave the questions open. In their turn to representative government, the former communist countries have clearly chosen a direction different from that pursued since the end of World War II. But the turn is still too recent to enable us to identify new modalities of management specific to the environmental area. Rather, the essays have presented the anomaly of weak and collapsing economies and government administrations that despite their rhetoric have not made an incisive break with old environmental policies and institutions. On the one hand, there is passage of new legislation to meet the new conditions, but no new legislation can be put in place until new economic institutions and mechanisms have stabilized into some kind of permanent order. Some countries have formed environmental ministries where there were none before. Many have instituted pollution payments, but in general all seem to have entered a protracted period of waiting.

Nevertheless, certain trends do emerge from this period of flux. First is the generally positive response to the Western model of environmental management. Kozeltsev and Vebra's essays, in particular, highlight the investigation of Western concepts and modes of regulation and suitable ways to adapt them to specific domestic circumstances. Kozeltsev shows how risk assessment can be creatively applied to Russian conditions, while Vebra gives us a list of generally recognized environmental principles and practices that are now being incorporated into Lithuanian law. Fisher stresses the role that western NGOs can play in developing permanent environmental organizations in the region. Peter persuasively argues the need to base sound environmental management on Western economic market models.

But this positive attitude towards Western pollution control efforts is offset by a second tendency. The essays convey a strong sense of inadequacy and uncertainty expressed in doubts that the former communist countries will in fact be able to realize the Western model. All are skeptical of any immediate possibility of improvements in environmental management. All stress the enormity of the problems. Indeed, each chapter tends to overwhelm us with its recitation of difficulties, so that we lose confidence in the new democracies' ability to confront them. While the incorrectness and injustice of the former regimes are never questioned, there seems to be little faith in the capabilities of democracy and the market economy to remedy the situation.

In part this doubt may stem from the general lack of knowledge in all the countries about the workings of democracy and the market economy. To peoples born into rigid hierarchical systems, the horizontal communication based on self-assertion and individual freedom and responsibility that is the essence of both democracy and a market economy is understood, if at all, imperfectly, and grasped with difficulty. In part it is the product of rapid economic collapse, with its resulting fall in living standards and rising unemployment, and in part it must be attributed to the attitudes and behaviors toward and about management and administration inculcated by several generations of communist education, informed in most circumstances from traditional bureaucratic structures.

Peter and Seserko both stress the deep-rootedness of negative managerial behavior. Seserko is particularly eloquent in his depiction of the ability of the management of large state-owned enterprises to utilize every type of argument and tactic to persuade elected officials to go slow in or desist from embarking on serious pollution control measures. Yet, given the candid recognition of the formidable obstacle presented by the ongoing power of the industrial bureaucracies, the chapters provide little expectation that under new political and economic conditions the situation will soon change for the better. The picture is all the more depressing because it refers to the economic and social elites of East European and Commonwealth society. If elite behavior does change, the prognosis is that it will take twenty years, or until the children now in school reach maturity. Can any of the countries afford to wait so long?

Equally disturbing is the fact that the public is also not viewed as a positive source of change. Each essay presents a rather distressing picture of considerable popular ignorance, a low level of public awareness of environmental issues, and highly individualistic leadership of environmental groups. Where Fisher correctly argues that the East European populations of the nineties are more aware of environmental degradation than the American public at the beginning of the U.S. environmental decade of the 1970s, he emphasizes the need for organization and mobilization from the outside to turn that awareness into a political force.

The result of such analysis is the search for a deus ex machina in the form of material, financial, and organization aid from the West. The risks in counting on such a strategy are enormous. In 1991, DM218 billion in public funds were transferred from western to eastern Germany, and estimates of the total cost of German reunification are now over a trillion DM.[1] Another $13 billion went to Russia to house and resettle the Soviet troops leaving Germany. Estimates of the amounts needed to rehabilitate the former USSR and Eastern Europe run into unimaginable sums. The Marshall Plan pales before such considerations. Large-scale financing in the amounts needed is clearly not available. The World Bank set aside $2 billion to $3 billion to provide assistance during 1992–93. While this amount represented a considerable portion of the bank's annual lending, over the same timeframe Russia was asking for $9 billion.[2] The package that the West was finally able to put together, again largely for Russia at the expense of the other CIS states, was $24 billion.[3]

In its aid policy, the West has chosen to emphasize technical assistance and the encouragement of capital investment. However, technology and managerial skills are not transplanted into a vacuum, and the experience of one country cannot be transferred intact into another national setting. In the absence of a comprehensive and comparable environmental legal framework and appropriate economic infrastructure, the West may prefer to export to Eastern Europe and the Commonwealth republics those industries and technologies that are most polluting. There are precedents for such actions. In the 1970s Romania's chemical production expanded more than five times as a result of its imports of Western technologies. In the late 1970s, Romania, along with several other CMEA countries, became an exporter of chemicals and chemical products whose production was banned or experiencing severe regulatory restriction in Europe or the United States.[4] It will be recalled that transborder pollution from Romanian chemical plants sparked the first major environmental protest in Bulgaria. A mining company that anticipates having to secure 140 permits in order to open a mine in California might well consider transferring its operations to a comparable site in Eastern Europe, where only five permits might be required and termination procedures are less rigorous. If such eventualities occur, then the West could find itself an integral contributor to the worsening of the environmental problem rather than the desired provider of its solution.

Again, in their rush to assist, international lending institutions could well lower their environmental criteria to facilitate priming the East European economic pump. While the European Bank for Reconstruction and Development and the World Bank have earmarked remedial environmental monies and have made loans dependent upon fulfilling environmental stipulations, past bank practice, coupled with the dismal record of past East European and CIS governments in implementing environmental programs, does not encourage confidence that current policies will be strictly enforced or implemented.

The new social systems of Eastern Europe and the Commonwealth are highly vulnerable to surprise. As fragile democratic governments face increasingly dissatisfied voters, they may decide that the better part of wisdom is to encourage Western investment and joint ventures no matter what the environmental cost. Moreover, East Europeans and Mikhail Gorbachev share the same dream of a common European home. European integration in this context means adopting the affluent life-style of the parent culture. In the face of economic uncertainty, public pressure may combine with the transformed bureaucracies to choose a prepackaged solution. The example of the West German take-over of East Germany is a case in point. In the race for a place in the global markets and an immediate higher living standard, East European and Commonwealth societies may opt to forgo any attempt to develop domestic solutions for immediate economic gains in the form of "goulash capitalism." With the world on the threshold of a new stage in technological development, the multinationals are anxious to push their products on the vast, virtually untouched East European and Commonwealth markets. Once the trappings of a consumer society are in place in the East, it may be more difficult than it is now in the West to transform the life-style to do without them.

The conclusion that suggests itself is that to orient the new directions in environmental management solely on Western models and Western assistance may result in mitigating social frustration through continued and increasing environmental deterioration. At the end of the 1980s, vast numbers of people from the Oder to the Pacific became aware that they were living under the threat of environmental catastrophe. They were able to exploit that threat to change their political and economic system. The threat has not decreased in succeeding years. What has increased is the struggle for domination of the economic and political sectors of society within the East European and Commonwealth elites. These are exploiting the danger of unemployment and lowered living standards in order to mobilize popular support for their interests, thereby deflecting public interest from the urgency of environmental remediation.

The predemocratic domestic environmental movements were able to develop their own individual philosophy, organization, and interaction with the international world. If they could succeed in a climate of censorship, oppression, and police brutality, there is reason to expect that they will find a way to use their experience to develop successful modes of operation in an open society. The path of environmental activists and practitioners to Western capitals is well worn. Up to now, the new directions in environmental management in the former communist countries have been largely passive. Social transformation and adaptation to new conditions require active learning. The longer East European governments put off their environmental problems, the harder it will be to address them. In the 1980s, public pressure organized and maintained by domestic forces with only limited external support produced nuclear moratoriums and government abandonment of important energy projects. That experience needs to be repeated in the 1990s if the new directions in environmental management are to become an integral part of the region's economic and social development.

Notes

1. "Kohl's Debterdammerung?" *The Economist*, April 4–10, 1992, pp. 57–58.
2. *Christian Science Monitor*, January 24, 1992, p. 4.

3. "Betting on Boris," *The Week in Review*, Section 4, *The New York Times*, April 4, 1992, p. 1.

4. For a discussion of pollution and comparative disadvantage, see H. Jeffrey Leonard, *Pollution and the Struggle for the World Product: Multinational Corporations and International Comparative Advantage* (Cambridge: Cambridge University Press, 1988). For information on Romania, see pp. 147–55.

Index

About the Editor

Barbara Jancar-Webster, Professor of Political Science at the State University of New York at Brockport, is a specialist in the environmental policy and political-economic systems of East Central Europe and the former Soviet Union. She has conducted field research on these issues and is the author of numerous articles, chapters in books, and papers. Her recent publications include: *Environmental Management in the Soviet Union and Yugoslavia: Structure and Regulation in Federal Communist States* (Durham, NC: Duke University Press, 1987), for which she won the International Studies Association Sprout Award in 1990 for the best book in the area of international environmental policy; "Technology and the Environment in Eastern Europe," in James P. Scanlan, ed., *Technology, Culture, and Development: The Experience of the Soviet Model* (Armonk, NY: M.E. Sharpe, 1992); "Chaos as an Explanation of the Role of Environmental Groups in East European Politics," in Wolfgang Rudig, ed., *Green Politics Two* (Edinburgh: Edinburgh University Press, 1992); and "US/East European Environmental Exchange," *International Environmental Affairs* 2, no. 1 (Winter 1990).